I Watch Therefore I Am:
The Political Economy of
Chinese Television Advertising

Liu Zixu

CANUT INTERNATIONAL PUBLISHERS

Istanbul - Berlin - London - Santiago

Selected Outstanding Project of Scientific and Technological Activities Funded by the Ministry of Human Resources and Social Security of the People's Republic of China

I Watch Therefore I Am: The Political Economy of Chinese Television Advertising
Written by Liu Zixu
Copyright © Liu Zixu, 2019.

Canut International Publishers
Canut Intl. Turkey, Teraziler Cad. No.29. Sancaktepe, Istanbul, Turkey
Canut Intl. Germany, Heerstr. 266, D-47053, Duisburg, Germany
Canut Intl. United Kingdom, 12a Guernsay Road, London E11 4BJ, UK
Copyright © Canut International Publishers, 2019
ISBN: 978-605-9914-78-9

www.canutbooks.com

About the Author

Liu Zixu, PhD in communication and media studies from the University of Massachusetts, Amherst, USA, Assistant Researcher at the Academy of Marxism, Chinese Academy of Social Sciences, and Deputy Editorial Director of *International Critical Thought* published quarterly in English (launched in 2011, by Routledge). His research mainly focuses on the political economy of communication, media studies, culture and ideology. His major publications include: *Fanaticism: Uses of an Idea* (by Alberto Toscano, Translation into Chinese), "The Historical Contribution of the October Revolution to the Economic and Social Development of the Soviet Union—Analysis of the Soviet Economic Model and the Causes of Its Dramatic End" (co-authored with Cheng Enfu, *International Critical Thought,* 2017), "Once upon a Time in China—Nationalism, Modernity, and Cinematic Representation" (*Frontiers of Literary Studies in China,* 2014).

Address & E-mail: No. 5 Jianguomen Nei Dajie, Academy of Marxism, Chinese Academy of Social Sciences, Beijing 100732, P. R. China; liuzixu@cass.org.cn

Publisher's Foreword

In this well-written and engaging book, the author begins with a meticulous investigation of the basic facts of the television advertising industry in China: its institutional lay out, content, and audience. The author Liu Zixu, the deputy editorial director of *International Critical Thought*, from a Marxian viewpoint and sharp critical eyes, draws upon the distinction made in Chinese television advertising between the working class and what could be called the "watching class," and suggests that the advertising in contemporary China is fundamentally an ideological apparatus, which educates not only for new life styles but also for a new social order. For that reason, it must be treated as an act of *the political*—a concept that has not been clearly defined in the existing literature of political economy of communication. The author has carefully reviewed numerous scholarly works both from China and West, when developing his analyses. Shifting the focus towards the very existence of advertising, Liu Zixu discusses the political and ideological conditions and background that have made advertising possible in contemporary China, and look at advertising as a field of ideological and political contention in which socialism and capitalism are in constant struggles. In fact, what the products of the Chinese television advertising industry reveals is the process in which a socialist system hosts capitalism and by so doing becomes its hostage, and in which critical intervention becomes necessary in order to bring socialist relations of production back to the discussion. Liu Zixu, suggests: in this sense, the banal and self-deceptive critique of China's "communist" authoritarianism as suggested by some domestic and foreign studies doesn't hold water, while in the meantime we must be cautious about the critique of China's capitalism, which easily misses the struggles against capitalism by various political forces in China at the state, collective and individual level.

Daivja Jindal

September 2018, London

Contents

Chapter 1. Leading Questions

Three young men, one pop singer, one motorist, and one Olympic sprinter champion. Three girls from a pop band. Two apartments across the street. What chemistry can we expect between them?

This is not a pitch for any movie or drama series. This is a Coca Cola com- mercial, which was aired on August 9, 2005, at 9:00 pm, on Chanel 1 of China Central Television (CCTV1). What is obvious about this particular ad is that even though it was not a prime time drama, it was actually presented as one, with the appearance and all the key elements of it: stars, plot, narrative, suspension, and of course, a happy ending. The commercial lasted five minutes. Coca Cola bought out the whole slot for this commercial only and the transition between the prime time drama and the commercial was seamless.

Yes, five minutes. It is certainly not a common practice, not in China, not in any part of the world (that is, if we don't consider the fact that programs are themselves advertisements in the form of product placement or *100 Best Commercials of the Year*), but the very event of a five minute commercial deserves tremendous attention precisely because it should not be considered to be an exceptional case in spite of its appearance of temporal uniqueness. Like all "successful" commercials on prime time television, it completely blurs the boundary between program and advertising. The meaning of such an event deserves even more attention if we realize that some new popular genres such as online drama can be but five minutes in length.

If, as some studies show, that advertising has experienced different stages (Leiss, Kline, and Jhally, 1997), and China once lagged behind in such development (Ha, 1996; Sinclair, 2008), then this ad of Coca Cola is undoubtedly a piece of evidence that advertising in China is now ready to catch up with its western counterpart and enter the stage of "totemism" (Leiss et al., 1997, p. 344). The Chinese market has entered what Naomi Klein (1999) described as the age of branding, with manufacturers, branding companies (advertisers), media, and audience/consumers well on board.

In order to fully grasp the significance of what was just said, let us go back in time to January 1979, when the first commercial appeared on Chinese television since the establishment of People's Republic of China in 1949. Back then, no one had the tiniest clue that it would have any significant impact on the structure of the broadcasting media as well as our everyday life. In three decades, it had been considered a capitalist tool and was still not widely acceptable on Chinese television in the decade following the reform and opening-up.

Such dramatic experiences of the media industry are certainly not exclusively Chinese. Tunstall (in Jenus, 1980) presented 3 changes that national media systems, especially those in developing countries, have undergone as a result of this process of transnationalization of advertising: (1) the media industry itself has grown; (2) the commercial sector of the media has grown relatively faster than the non-commercial sectors; and (3) the entire national media system has shifted from traditional political forms to commercial forms.

Tunstall seems to be simply speaking the obvious – anyway, the connection between the advertising industry and the mass media has been much talked about to the extent that it is a naturalized fact among the audience. However, if the same was said in China at the time of its first TV commercial, it would be guaranteed to be greeted with not only amusement but suspicion of sanity of the one who dared to speak of it. Yet 30 years later (we may as well say 20 years later, or even 10 years later if we cut in 1988, when the current structure of Chinese television was already predictable), we see the coke commercial on CCTV 1, taking over a whole slot with seamless transition from program to advertising. Today, the media system in China is no less commercial than any media system around the world. Some celebrate as they see history unfolding right in front of their eyes, while others are looking cautiously towards the future. In either case, the commercial system appears so natural to the Chinese audience as if it has always been like this since the very beginning of their memory.

In media studies, particularly in the United States, it is commonly acknowledged that advertising is historically connected with the development of a media system (e.g. Kellner, 1990; Mattelart, 1991). In this respect, one may find that things are a little more complicated in China. Apparently, the leap from television without advertising to television primarily supported by advertising revenue fits into the formula of transition from planned economy to a market economy. However, such an understanding leaves many questions unanswered. The first and the most obvious one would have to be: how did it happen – how did advertising get into Chinese television? The not so obvious one would be: did it get in because it is simply the natural result of rational economic act in a free marketplace? It should not be forgotten that 40 years ago there was no such thing as advertising on Chinese television—the so called market behavior had to be made possible first by an initiative at the state level. That is to say, China, more visibly than any other countries, presents a perfect case to trash the idea that market is the result of "free choice" by the so called "economic men." If so, can we still believe that advertising, as the primary articulation of the marketplace, is an economic act in its pure sense, when in fact it appears to be a completely parasitic existence, contingent upon the political initiative at the state level?

To ask the above question is to ask what happened since 1978 that brought China to where it is today. And don't forget that advertising was long considered in the official discourse as something exclusive to Western capitalism (or at least so in the early 1980s); and that the idea has never completely disappeared that "westernization" and "bourgeois liberalism" are something that we must resist. In such a context, where is the line to be drawn between one "westernization" and another? Where did the unfolding history, no matter how short and fast moving it may have appeared, turn its direction? What has happened that makes it possible for the rhetorical shift towards commercialism?

These questions could be answered by looking at any chosen aspect of Chinese society, but none so visible, so despised yet in the meantime so happily embraced as television advertising. How has the institution of television changed? What happened that has made advertising the most prominent element for the Chinese television industry, its content an integral part of everyday life of ordinary citizens and its logic the defining principle in contemporary Chinese society? Where does advertising fit in these drastic yet seemingly "natural" changes, socially, culturally, and ideologically? Debates over information flow and changes in communication infrastructure at the global level suggest that advertising functions as a means to open markets for transnational corporations, and that it changes the media system of third world countries. Before jumping into this kind of discussion, we should keep in mind that from 1978 (the beginning of the reform and opening-up) to 1992 (Deng Xiaoping's inspection tour in Southern China during which he gave a series of speeches that had the effect of tabling debates about the socialist vs. capitalist nature of the reform and focus on economic construction in its concrete forms), China was not seen to be genuinely open to the outside world, and in the present case, to transnational advertising and whatever changes it may bring about. If we have to accept the fact that advertising in China must have been initiated from within, then what else can we say about the interaction between the global and the local, and about the consequences of such interaction?

Studies of advertising in China can rarely ignore its geo-political implications. Some focus on the impact of transnational advertising on the socio-economic development in China (for example, see Herman and McChesney, 1997; Wang, 2000), others compare Chinese advertising with its Western counterparts and explain their differences from a cultural perspective (see Chapter 2 for analysis of the literature concerning the content of Chinese television advertising). Still others approach similar issues in other "geo-linguistic" context with a "peripheral vision" (Sinclair et al., 1996), which tries to break away from the deterministic view of cultural/media imperialism with the West in the center and "analyze in a more nuanced way the intricate and multi-directional flows of television across the globe" (p. 5). While acknowledging the hierarchical structure of global political economy, I try to understand Chinese television advertising not as mere juxtaposition of a geo-political entity and a foreign idea of economy, but rather as part of the interaction between the political and the economic. The rationale is simple: the center and peripheral are both part of an integral whole of global capitalism.

In actual practice, such understanding is obtained on the basis of an ideological analysis at the micro level by asking how it affects people's view to have a television primarily supported by advertising, as compared with one without it. Indeed, television advertising may tell a lot about Chinese society when we examine the perception of it by the audience, who had never seen a TV commercial 40 years ago, yet cannot imagine a television without ads today (this will be elaborated in Chapter 6). It suggests the process of the enculturation of the audience into a consumer culture, which in China means incorporating different generations with different experiences into a new commercialism that homogenizes in different ways than the old "political" propaganda.

This will inevitably lead to questions that move beyond the micro analysis of television watching and consumer culture. With the economic (and cultural) realm more and more defined by advertising, a situation that has not been genuinely changed but rather reinforced by the emergence of the "new media" (internet and smart phone), what can be said about the notion that China has a "socialist politics" and capitalist (market) economy? What is the problem with such a dualism that keeps such things as advertising on one side (the economic) but not the other (the political)? What does it mean to the long tradition of debate over base and superstructure when the economic changes obviously have not been responded with corresponding changes at the level of superstructure? Should we look at it as a short term compromise like Lenin's New Economic Policy? To borrow Samir Amin's term, does it represent a "Thermidor" or "Restoration" (Amin, 2017)? Or, does it mean that changes in the superstructure had taken place even before changes in the economic base, albeit in a gradual, complex and incomplete manner? What theoretical significance can we possibly obtain in bringing up a seemingly obsolete Marxist proposition of political economy?

Critiques of advertising are not rare at the global level in the past three decades along many different lines such as the process of meaning production (Williamson), the impact of American advertising (Tunstall, in Jenus 1980), representation (Killburne, 1999), and the economy of watching (Jhally, 1990). What does a study of Chinese television advertising contribute to this repertoire? What would be the implications of investigating television advertising within an already loaded geo-political prefix? At the most fundamentally level, what ideologies make it possible for one to talk about a homogenizing process of globalization on the one hand, and upload a project with geopolitical and cultural uniqueness on the other?

The critiques mentioned above have undoubtedly enhanced the understanding of advertising and its political consequence, but looking at Chinese television advertising with their perspectives inevitably keeps one within the realm of either the economic or the cultural. The question is, would it be more productive to assume that commercials should also be an essential part of ideological power? If television advertising is ultimately an economic act, then what can we achieve with a political economy of television advertising? Is there something that is fundamentally "political" in advertising, or do we have to live with the faith of the old school political economy, i.e., by talking about the *economic*, we are, by default, talking about the *political*? These questions will determine the way that I look at the basics of Chinese television advertising. They contain the reason why I choose to juxtapose political economy with television advertising.

For one thing, as Althusser suggests, understanding of a part is not possible without the understanding of the whole. Changes in advertising cannot be possibly understood without linking them to the environmental changes in Chinese society as a whole. That is to say, the current project will be looking at advertising as an articulation of the whole ideological terrain which plays a determinable role in the chain of production of television advertising. That is to say, advertising itself is part of the forces that have brought about changes in a much broader context than television watching. In short, I am looking at the expressions of a new social order in contemporary China, and advertising enables me to cut into the joint from a very convenient angle in terms of its role during the course of the ideological transformation and reconfiguration in contemporary China, and the displacement of political problems to the economic dimension.

Obviously, this study is not intended to be merely a documentary of Chinese television advertising, nor is it going to be just a hypothesis driven content analysis. The ultimate goal is to address some critical questions concerning social structure and ideology in contemporary China, drawing attention to the complexity of political conditions regarding its ideological transition, which has not received much attention of the intellectuals in the West and East alike.

Indeed, in cultural studies, television programming has often been considered to be a source of ideological power (See Lewis, 1991, pp. 66-67). I do believe that in contemporary China, as in the United States, effective political persuasion is largely embedded in entertainment, which, though apparently "opposite" to the traditional political propaganda, fulfills the function of political education without provoking people's resentment against the old "socialist" discourse. By the same token, television advertising in my analysis is not only the result of a political initiative but also a state apparatus itself – it functions to educate consent and advocate for a new social order. I insist, as Laclau (1996) does in *Emancipation*(s), to remain on the political-ideological field as opposed to a neutral or objective cultural observation.

Media (printing or electronic) institutions in China have been historically considered to be part of the political system, and still so in many ways. In the meantime, advertising, which has been regarded as something purely economic, was first banned (before 1978), and then restricted by state policies. For example, foreign ownership of advertising agencies in China, just like that of television stations, has been prohibited (Wang, 2000, p. 95). Such restrictions have experienced changes after China became a member of WTO, which is also considered to be a purely economic organization (Wang, 2003, pp. 23-24). After 2002, China still prohibited foreign ownership of media but began to allow existence of foreign advertising agencies (first in the form of joint venture with local partners, and then as a wholly foreign owned enterprise since 2005), even though the latter is much more effective than propagating a new ideology. Despite of all these political implications of advertising, existing studies of political economy of advertising are more economic than political. That is to say, although they look at advertising from a political point of view, they ultimately retreat to the position that advertising is fundamentally an economic, or cultural phenomenon, which has certain political implications (I'll further discuss this point later). While there is certainly a legitimate reason for such a stance, I would like to take a much more explicit position, that advertising is a political act, and none other than a political act. What I am addressing here is not the meaning of specific advertisements, nor advertising as the force that shapes the structure of the media industry, but the very existence of advertising in a socialist state under transformation.

6

Critique of television advertising in China, therefore, is about the conditions that make the very act of advertising possible on television, which was once a propaganda machine of the "socialist" state. These conditions involve both state and civil society, which are often perceived as opposing forces in China. Drawing upon some well know cases of resistance in China since 1978, I will try to locate not only contradictions, but also the collaborations between the forces of the state and civil society.

To that end, the present study will, before everything, deal with the basics of Chinese television advertising. First, it begins with an institutional analysis that accounts for the contextual factors for Chinese television advertising, i.e., the ways that Chinese television and the advertising industry have been shaped by a series of interactions with the state. Second, with concrete evidence from content analysis, this study will analyze the patterns and values that prevail through television advertising, which will be illustrated by analysis of specific commercials in terms of their narrative structure, persuasive interest, and prominent images. Third, the analysis of the audience of Chinese television advertising from the perspective of political economy will elaborate on how the audience constitutes the axis of the entire media industry and advertising industry. The investigation of these basic elements about Chinese television advertising will culminate in an ideological analysis that explicates how advertising in Chinese television constitutes a social force that is at the same time defined and constitutive of a new social order of Chinese society. The following is a sketch of the contents of each of the following chapters.

Chapter 2 will review some literature in a few different areas that will shed light on the present study from different angles. First, there is an evaluation of the existing literature on the content of Chinese television advertising, so as to be clear about how the particular issues of advertising in China has been treated in the academia. It is followed by a reflection upon the implications of the history of broadcasting media in relation to advertising. Research on the political economy of communication will be carefully examined, and questions unanswered here will be picked up again in later chapters. Questions raised in these two sections will lead to the theories of ideology and the framework for an ideological critique based on a revisit to the base/superstructure debate within the Marxist tradition and its implications to the current study.

Chapter 3 examines the structural transformation of Chinese television in the three phases of its development, namely, 1978-1989, 1990-1992, and 1993-2007. It provides information necessary for the understanding of the dominant form of advertising medium in China today. Its initial development and transformation in the reform era, interactions with what Herman and McChesney (1996) call the global media, and foreign programming on Chinese television, etc., will be discussed.

Chapter 4 introduces the evolution of the social environment of the advertising industry in China. It includes a brief history of advertising in China, from its beginning as a foreign concept and practice to its return to the economic life in 1979 and its development in sync with that of the television industry. Three stages of changes in the regulations of advertising in China will be discussed, as well as the implications of these regulations. The object of analysis in this chapter is in fact the conflicts and coordination among various social forces during the process of the establishment of a new social order. The theoretical departure point (television and advertising as part of the "ideological state apparatus") means that the analysis here will necessarily be different from the self-claimed "objective" observation of Chinese television advertising from the mainstream academia.

Chapter 5 is on the content of Chinese television advertising. In this chapter, I will demonstrate the most manifest values that the commercials on Chinese television display and discuss prominent issues illuminated by such demonstration in regard to age, gender, race, class, and urban-rural differences. It will illustrate in the most straightforward manner some important aspects of the dominant ideology in contemporary China.

Chapter 6 focuses on the audience of television advertising in China. Based upon data collected from focus group interviews, I will move away from the meanings of messages towards the consuming behavior of the audience in relation to television advertising. This chapter will highlight the educational function of advertising as what Althusser calls an ideological state apparatus.

Chapter 7 will be the longest chapter that includes all the major arguments—both theoretical and empirical—of this project. Following the chapter on the audience of television advertising in China, it revisits the issue of watching as labor and tries to develop the idea by making a further distinction between the real working class and the working class created during the viewing process, which I call the "watching class." This will lead to a discussion about the experiences of working class Chinese since 1978, which reveal the same political conditions that have made television advertising possible in China. The role of the state will be further discussed in terms of its relationship with civil society and its role in the establishment of a new social order in China. To link all these with television advertising, the argument is simple and straightforward: the object of analysis in this book—advertising that aims to promote consuming products, cultivate new life style, and educate different way of thinking—is a part of the changing mode of production, which has led to the transformation of a whole nation to a system in which subjectivity is constituted on the basis of a dramatically different relationship with consumer products.

8 Chapter 8 expounds the conclusion of this study. After a brief summary of what has been done in previous chapters, I will present critical reflections upon two key concepts, namely, the concept of "the political" and the concept of "cultural difference." Ultimately, I hope to redefine the parameters of inquiry in regard to the loaded term of Chinese television advertising. This chapter will also list some important limitations of this project, which, although cannot be immediately solved within the scope of this study, nonetheless opens up the possibility for some future research in more than one direction.

Chapter 2. Theoretical Considerations

Let me begin this chapter with a clarification. While China has demonstrated some peculiar characteristics in the development of its television industry and advertising industry, as well as the connection between the two, it would be a very bold theoretical (and political) statement to look at it as a particular case of merely regional significance and therefore requires completely indigenous theories to account for its uniqueness. Indeed, the very tendency to divide both the subject of a study and its theoretical foundations in a geopolitical way suggests an already existing ideological orientation that deprives these studies from potential theoretical depth and analytical rigor.

This is not to legitimize the primary reliance on "Western" theories in terms of the analytical framework of this study. For one thing, the dramatic development of both the advertising industry and the media industry in China began since 1978, when China started the reform and opening to the outside world, *and* when global capitalism was gaining new momentum under neo-liberal incentives. I will elaborate on this in later sections. It suffices here to say that the development of the television and advertising industry in China respectively, as well as the connection between them, must come to terms with the neo-liberal logic that started to dominate and shape the structure of cultural production in the West since early 1980s, and the understanding of the latter necessarily becomes part of the context for the analysis of the former. For another, the studies on television advertising by Chinese scholars within or outside China have offered more data than theoretical inspirations for further understanding.

In reviewing the literature regarding the Chinese television advertising, I will move from the particular to the general. First and foremost, I will look at the studies of the content of Chinese television advertising, which has experienced a development from zero to more mature ones in both theoretical and method-ological terms only after the year 2000, and the presuppositions in such studies are of more inspiration than their conclusions. After that, I will put television advertising in its historical context, and obtain a perspective that looks at the relationship between broadcasting media and advertising, which will enable me to look at Chinese television advertising in its proper media context as a constitutive element of such context. Most importantly, I will reflect upon the critiques of advertising from two perspectives, namely, the political economy of communication and theories of ideology, to establish an analytical frame-work that enables me to examine advertising as an apparatus, as well as the broader political context that makes the very existence of Chinese television advertising possible in the first place.

2.1 The Idea of Content Analysis

Neuendorf (2002) defines content analysis as "the systematic, objective, quantitative analysis of message characteristics" (p. 1), which can be descrip-tive, inferential, or predictive. With a message as the unit of data collection, such analysis aims to summarize (in a quantitative way) details of character-istics of messages in human communication (interpersonal, group, or organi-zational), and make inferences to the producers, audience, and effects of the message (pp. 52-55). It should be noted that although content analysis relies on the "scientific" method (with rigorous procedures of an "a priori" design, and concerns with reliability, validity, and hypothesis testing), every human inquiry is by nature subjective and objectivity is only what is socially agreed upon (pp. 9-25).

There are researches, as suggested by Neuendorf (2002), which connect content analysis with audience research. Normally these kinds of studies are quantitative on both ends and commercial in nature, linking for example evalu-ations of advertising features to "audience recall, readership, and evaluations of ads" (p.55).

Before moving on to the case of Chinese television advertising, one content analysis project is particularly inspiring to the current study. In presenting the Cultural Indicators Project, Gerbner et al. (1973, 1994) summarize it as a three-pronged research strategy, namely, institutional process analysis, message sys-tem analysis and cultivation analysis. All three are more or less relevant to the present study. What I want to highlight here is that for cultural indicators proj-ect, the results of their content analysis projects have been consistently useful in the next stage, namely, cultivation analyses, especially in comparing images in the world of television and viewers' perceptions of the world in reality.

For example, through content analysis, the cultural indicators group found out that "the most frequently recurring features of television cut across all types of programming and are inescapable for the regular viewer," and "there is no evidence that proliferation of channels has led to substantially greater diversity

10

of content" (Gerbner et al. 1994. in Bryant and Zillman, 2002, p.19). The importance of such findings cannot be exaggerated. They provide a conceptual basis and reference for comparison for later cultivation analysis in particular and research on television in general. More importantly, they completely reshaped the understanding of the interaction between audience and television in terms of the shift of emphasis from short term, change oriented "effects" to long term, ideology oriented conceptions of social reality.

Although advertising is not the central concern of the cultural indicators project, it does lead to the speculation of the possibility that heavy viewers watch more commercials on television, and the influence of advertising on the audience overlaps that of television programs in terms of their perception of social reality. The important implication of such perspective is that television advertising should not be considered to be merely "commercial" messages, but a form of enculturation, which, like other forms of television programming, cultivates a "mainstream" among the television audience.

Now I will turn to the case of Chinese television advertising, with the recognition that its content has everything to do with the formation of a new value system in cotemporary China. Two things are especially prominent among the existing literature on Chinese television advertising (by Chinese scholars or otherwise, within China or abroad). One is that most studies are industry related in terms of their basic assumptions and target audience. Among most Chinese researchers, advertising research seems to be considered an effort to help the industry and thus contribute to economic development (see, e.g., Cheng 2017; Nie 2017; Zhao, Yin, and Zeng 2017; Li, Zhao, and Lin 2017; Wang 2016; Xu and Yan 2016; Dong and Liu 2016; to list just a few most recent ones). The other is that "globalization" is the eye-catching background that sets the tone for any related discussions. The most observable consequence is that comparative study is a major category and cultural values conveyed in US and Chinese commercials respectively are of primary concern. This is particularly visible among Chinese scholars living and studying abroad (e.g., Cheng and Schweitzer 1996; Ji and McNeal, 2001; Zhou et al, 2005), though the Chinese researchers at home also share this topic (see, e.g., Dou, Sun and Lin, 2012). I will elaborate on this point below.[1]

11

Both are understandable. If China is now in an era of "transition" towards a market economy and commercial culture, such transition should be reflected in the content of (television) advertising (just like it is reflected in the content of television programming), which has gradually become the defining element of the new era. Most importantly, given that this "transition" has been inevitably

---

[1] There is actually a new tendency in the new millennium that, with the rapid development in information and communication technologies, the concern of advertising research in China has been shifting towards the adaptation of the traditional ways of advertising in the new media environment, and how traditional forms of media such as television may survive under the impact of the (mobile) internet (see, e.g., Wu and Wang 2007; Gao 2014; 2014; Fan 2016; Wang Donglan 2016). This is not the focus of the present study but does deserve a note.

intertwined with the opening to the West, such a reflection would doubtlessly be contextualized by the interaction between domestic and foreign advertising. In some sense, scholars are doing nothing but speaking the obvious.

That is certainly not the path that the present study is taking. With no intention to serve the advertising industry, the present study will digress from the above two existing routes. I will not deny the legitimacy of such comparisons between domestic and foreign advertisements on Chinese television in terms of their values (such as family, friendship, social status, success) articulated through visible codes regarding traditional Chinese and foreign/global characteristics. But this study is intended to move beyond concrete messages and their meanings. It will not only look at the messages of television advertising, but the very existence of advertising and the ideologies that makes possible the availability of the "new" "economic" practices and "cultural" codes. The highlight is therefore not how Chinese culture and Chinese practices differ from its Western counterparts, but rather what is missing in the comparative studies: the recognition of the same underlying logic in apparently antithetical values such as nationalism and globalism.

For example, Zhou et al. (2005) examine manifest characteristics and values in television commercials in the U.S. and China. Through the exposure of visual discrepancies in different cultures, they try to reveal the diverse means of visual manipulations, and, on the practical side, enlighten international marketers who conduct culturally based advertising campaigns, which have proved to be more effective than "generalized" advertising campaigns designed for a universal market.

Ji and McNeal (2001) have conducted a content analysis of children's television commercials from China and the U.S., and describe the underlying reasons that lead to the differences between the two sets of commercials. They conclude that Chinese children's commercials reflect China's traditional cultural values, but there was a shift of power in Chinese society from the elderly to the young due to the one-child policy during the past two decades. In the meantime, evidence is found that Western values have "crept into children's commercials in China."

Almost inevitably, though in most cases inadvertently, studying the content of television advertising will touch upon the issue of the audience. The cultural values embodied in television commercials can be easily conflated with values that the audience holds. For example, Zhou and Belk (2004) use what they call a "reader-response" approach to study Chinese consumer readings of global and local appeals in television and print ads. What they use for comparison is not Western and Chinese commercials, but rather commercials with "global" or "local" appeals in terms of the "locus of the brand names, images, model nationalities, settings, and stylistic elements of advertising," regardless of an advertised product's country of origin. In the same time, however, the authors do admit that often times "global" is the synonym of "Western" or "American".

Tremendous effort has been spent to find categories that may generalize about Chinese and American cultural values as observed in television advertising in the two contexts. In 1996, Cheng and Schweitzer (1996) conducted a content analysis of 1,105 Chinese and U.S. television commercials from 1993 and identified eight cultural values dominating either Chinese or U.S. television advertising. They found that Chinese commercials resorted more often to symbolic cultural values while U.S. commercials tended to use both symbolic and utilitarian ones. Specifically, "modernity" and "technology" were most dominant in Chinese advertisements.

In 1997, as an update of his 1996 study, based on Polly's (1983) typology of cultural values manifest in advertising, Cheng conducted another content analysis of Chinese television commercials. There are 31 cultural values defined in his study, falling into two major categories. The first one is "utilitarian," referring to those emphasizing product features or qualities, such as "economy," "effectiveness," and "safety." The second one is "symbolic," referring to those suggesting human emotions, such as "collectivism," "enjoyment," and "social status." He found that "modernity" and "technology" continued to be dominant cultural values among Chinese television advertising in the 1990s, followed by "youth" as the third dominant cultural value. In the meantime, both the supposed values for the Western culture ("competition," "enjoyment", and "individualism") and the supposed values for Chinese culture ("courtesy," "patriotism," and "tradition") occurred significantly more often in 1995 than in 1990. Overall, Chinese television advertising has come to portray more symbolic values and fewer utilitarian values.

13

While Cheng's categorization of 31 cultural values serves as a very good reference for designing coding schemes, there are also serious problems that undermine the whole foundation of his study and others of the same kind. In exposing the prevalence of such values as modernity, technology, and youth, he suggests that Chinese advertising has come to target young consumers more than other demographic groups, and concludes that Chinese television advertising is promoting things that are new and "encouraging change rather than maintaining the status quo." Demographics aside, the perception of the older generation or "tradition" as status quo is naïve and has no connection with the social reality in contemporary China. In the same study, both "tradition" and modernity, as two supposedly antithetical categories, are presented as frequently portrayed in Chinese television commercials. Such a coexistence of "traditional" and "western"/modern values requires more careful reflections than the simple equation of the old to "status quo" and the new to "change," and the linear progression from one to the other. The foundation of such labels as "semi-traditional" and "semi-modern" culture in China is theoretically ill grounded and empirically insufficient. These dichotomies or semi dichotomies miss not only the inherent hybrid nature of both Chinese and Western cultures, but also the "status quo" in its real sense, status quo in regard to the economic and political structure in China, rather than to the superficially constructed categories of "culture" and "tradition" for the sake of convenience. In the meantime, the seemingly innocent observation of "cultural differences" in Chinese and American advertising (implicitly present even when Chinese advertising is the only concern) cannot conceal the preexisting cultural hierarchy as seen in the no-need-to-define concepts of "status quo" vs. "change," "youth" vs. "old," and "tradition" vs. "modernity." Without a clear understanding about the nature of the status quo and modes of modernity in China, this kind of study confuses more then it clarifies.

Such is the situation in the studies of Chinese television advertising – the scarcity of independent scholarly work accompanied by heavy focus on solution-for-the-industry and comparative analysis. It is not that all these studies are of no significance, but the collective recognition of the obligation to find solutions for the industry and cultural differences reveals less about the actual subject of study than the social context for both television advertising and the related scholarly works. And the appearance of new media does not seem to trigger any substantial changes so far.

Based on these previous studies and the reflections upon the dominant mode of contextualizing Chinese television advertising, namely, the dichotomy of Chinese vs. West in terms of cultural values manifest in commercials, I intend to proceed with the following research questions.

Before entering a possibly fruitless discussion about the cultural differences in Chinese and Western advertising, can we begin instead with the question about their sameness? Specifically, what are the features of television commercials that cut across both Chinese and foreign commercials on Chinese television (for example, gender role)? What are the implications of such similarities between the global and the local, for advertisers and the audience, respectively? That is to say, taking a step back from the struggling with the superficial meanings of individual or an ensemble of individual commercials, what can we say about the sameness between advertising in different cultural context in terms of their very existence and the politico-ideological conditions of such existence? Moreover, scholars (e.g., Cheng, 1997) routinely attribute the "cultural" changes in Chinese television advertising to those in the broader economic environment, though never taking such a proposition in a seriously elaborative way. From the perspective of political economy in this study, what can we say about the political aspect of television advertising, about its political relationship with the "broader economic environment" and perhaps more importantly, with the newly emerging ideology of commercialism in the socialist China?

Obviously, these questions cannot be answered by content analysis alone. The questions in regard to the role of advertising in the new ideology, while stemming from the process of content analysis, lies beyond its scope and must be addressed with a different perspective and theoretical framework, to which I will come back later.

Before I move on, I want to point out that there has been debates within the advertising industry and related researches over the advantages of "global advertising" versus the localized approach. In the meantime, there has been rather heated discussion in China concerning whether it is culturally proper for global brands to use local names and appeals in advertising and for local brands to use non-Chinese names and appeals. The content of these debates is far less important than their very existence. Researchers have already shown that, in the Chinese market, both foreign and local advertisers use a combination of global and local approaches (e.g. Zhou and Belk, 2004; Yin, 1999). The debate in China is nothing but a call for a clear distinction between global advertising and local advertising under the guise of a taken-for-granted national identity and cultural tradition. These debates, instead of solving any problem, have become part of the problem that they try to tackle. They themselves reveal more than their conclusions do. As far as I see, they all result from the same anxiety and sometimes confusion on the side of advertisers who are struggling between "standardization" and "specialization." As such, they reflect a new social order without which there would be no conditions for such anxiety and such debates, and for that reason they must be included in the present study that tries to investigate the ideological (re)articulations in contemporary China.

In addition to content analysis, semiotic analysis also looks at the messages of advertising, albeit from a different approach. For example, Barthes (1988) suggested that we adopt a method from (Saussurian) linguistics and examine how an advertisement is constituted at the semantic level (pp. 173-178); Williamson (1978) elaborated on the way that advertising produces meaning through the juxtaposition of unrelated images from two different systems of signifiers such as that of the products and celebrities; Kilbourne (1999) dissected verbal and visual messages of advertisements to demonstrate the devastating effect of advertising on our values, relations and civic life. Individual messages of advertising, however, are not the central concern of this study, and literature in this aspect will be dealt with only when such need comes up occasionally in later discussion. I will now move on to the institutional relations between television broadcasting and advertising, as well as the role of the audience in this relation.

2.2 Critical Reflections: Broadcasting, Advertising, and Audience

It has been well documented by scholars of media studies (e.g., Janus, 1980; Jhally, 1990, Chapter 3; Leiss et al., 1997, Chapter 5; O'Donnell, 2007) that an undeniable relationship exists between television and advertising to the extent that the structure, content, and goal of programming are all shaped by the need of advertisers who are the major source of revenues for the television industry.

Such a relationship has been a naturalized one among the audience. One implicit conclusion in the above section is that most previous studies of the content of advertising take its existence as a given fact. By focusing on the most effective way to address cultural difference as a marketing strategy, they implicitly constitute a defense of the legitimacy of advertising, which is considered to be a definitely positive element in the social and economic development in modern China.

With this sophisticated, powerful, and naturalized commercial system of television, surely the only thing that seems to require scrutiny is the message itself. The claim of Livant (1981b) about the study of mass media in general may well apply to the study of advertising in particular: "practically every study, both radical and mainstream, focuses on these messages – there composition, flow, production, reception, behavioural effects, and so on. Similarly, discussion of the impact of the new communications technology, which it is claimed will increase the number of channels available to the audience, is nothing less than a discussion of messages, for a channel is fundamentally a flow of messages" (in Jhally, 1990, p. 68).

Not everyone is complacent with this "natural" existence of advertising. Some scholars took insights from political economy, which could be considered to provide a theoretical ground for a general break away from the message centered approach to the study of media and advertising. A side note: the tendency (to focus on the message) is so strong that even the most critical scholars in political economy of communication cannot help but primarily focusing on the impact of commercial media on the content being presented (for example, Schiller, 1989; McChesney, 1999). Two general tendencies could be observed in the political economy of media/advertising. One takes a historical perspective and investigates the institutional history of media in relation to advertising, and the other returns to some fundamental concepts of Marxian political economy to reveal the secret of "commodity form" in advertising.

2.2.1 Implications of the Early History of Broadcasting

Within the Chinese context, the naturalization of advertising and the nearly compulsive comparison with the US television advertising is actually a logically consistent move. Who else but the U.S. not only created but has exported the ideal model for a "market economy" in which advertising is nothing but the product of an "objective' economic law? Such idolization of a commercial model of broadcasting is easily seen at the global level. One obvious fact about the broadcasting industry around the world is that although most systems began as some form of public service funded through general tax revenues, they all end up as (or are on the way towards) commercial media serving corporate interests, with advertisers as their major source of revenue (See Jenus, 1980, Chapter 3; Herman and McChesney, 1997, Chapter 5).

Television was hailed as the ideal medium for advertising since the very beginning of its inception (Jenus, 1980, p. 37-39), and it has been clearly so later at the global level with transnational corporations. Even with the dramatic development of new media technologies such as the internet, smart phones, and mobile internet, and despite the fact that Chinese Internet subscribers exceeded 200 million in as early as 2007 and 700 million in 2016, television remained the most powerful advertising tool in the three decades since the reform and opening up with a loyal audience of over a billion and a growth rate that is much higher than that of the GDP[2]. The dominance of television on advertising was seriously challenged in 2014, when it was reported that the revenue of online advertising (RMB 150 billion Yuan, about 23 billion US dollars) exceeded that of television (RMB 120 billion Yuan, about 20 billion US dollars).[3] In 2015, the growth rate of television advertising was lower than that of GDP in the first time since the early 1980s,[4] and the internet became the dominant source of advertising revenue, which amounted to about RMB 210 billion Yuan, higher than the total advertising revenue (RMB 174 billion Yuan) of all the four traditional forms of media, i.e., newspaper, magazine, radio and television, and far exceeding that of television (RMB 122 billion Yuan).[5] In the same year at the global level, the online advertising revenue ($ 42.8 billion) in the United States first exceeded that of television ($ 40.1 billion), and it is estimated that total online advertising revenue of the world will exceed that of television in 2017.[6] While fully recognizing the impact of the internet and mobile internet upon traditional forms of media, two points must be made clear. First, the dramatic development of new technologies and the tremendous increase in the number of netizens in China (688 million in 2015) by no means eliminate the important of television in people's everyday life. In 2014, the size of television audience was still as large as over 1.2 billion, with an average daily viewing of 157 minutes.[7] Such a huge audience scale and rather long viewing time undoubtedly constitute a large and valuable business

17

2 "Statistics of Chinese advertising revenue in 2005-2014, http://www.qianzhan.com/qz-data/detail/149/151201-22e4edb9.html.
3 "Internet Advertising Revenue Exceeding that of Television," http://www.admaimai.com/news/ad201505062-ad122166.html. The report has not been officially verified, but the tendency of rapid increase in online advertising is quite obvious. Similar report could be seen in "Chinese Online Advertising Revenue Expected to Exceed That of Television in 2016." http://www.techweb.com.cn/data/2014-08-11/2062915.shtml. Accessed September 15.
4 "Analysis of the Advertising Revenue and Future Market of Radio and Television in 2015." https://sanwen8.cn/p/1f8wnS0.html. Accessed September 15.
5 "Data: Radio as the only Traditional Media That Had an Revenue Increase in 2015." http://www.360doc.com/content/16/0626/09/27794381_570807304.shtml. With reference to the *Blue Book of the New Media: 2016 Report [No. 7] on the Development of the New Media in China*, by the Chinese Academy of Social Sciences.
6 "Revenue of Advertising on the Internet Will Exceed That of Television A Year Earlier Than Predicted." http://tech.qq.com/a/20160321/049907.htm.
7 "Internet Advertising Revenue Exceeding that of Television," http://www.admaimai.com/news/ad201505062-ad122166.html.

resource. Second, the momentum of the growth in online advertising comes mainly from social network, video sharing and search.[8] As one of the major source of revenue, web video is closely related to television shows in both its form and content, while its advertising is obviously structured, produced and presented in basically the same way as television commercials. Besides, the continuity between television and new media forms in form and content means that the study of television (advertising) and the new media (advertising) inevitably share the same theoretical repertoire. In structural sense, the broadcasting media laid the foundation for all later forms of new media. For that reason, an investigation of the "natural" marriage between advertising and television and the social and historical conditions that made such marriage will not only help us understand the essence of advertising as a social force, but also constitute a necessary prerequisite for the understanding of the communication process under the new media context. To that end, a historical perspective is essential, and we need to go back in time.

A look into the early history of US broadcasting industry, whose model dominates the world today, may shake the ground for this taken-for-granted perception of the relation between television and advertising, and of the often mystified role of government intervention in the world of liberal democracy. Two case studies may be quite illuminating about radio broadcasting – the broadcasting medium that provided all structural fundamentals for television. Ever since the commodification of the airwave in the radio age, not much has changed to the basic model of broadcasting, even in the age of "new media" today.

In "Selling the Air," Streeter (1996) describes the historical development of the US broadcasting system, arguing that the establishment of commercial broadcasting is not a natural result of economic or technological necessity; rather, it was created by a series of government policies that favored large corporations and eliminated the non-profit broadcasters out of the stage. In exploring the underlying logic of the regulatory agencies at the early stages of radio broadcasting, Streeter adopts the notion of "corporate liberalism" to illuminate that it was the corporate liberal philosophy that led the government agencies towards a pro-corporation stance and the regulations thereafter.

In examining Radio Acts of 1912 and 1927, and the Communication Act of 1934, which constitute the defining moments in the broadcasting history in America, Streeter finds that two concepts stand out as the guiding principles for government intervention in the early years of broadcasting – public interest, and technological necessity.

Contrary to the current popular perceptions, the structural model of radio (and television) broadcasting is everything but a market decision. Advertising was seen as a completely absurd idea in the early years of broadcasting. For the government and the Navy, it was a technology that has to do with national

---

8   "Internet advertising around the world will exceed that on television in 2017, earlier than expected http://tech.qq.com/a/20160321/049907.htm.

security and therefore had to be monopolized. The only problem is: who is going to hold the monopoly, government, or large corporations? For Streeter, the 1912 Act is crucial in the history of broadcasting in many aspects, the most important of which is that it established the privilege of large corporations in the access to the spectrum. The act was a legal effort to bring air spectrum under the control of the Navy and the commercial operators (Marconi Company mainly) (Streeter, 1996, p. 78). It was not the cooperation between the government and the private, but between the government and a specific portion of the private sector. Amateurs, radio hobbyists, small entrepreneurs, and non-profit operators, are "banished to a spectrum wasteland" if not eliminated completely.

The 1912 Act and the official interpretation of it also implied the beginning of a new ideology: the ideology of "public interest" and "technological necessity," as different from the ideas of classical liberalism such as "individualism," "rights," and "free enterprises." The government intervention is entirely based on a discourse of "airwave crisis," or "spectrum chaos," which legitimized the regulation as neutral and the monopoly as a technological necessity. Apparently, in the 1912 Act, large corporations (Marconi Company in particular) were not considered as "individuals," but rather an entity which, like the government, is capable of fulfilling the task of serving the public interests, and therefore is trustworthy to be granted privileges in the access to spectrum. The distinction between corporations and individuals, between large corporations and small ones, is confusing. It set up no criteria as to define which corporation would best serve the "liberal goal."

19

The 1912 Act stipulated that broadcasters must have a license in order to operate legally, but said nothing about the rejection of an applicant of license, which means anyone could obtain a license. With the booming of radio broadcasting in the early 20s, the licensing system of the 1912 Act needed to be revised to solve the problem of interference among broadcasters. Big corporations, for obvious reasons, desired to cut the number of stations and obtained a monopoly status in the new industry.

Under such a circumstance, the 1927 Act repeated the discourse of public interest and technological necessity, and confirmed the commercial practices in radio broadcasting and the ideological legitimization since the 1912 Act. The only difference lies in the fact that radio was no longer just a means of point to point communication, but was now becoming a broadcasting service which could reach numerous ends at the same time.

The most significant part of the 1927 Radio Act was the non-ownership clause, which intended "to maintain the control of the United States over all the channels of radio transmission; and to provide for the use of such channels, but not the ownership thereof, by individuals, firms, or corporations... no such license shall be construed to create any right, beyond the terms, conditions, and periods of the license" (Streeter, 1996, p. 97). That is to say, broadcasters used the channels to serve the public interest, but had no right to own them.

Two major problems existed in this clause. First, the term public interest had never been defined, and the government agencies assumed that the licensees would have control of what they transmit through the air. However, when it comes to the fact that direct advertising on radio brought about huge profit for broadcasters, there is a tendency to make a connection between commercial interests and public interests even though the majority of the public was fervently against advertising on radio. Under the name of technological necessity, the 1927 Act reaffirmed the principle that commercial broadcasters better serve the public interests by assigning clear channels to big broadcasting companies, and thus marginalizing the non-profit broadcasters.

Another more crucial contradiction became obvious when the ownership clause is connected with the licensing policy. Although broadcasters could only use the spectrum but not own it, they could actually sell their licenses. Since the 1927 Act closed the application for new licenses, the only way to have license is to buy a broadcast station, and hence the license. The consequence of this practice is that licenses started to have an exchange value. Technically, this exchange value cannot be separated from the airwave. It subtly changed the meaning of both the license and the spectrum. A license started to obtain property features, and so did the spectrum—the commodification of license to use the spectrum gave the spectrum itself a property feature which could be bought, sold, and finally, owned by a private party.

According to Streeter, the 1927 Act finalized the ideological take over of American broadcasting. The following years were merely the refinement of the discourse of public interests and technological necessity. As a landmark in broadcasting history, it created the ideological and subsequently the material condition for advertising through broadcasting media. Once established, the commercial ideology became self-prophetical: indeed, advertising was self interest rather than public interest, but it was inevitable since broadcasting wouldn't survive without it. And since commercial broadcasting was doing so well, it certainly was the only natural way for radio broadcasting.

However, the broadcasting policies and their consequences in Streeter's description were not as consistent as he believes to be. For example, the 1912 Act, as Streeter points out, established a government-corporate monopoly. However, the absence of rejection to license applicants and the so called "spectrum chaos" before 1927 accidently created an "open" market for radio broadcasting, either commercial or non-profit, and it to some extent implies that the foundation for the monopoly of commercial broadcasting, if any, was far from being solid.

The same problem exists in his analysis of the 1927 Act. Despite Streeter's insistence on having the 1927 Radio Act as the watershed for the establishment of an advertising supported broadcasting system which was accepted as the only possible system after the 1927 Radio Act, commercial broadcasting up to this point, however, was far from being homogenizing. The major source of revenue for radio companies did not come from advertising, but from selling radio sets. Not until 1923 did the first weekly advertiser appear on WEAF (Head, et al., 2001, p. 31), and it took many years of struggle after that for blatant advertising to become an "acceptable" practice (McChesney, 1993).

In McChesney (1993), the 1927 Radio Act as a watershed event assumes completely different features from the one in Streeter's description. His argument is that the commercial broadcasting in the US did not appear until after the Radio Act in 1927, therefore the 1927 Act was actually not the end, but the starting point of public debate over regulation. Two things support this argument. First, "the unprofitable status of broadcasting was emphasized by the FRC and the networks themselves as late as 1928 and 1929," when "only 4.3 percent of the stations in the U.S. were characterized as being 'commercial broadcasters" (p. 15). Second, rather than the consistent support for commercial broadcasting as in Streeter, the context before the 1927 Act was a strong opposition against direct advertising on radio. In fact, the regulation and the frequency reallocation that legitimized the advertising supported broadcasting did not come until the General Order 40 in 1928. It certainly could be argued that the pro-corporate tendency existed before 1927 (how could it be otherwise?), but the significance of McChesney's distinction is that it highlights the clearly felt uncertainty as well as the controversy in the field of radio broadcasting in terms of its operation. The resentment against advertising and the debate over regulation illuminates the process in which public opinions were neglected and commercial broadcasting was favored over non-profit broadcasting for the sake of the interests of a specific private sector of the society.

For McChesney, there was a consistent contradiction between commercial broadcasting and non-profit broadcasting. The 1927 Act created a temporary FRC to allocate licenses under the principle of the public interest, convenience and necessity. The FRC, however, simply "attempted to accommodated the existing 733 stations through the sharing of the ninety frequencies" (McChesney, 1993, p. 20), which means large corporations with more powerful equipment would be in a privileged position within the existing system. Besides, most of the stations set aside for clear channels were licensed to NBC affiliates. In Streeter, this is the product of an established order, which already dominated before 1927. McChesney, however, considered it to be the very beginning of a battle in which there were distinctive winners and losers. In this sense, there is no "liberal consensus" over such concept as the "public interest" around 1927. Instead, the debate was all about public interests, which focused on specific problems of direct advertising on commercial broadcasting, and the survival of non-profit broadcasting. The real consolidation, according to McChesney, began in 1928, when the FRC, questioned for its first year performance, generated a permanent plan of spectrum reallocation and put it into effect in 1928. It was this reallocation that started to generate the so called "status quo" of commercial broadcasting. This status quo, however, was not established through consensus – but rather, as McChesney implies, through the small pro-corporate group of FRC members who had no idea of protecting the "public interest" from the selfish goals of the commercial broadcasters (McChesney, 1993, Chapter 2). Again, the commercial interests were conflated with public interests, and the whole process of regulation was (re)presented as a neutral and technological procedure so as to legitimize the expansion of commercial broadcasting. Unlike Streeter, McChesney suggested that the ideological closure, as well as the burgeoning of radio as an advertising medium (p. 34), did not come until after the Communication Act of 1934, when the issue of non-profit vs. commercial broadcasting, and of regulation on commercial broadcasting was finally removed from "the range of legitimate topics that could be addressed by Congress and the public in subsequent years" (p. 188). Short lived and one sided as it was, the battle over public broadcasting in the U.S. clearly demonstrated an undeniable fact – the "market" that we know never exists without government intervention, and "free" market is nothing but the expression of the post-intervention "status quo."

The implication and relevance of this rather lengthy summary of early broadcasting history in the U.S. is not very hard to articulate. When technology made its existence possible, the new form of broadcasting—television—completely adopted the existing system of radio broadcasting, i.e., advertising as the only natural way of funding. As US historian of radio and television boradcasting Erik Barnouw has noted, in the brief period between 1928 and 1933, "almost all forms of enterprise that would dominate radio and television in decades to come had taken shape" (in McChesney, 1993, p. 30). This is also the reason why this early history of broadcasting is of tremendous significance to the studies of the "new media" today.

Let us not forget about the focus of this project. This not so "natural" history of the commercial broadcasting in the U.S. tells more if we turn our attention to the Chinese context. After about two decades of struggle, by mid 1930s, i.e., after the 1934 Act of Communication, radio in the U.S. became an advertising medium, and consensus was reached at least within FRC that "Without advertising, broadcasting would not exist" (McChesney, 1993, p. 27). This should sound very familiar to the audience of Chinese television. Despite all the differences (cultural, economic, and political), the two decades of reform and Opening-up in China since 1978 generated some expressions that echo in a verbatim way what was said in the 1930's America (I will come to this in Chapter 7). Under the circumstance that a commercial system of broadcasting is being established and consolidated, we can observe an interesting consistency and continuity between the neo-liberal discourse today and that of "corporate liberalism" in Streeter's investigation.

Other than what is already known as mentioned above, this revisiting of early broadcasting history reveals some not so obvious problems with "critical" scholars in the political economy of communication. I would call them the problems of idealism – not in the sense that conservatives use to call the "unrealistic" radicals, but in the sense that Marx use to describe those who refuse to come to terms with the concrete material conditions of social consciousness, even though many claim to take a Marxist/materialist perspective in studying communication and media.

In Streeter (1996) for example, the theoretical foundation for the whole discussion on early broadcasting is the concept of "liberalism." American broadcasting, according to Streeter, can only be explained as the outcome of this "nearly century-long, deliberate social and political effort to put the liberal principles of the marketplace and private property into practice in the field of electronic mass communication" (p. 26). Unlike the traditional liberalism that emphasizes individualism, Streeter argues that this liberalism as is seen in the early history of broadcasting, was not formalist, but functionalist – "there was little talk on absolute rights, property and contract," and "radio was not a realm of autonomous individuals, it was a system that if properly organized could fulfill beneficial social functions such as public safety, the national interest, and the furtherance of technological and economic progress" (p. 79). Streeter calls this system "corporate liberalism." It involves a "hierarchical distribution of power" and an "alliance of corporate and government elites," which are necessary for the construction of corporate America.

There is nothing wrong with it. The question is, then what?

Streeter points out the for-profit nature of corporate liberalism in the choice of large corporations as better serving the public interest, thus equating public interests to commercial interests. In doing so, he seems to insist that the decision makers, the regulators, and consequently the policy itself, had a sincere goal of serving the public interest, and of solving the tension between the individual rights of free enterprises and the social good of corporate monopoly.

The root of this problem is the idealist turn—the replacement in his theoretical framework of the Marxist notion of "bourgeois consciousness" with "liberalism" (or corporate liberalism as its updated version in the 20th century). The reasons for such replacement are rather bewildering—that the word "bourgeois" implies the base/superstructure model, and "create a distance between its user and the values being critiqued" (p. 27). Liberalism, in contrast, is a term that helps maintain the awareness that "one works from within culture, not outside it" (p. 27). Streeter did not give up the analysis of material conditions from which ideas emerge. In fact, his entire book is about concrete social conditions in which corporate America and commercial broadcasting are constructed. However, attributing all those specificities ultimately to a "cultural" idea of "liberalism" compromises the most insightful idea that he has had in the book: that the corporate America is a "political, not just economic, achievement" (p. 39). Now, the only explanation that is available for all those self-contradictions in the Radio Acts regarding property, ownership, and the public interest, is that they represent the conflict between "liberalism in practice" and "liberal aspirations" (p. 27).

23

Apparently, McChesney does not believe that corporate and government elites are by any means sincere about protecting the "public interest," but he is subject to the same "idealist" problem as Streeter is. In McChesney, "democracy" is the end rather than a tool. The universalist moral claim of democracy, however, is not intended to deal with the real condition that made possible the corporate media system. The structural change in the media system, or the democratization of media in the U.S. is supported, discursively, by what Rey Chow (2002) calls a concomitant culture of protest, which, in the case of McChesney's approach to the media system, is perceived to be achieved within the realm of communication through following a "democratic" procedure to bring about an "alternative" media system (see McChesney 1993, 1999). Ironically, all the promises about examining the social material conditions in which the corporate media system has been constructed end up with missing the most obvious one. As Drinot Silva (1973, in Jenus 1980) points out, the interdependency between the media and their advertising sources is determined by their existence within the capitalist economy. Jenus (1980) sums it up quite well – "the mass media only fulfill their function for the capitalist mode of production in so far as they make advertising viable" (p. 33).

Here is the problem with many "critical" scholars—by reducing both the economic act of advertising and the political act of the creation of market to the idealist notion of "liberalism," or "democracy," the terms of political economy are used in a way that completely ignore the root, condition and goal of those terms. Starting as a critique within the parameters of political economy, many end up with avoiding the real political agenda of political economy. The conclusion to bring media back to its position of vanguard of democratic participation is based on the assumption that a capitalist mode of production is able to generate a not-for-profit media system, which is structurally different from the existing one. It is a political economy without the political – a pious discourse without piety. The idea of the "political" simply means government intervention through policy making. Many, like Streeter and McChesney, begin with institutional/policy/political economy, and end up with the idealist notion of liberalism or universalist moral claim.

2.2.2 Further Critique: Television, Advertisers, and Audience

While some scholars in the political economy of communication take off to examine the political aspect of media but end up as being non-political, others return to the traditional Marxist economic terms and turn out to be more conscious of the political agenda of Marxist political economy. In these scholars, the political economy of communication constitutes an effort to break with the "consumer model" of communication, which, despite a wide range of different focuses, is essentially a message-centered approach (See Jhally, 1990, p. 68).

Garnham (1979, p. 145) points out that Marxist analysis of the content of mass media looks at its subject as purely ideological, as part of the superstructure, and therefore not subject to a political economy analysis. Such a narrow focus makes it difficult to truly understand the dynamics of cultural spheres. He argues that the latest development of capitalism—the commodification of culture—has increasingly drawn communication into the realm of commodity production and therefore one must examine it as it is—a realm where capital reproduces itself, a subject of political economy.

Smythe (1977; 1980) argues that the realm of communication constitutes a blind spot of Marxist political economy. His political economy of communication and media begins with the commercial context in which television's reality is represented, and he pushes the envelope of what can be studied in political economy by introducing the idea that mass media produce audiences as commodities for sale to advertisers, and the audience labor for advertisers to assure the distribution and consumption of commodities in general. This is perhaps the most important development in the political economy of mass communication, in that Smythe corrects the taken for granted notion that television network sell programs to make profit by pointing out that transactions take place between advertisers and networks, and the commodity in exchange is not the message (program), but the audience. Furthermore, the time when the audience watches commercials is in fact not a leisure time, but the time when they are at work.

These perspectives has led to a breakthrough in the political economy of communication in that they made it possible to look at media programs as commodities with both use value (meaning) and exchange value. Particularly, the exchange value of the media content sheds light on its role in the chain of production. The network uses the program to get the audience to work for the advertisers. We are getting closer to the truly exploitative nature of mass media within a capitalist mode of production.

This, according to Sut Jhally, is to move beyond the message centered approach towards an audience centered approach. What he means is that focusing on messages misses the real creator of value in the process of advertising on broadcasting media such as television. This exchange value of program (and the audience) is something that the media industry has long recognized. As early as the 1920s, CBS president William Paley paved the way for the evolution of the broadcasting industry by making the decision to give "free" (un-sponsored, or non-advertising supported) programs to CBS affiliates, in exchange for a guaranteed coast to coast audience for the advertiser of a sponsored program that CBS provided to its affiliates (see Jhally, 1990, pp. 69-71).

Inspiring as they are, Garnham and Smythe's conceptualizations remain ambiguous, and therefore insufficient, on a few important aspects that must be theorized with lucidity.

First, for whom does the audience work? Smythe's answer is the advertiser, that the audience is engaged in an act of self-marketing of commodities in general. If this is the case, then Smythe is simply falling back to the orthodox Marxists who would insist that all surplus value of a commodity – for example, a pair of shoes – is produced by factory workers, which is realized by consumers at the time of buying. Advertising only functions to reduce the cost by speeding up circulation, and there is nothing to explain about the audience in the whole process. The labor of the audience, as Smythe calls it, is then nothing but a nominal thing, a labor that does not produce any value. Such a self negation is obviously far from satisfactory.

Secondly, in Smythe, the audience is at the same time a commodity sold by mass media to advertisers and the producer of this commodity. This dual identity of the audience, i.e., as both a commodity and its producer, has its root in Marxian political economy, and is by no means insignificant, although such significance was not picked up by Smythe himself. I will come back soon to this point. Questions remain as about which particular aspect of the audience is being sold to advertisers as a commodity. It is undoubtedly worth further exploration.

Jhally (1990) addresses these two questions in a rather forcible way. Picking it up from where Smythe left off—the use value of messages (the content of television programs) conditioned, contextualized by their exchange-value – he argues that it is the audience's watching time that is sold to advertisers as a commodity. It follows that in their watching, the audience turns the commercial time into labor time. What they produce is their watching time as a commodity. Program time is therefore the compensation for the audience labor, i.e., their wage. As labor, the audience watching can be subject to the same Marxian analysis of the production of value that equals the production and purchase cost of programs, and most importantly, surplus value that amounts to the profit of network broadcasters, both paid by advertisers. It must be remembered, Jhally reminds us, that this watching as labor is not meant to be a metaphor. Watching commercials on television is in every sense an extension of factory labor, thus must be understood in its concrete and existential way (pp. 71-90).

Jhally partially solves the ambiguity in Smythe's analysis. That is, it is not the audience per se, but rather their "objective watching time" that is produced as a commodity and sold to advertisers. In such process, the audience is working for the media network which compensates them with programs as the wage for their labor.

This is undoubtedly illuminating, but the first question, i.e., the one raised by orthodox Marxists, is only partially answered. Does the audience really produce surplus value through their watching? Is it true, as Lebowitz (in Jhally, 1990, p. 115-117) (and even Smythe, if pushed far enough with his own logic) would argue, that there is no mystery in the audience watching since they participate through the act of buying? Is the cost of advertising nothing but a cost of speeding up the process of circulation and reducing the cost of production?

Do industrial workers indeed produce all surplus value of a commodity, and is there indeed nothing happening and therefore nothing to explain in the watching behavior of the audience? Jhally did not offer a direct argumentative response to the critiques of this kind, but rather used them to highlight his own approach (p. 119). He does, however, end with a hint that "human activity (watching) as a power" is missing in the critique of orthodox Marxists.

I will return to this point and try to answer the question posed by orthodox Marxist in Chapter 7. Here I wish to conclude this section by pointing out that subjecting advertising to the analysis of political economy should not be confined within either the level of superstructure (as in Garnham's critique of some Marxist view of media content), or the level of economic base for the sake of analytical convenience. In the Chinese context, easily observable is the synchronizing development of the television industry and advertising on television, the transformation of a propaganda machine into a commercial monster, and the perceived struggle between the marketplace discourse and the political control. All these makes a simple cut between the base and superstructure superficial and non-productive. The very idea of political economy stipulates that we stick to the political in analyzing an economic act. To that end, I will bring ideology back to the political economy of communication, and by doing so, bring the concept of "political" back to political economy.

2.3 Thinking about Advertising: The "Rediscovery" of Ideology

Two things remain to be clarified. First, studies in the area of political economy often end up with critique of the corporate influence on the content of media. Even though effort has been spent to point out the non-overt influence, the function of media as an ideological apparatus is not clear in a theoretically rigorous way. This is even more prominent in the study of advertising as both a discourse and an institution. Second, it has been repeatedly emphasized that the base/superstructure model is insufficient in understanding media, but the subsequent critique is even less illuminating than where it begins, with either a simple list of policies (government intervention) or the idealist turn to universal moral claim.

So far it appears that more insights have come from the literature in the political economy of communication that focuses mainly on the "economic" aspect in bringing media into the realm of production and examine it from a materialist perspective. Those who claimed to focus on the political aspect often turn out to be rather ambiguous or self contradictory in terms of their political agenda. Now I am going to present a theoretical framework that enable me to look at it from the political aspect, on the basis of reflections upon the Marxian proposition of relations between base and superstructure. A critical perspective will be gained in understanding the relations between objects and subjects through exploring the idea of determination (Marx), hegemony (Gramsci), Ideological State Apparatuses (Althusser), and politics of Culture (Williams). In the meantime, I am sure that the social changes in contemporary China will provide a good case to add new insights into an old proposition.

2.3.1 Marx: The Issue of Determination

For Marx himself, the civil society is the real basis of the state and the social basis of the human being cannot be overemphasized (see *On the Jewish
Question*, in Marx, 1964, pp. 1-41). The Marxian approach to ideology takes
as its departure point the "real" premises, namely, men, not in any fantastic
isolation and rigidity, but in their actual, empirically perceptible process of
development under definite conditions. The production of ideas, conceptions,
and consciousness is thus directly interwoven with the material activity of men
and their interaction (Marx, 1970, pp. 48-49). "It is not the consciousness of
men that determines their being, but on the contrary their social being that determines their consciousness" (Marx, 1996, p. 160). Under such a perspective,
neither thoughts nor discourses in themselves form a realm of their own, they
are only manifestations of actual life, in which all struggles within the state are
"illusionary forms" of class struggle. Marx (1996) expresses it most clearly in
the *Preface to A Contribution to the Critique of Political Economy*:

> In the social production of their lives men enter into relations that are
> specific, necessary and independent of their will, relations of production
> which correspond to a specific stage of development of their material
> productive forces. The totality of these relations of production forms the
> economic structure of society, the real basis from which rises a legal and
> political superstructure, and to which correspond specific forms of social
> consciousness. The mode of production of material life conditions the
> social, political and intellectual life-process generally. It is not the consci-
> ousness of men that specifies their being, but on the contrary their social
> being that specifies their consciousness. (Marx, 1996, p. 159-160)

28

In the present study, the assumption to begin with is quite clear: television
advertising is a domain where the symbolic (expression of social values) and
the material (the existence of an unprecedented amount of material production)
intersect. Therefore, an investigation of television advertising has to come to
terms with the distinction between the symbolic and the material, which might
as well translate into the distinction that Marx makes between the (economic)
base and (ideological or political) superstructure.

Ideology in Marx is taken, at least on certain occasions, as an up-side-down
version of reality, an abstract and false thought and a failure to recognize the
real social conditions of consciousness. The relationship between the base and
the superstructure is described as direct, explicit, and definite: material production and its relations are the real foundation of society, which give birth to
state, legal and political formations, and explain ideology and its corresponding social consciousness. Such is the commonly distributed knowledge about
Marx and his theorization of social structure. Enough has been said about the
deterministic nature of Marxian notion of ideology. Let us look at Marx and his
theory as a whole.

According to Hall, this immediate correspondence between the base and superstructure, has its rhetorical purpose and should not be read independently of its historical and textual context. Nor should it be understood without reference to his more complex works such as *The Eighteenth Brumaire of Louis Bonaparte* or *Capital*, in which the issue of ideology is far more elaborated and far less deterministic. To read Marx as a whole rather than retreating to the "vulgar economism" is particularly important for a study about China. In China, a country established on the basis of and still (rhetorically) sticking to Marxism, talking about Marx or Marxism has gradually become the least fashionable act among ordinary citizens. "Leftism" as a political tendency is now the one that is officially declared dangerous and popularly abandoned. Such a transformation reveals some essential problems regarding the nature and role of ideology. If China has transformed into a state where market economy prevails—the socialist or capitalist nature of which has been an abundantly debated subject—and advertising has become a structuring force for social and cultural life, as I have observed, such a transformation obviously has not been a sheer economic one, not even primarily an economic one in the beginning. The establishment of the so-called "market economy" has required as much ideological shift as economic transition. In the meantime, the very existence of a Communist Party and a dramatically transformed socialist discourse immediately reject any simple conclusions regarding the social structure in China.

Therefore, a discussion of some later theorists is necessary who have discovered that Marx's works, once taken as a whole, provide much more complicated theorization of ideology as reflected in cultural production. Such development in theories of ideology will then constitute a departure point of this study in building up a theoretical framework in analyzing advertising as part of an ideological project and its viewers as collaborators in the production of meaning and is as important as the material production in this study.

2.3.2 Gramsci: Ideology and the Rule by Consent

Let me start by an immediate difference between Gramsci and orthodox Marxism. As some of Marx's works suggest, a revolutionary class obtains political power first in order to represent its interest as the general interest, and this power is an alien force existing outside them, of the origin and goal of which they (i.e., individuals) are ignorant (Marx, 1947, p. 54) and which they cannot control. Gramsci, however, picks up the less obvious and often discarded idea that every new class "achieves its hegemony only on a broader basis than that of the class ruling previously" (Marx, 1947, p. 66). Gramsci's focus on such notions as the civil society and social bloc lead to the theoretical development of hegemony in the sense that it takes place in both political and civil society, and therefore hegemony must be achieved before obtaining political power.

In developing the Marxist notion of hegemony, Gramsci provides us with an understanding of ideology different from the "false consciousness" in orthodox Marxism. In Gramsci (1992), neither economy nor political dominance can be the only determinant of hegemony, rather, they are only factors of it. It's true that to win hegemony there must be a fundamental/ruling class, but this ruling class has to be both leading and dominant (pp. 136-137). As opposed to the "vulgar economism," Gramsci argues that "intellectual" and "moral" leading must exist even before winning government power. Further more, hegemony is not merely an indication of class alliances (as in Leninism), but it "defines the complex nature of the connection between the mass of the people and the leading groups of society: a connection which is not only political in the narrow sense, but also a question of ideas or of consciousness" (Gramsci in Bennett et al, 1991, p. 199).

Hegemony must exist before the winning of political power. That is to say, it must experience a development, a process of formation in which political/coercive power is not the determining aspect. According to Gramsci, this formation is brought about by ideology, which has a much more complex composition than it is commonly perceived. He begins with the notion that "all men are philosophers" and are capable of critical thinking. Philosophy is contained in language, common sense, and folklore. There is equal possibility for people to criticize their own conception of the world, accept new conceptions, and thus add new content to their "common sense" or "popular belief". A particular philosophy, for example, Marxism, would cultivate the common sense of the mass of people and brought about a critical self consciousness, which could be further developed into a unified/collective consciousness. Ideology, in Gramsci, undoubtedly contains political factors that ensure "the relation between common sense and the upper level of philosophy" and consequently, it links the "elite" with the "mass of people" and keep together the leading and the led. Thus, a philosophy becomes dominant by "rearticulating the hegemonic principles" (see Mouffe in Bennett et al., p. 231) of the ideological elements in the common world view. Obviously, ideology is not philosophy, but the philosophy transformed into common sense, which functions to bring about the intellectual and moral hegemony through the disarticulation and rearticulation of hegemonic principles.

Then what does all this have to do with advertising in China or other parts of the world? What concerns the current project is that culture in Gramsci is not subordinate to politics and must change accordingly, rather, it is something as decisive and indispensable as the coercive dominance of the political power. This "utmost importance" of culture and "crucial link" between culture and politics is a radical break away from both the "liberal idealist tradition" in which culture is "apolitical," and the "vulgar materialism" as Gramsci called it, which asserts that culture (and even politics) is a reflection of the economic base of a society. Looking at television advertising in China from this perspective, there must be an awareness of both the restrictions over it in economico-political terms and the autonomy of the commercial culture that it cultivates, so as to understand the struggle for hegemony between different social forces at the discursive dimension. That is to say, one must be reminded that as someone who is constantly referred to by scholars in cultural studies, Gramsci in fact never leaves the terrain of the Marxian proposition regarding social consciousness. It is obvious that in Gramsci, isolating either base or superstructure is a flaw in both theory and practice. His emphasis on culture and rule by consensus is achieved on the basis of the notion that ideas are material forces that do not just appear.

Closely related to the above conclusion is the role of intellectuals who are regarded by Gramsci as "the entire social stratum which exercises an organizational function in the broad sense," and as functionaries of the "center of formation, irradiation, dissemination and persuasion" of ideas. The role of intellectuals is obviously instrumental as the "dominant group's deputies exercising the "subaltern functions of social hegemony and political government" (see Gramsci in Bennett et al, 1991, pp. 210-214). In this sense, the institutional location of intellectuals, i.e., the "educational apparatuses" (see Althusser, 1971), seems indistinguishable from the state in terms that they both "educate" to obtain consent from subordinate classes. Perhaps that's why Gramsci needs to introduce the distinction between "civil society," which constitutes the part that overlaps with the educational apparatuses, and the "political society" to explicate the concept of the state. Such a perception of the relation between state and ideology will be further illuminated by Althusser, to whom I will come in a later section.

This idea that hegemony includes both political dominance and popular consent, and that equilibrium between the civil society and the political society is always temporary, implies the possibility of social change at the intersection of discourse and ideology. Fundamentally, this is a theory of praxis based on the understanding that cultural intervention in civil society is where political action begins and where intellectuals have the opportunity to disarticulate the dominant ideology. Speaking about dominant ideology and civil society, I would like to add that in contemporary China, these two concepts have different appearances. The implications from Gramsci will undoubtedly shed light on the relationship between the "dominant" ideology (the socialist discourse) and the leading "ideology" (the discourse of marketplace) and the role of intellectuals in contemporary China, which will be elaborated in the concluding chapter as an extension of the discussion on advertising and ideology. Besides, the notion that philosophy, and by the same token politics, is contained in language, common sense and folklore leads to the reflection about the construction of a collective consciousness in China since 1978, not only in terms of what is to be mostly valued, but also in regard to the most fundamental question about what is politics and what is political.

2.3.3 Raymond Williams: What is the "Base"?

The theoretical framework for the study of advertising necessarily involves a conceptualization of the positioning of advertising and the related "labor" in the process of advertising within a given socio-economic structure. Raymond Williams is particularly helpful in this respect.

Williams continues the critical reflection on the role of cultural practices, meanings, values, etc., within the context of the much debated issue of "determination" in regard to the Marxian notion of base and superstructure. What Williams tries to do in such works as *Culture and Society* and *The Long Revolution*, is to reevaluate the question of "base" so as to develop a different kind of theory of social totality. He takes the study of culture as the study of relations between elements in a whole way of life, which he relates to Lucas' notion of totality and Gramsci's notion of hegemony. In finding a way to study structure in particular works and periods, he tries to stay in touch with not only particular art-works and forms, but also forms and relations of more general social life.

Williams (1980) finds that the rigid, abstract, and static character of the base-superstructure methodology is weak in its capacity to give precise, detailed, and reasonably adequate accounts of actual consciousness, which is not just a scheme or a generalization but actual works, full of rich and significant and specific experience. First, the word "determines" is of great linguistic and theoretical complexity. Second, ideology in this framework is too weak as a simple reflection of the reality of the base, with the implication of the notion of an external cause which totally predicts or prefigures, indeed totally controls a subsequent activity. Lastly, while certain modifications have been conceived about the superstructure (a. delays in time, i.e. the famous lags, or the distance from the primary economic activities; b. mediation – something radically different from either reflection or reproduction, something more than simple reflection or reproduction actively occurs; homologous structures), the received notion of "base" has not been looked at with equal care, though it is the more important concept (pp. 31-33).

That being said, Williams suggests that we begin not from the proposition of a determining base and a determined superstructure, but from a proposition which originally was equally central, equally authentic, namely, the proposition that social being determines consciousness. This alternative approach to the old question contains a different understanding of all the three constituents of the proposition of orthodox Marxism, with attention shift to a field of mutually if also unevenly determining forces. To that end, Williams (1980) suggests:

> We have to revalue "determination" towards the setting of limits and the exertion of pressure, and away from a predicted, prefigured and controlled content. We have to revalue "superstructure" towards a related range of cultural practices, and away from a reflected, reproduced or specifically dependent content. And, crucially, we have to revalue 'the base' away from the notion of a fixed economic or technological abstraction, and towards the specific activities of men in real social and economic relationships, containing fundamental contractions and variations and therefore always in a state of dynamic process (p. 34).

This proposition of "social being determines social consciousness," which defines the relation between base and superstructure, is more compatible with Lucas' notion of totality as the whole of social practices that interact, relate, and combine in complicated ways. However, we must be cautious here about the danger of such a framework, namely, the complete abandonment of the realm of determination.

Williams solves the problem by sticking to the "intention" contained in the notion of totality, reminding us that "totality" has to be understood in combination with the Gramscian notion of hegemony, which "supposes the existence of something which is truly total" (p. 37). For Williams, hegemony has an advantage over totality, in the sense that the former maintains the facts of domination yet in the meantime avoids the weak sense of ideology as merely some "abstract, imposed set of notions" or the results of manipulation and overt training. That is to say, the framework that Williams adopts is one that looks at the "reality of social experiences" not merely as "secondary" or "superstructural," but rather as something that is lived at great depth, to the extent that it saturates the "consciousness of a society," and constitutes the "substance and limit of common sense for most people under its sway" (p. 37). The point is, intention is essential in the hegemonic process, experienced in the principles of specific structure and organization as the rule of a particular class, only that such a rule has "continually to be renewed, recreated and defended," and by the same token, challenged and modified. So far his understanding of hegemony is in line with Gramsci, but his underlying logic, i.e., the role of intention in hegemony and social totality has something divergent.

Williams is more interested in "historical" questions than "epochal" questions, i.e., more interested in the reciprocity between specific social practices of class nature and the ratifying effects at the ideological level. To achieve that "precise and delicate analysis" of historical process of specific moments of specific phases within capitalist society, Williams returns to the "base" level and extends the notion of productive forces. When base is the center of discussion, Williams argues, it often refers to the primary material production, which has important aspects missing since certain vital and basic productive social forces are too willingly dismissed as superstructure, for example, the process of art and thought (p. 35). This is the moment when Williams has to split a social totality into "social experiences" and the "reality" of social experiences, which he refers to social being and social consciousness, respectively.

For many involved in cultural studies and political economy of communication, Williams' works reflect, and to some degree has paved the way for, an effort to incorporate what Marx calls "non-productive" labor into the circuit of production. Quite obviously, as a Marxist, Williams is struggling with Marx's idea (p. 35) that artists and writers are not productive workers. What he does to keep himself within the Marxist framework is to revise that framework, temporarily abandon the degenerate form of base/superstructure proposition, and then broaden the concept of base to include the process of art and thought.

After that, he returns to the base and superstructure proposition, re-emphasizing the Marxian idea that certain kinds of ratifying theory, law, institutions, are very much part of the superstructure.

The problem is, if we extend the realm of base to include such social practices as thinking, on what basis can we make the distinction between thought and intention? In other words, if intention becomes the defining moment of determination in the realm of superstructure, as Williams suggests, on what basis do we NOT include practices within law and educational institutions – both considered to be superstructural so far—in the "base" as well? Ultimately, is there going to be a clear distinction at all?

Apparently, Williams' re-evaluation of base and superstructure bears visible influence on later scholars like Stuart Hall, as could be seen in the encoding/decoding model with the idea of determination defined as setting limits and exerting pressure. In empirical studies, the emphasis on intention in Williams is at the risk of missing the full range of meaning that audiences may produce out of advertising images. However, the notion of intention may lead to some interesting findings in the Chinese context. Even though it does not help explain the different appearances between dominant and leading ideology in China, his framework of analysis does provide a perspective to engage with questions regarding the relation between the intention of individuals, particularly that of the "organic intellectuals," and the intention of the state or the superstructural institutions within the state. In contemporary China, the intentions at both the individual and state level have been both explicitly articulated and contradicted by the existence of advertising. I will elaborate on this in Chapter 8. Now let us move on to a few concepts of ideology that will be crucial for later analysis.

2.3.4 Althusser: Ideology, Overdetermination, and Articulation

(1) Ideology and Ideological State Apparatuses

Althusser's development of Marx's notion of ideology should be located in a rather special intellectual context which, according to Hall, is marked by a "shift from the 'mainstream' to critical perspectives in terms of the movement from, essentially, a behavioral to an ideological perspective" (Hall, 1982, in Gurevitch et al). Hall's summary of this transition highlighted for us a connection between the philosophical development and the paradigm building for practical research in communications studies. Such development leads us to a better understanding of such terms as "mass society" or "mass media," which in turn feeds into the underlying assumptions of studies of advertising and its audience.

Althusser's central points constitute a structuralist twist of the Marxist notion of social formation through the reconceptualization of the following: the nature of ideology as imaginary, the distinction between state power and state apparatuses, and furthermore, between the Repressive State Apparatuses and the Ideological State Apparatuses, ideology in relation to the social totality, and the structure of totality as such.

Marx is often perceived as theorizing ideology (e.g., in *The German Ideology*) as an imaginary representation of the world, something like a pure dream, "a set of ideas and representations which dominates the mind of a man or social group" (Althusser, 2001, p. 108). Althusser discards this perception of Marxian theory of ideology for the reason that it is not "Marxist" due to its positivist orientation. Instead, he took the hints from *Capital* and developed a schematic outline for a genuine Marxist theory of ideology in general.

Althusser (2001) points out that instead of the *representation of the real world*, ideology is the *representation of the relation with the real world*, to be exact, with the conditions of existence in that world; and this relation is basically an imaginary one, which explains "all the imaginary distortion that we observe in all ideology" (pp. 109-112, emphasis added) This ideology in Althusser is an abstract term referring to a "non-historical reality," or an "omni-historical reality," with "immutable structure and functioning present in the same form throughout what we call history." In contrast with this "ideology in general" which has no history, are ideologies, which could be understood as the specific representation of the "ideology in general" at a particular time in history, and which, of course has a history of itself as well as a material existence (pp. 107-109). This history and material existence of "ideologies" is made possible by its connection with what Althusser calls the Ideological State Apparatuses (the ISAs)

Althusser restructures the superstructure in Marx's social theory. In Marx, every society is constituted by infrastructure (or economic base) and super-structure, the latter of which contains two levels: the political-legal (law and state) and ideology. For Althusser, all these are but integral parts of the state. The state in Marx actually refers to the state apparatuses, the concrete insti-tutions that realize the function of state power. Althusser distinguishes state power from state apparatuses, and conceived that the state (apparatus) exists as the function of state power. Within the state apparatuses there is another dis-tinction between the Repressive State Apparatuses (RSAs) and the Ideological State Apparatuses (ISAs). The later was defined as "a certain number of reali-ties . . . in the form of distinct and specialized institutions" (p. 96). The list of ISAs given by Althusser includes religious ISA, educational ISA, family ISA, Legal ISA, Political ISA, trade union ISA, communication ISA, cultural ISA, etc. The function of state apparatuses is operated through the interplay between RSAs and ISAs. There is no pure RSA or ISA, only RSAs "massively and dominantly function by repression" and "secondarily by ideology," while the ISAs function "massively and dominantly by ideology," and "secondarily by repression" (pp. 96-98).

Such a conceptualization of the structure of state is insightful when applied to activities at socio-economic level. On the one hand, the ISAs are crucial for the reproduction of the conditions of production, i.e., the reproduction of the productive forces and the existing relations of production. On the other hand, hegemony in Althusser contains two levels. First of all, political hegemony is ensured by the RSAs, and constitutes the political condition for both the reproduction of the relations of production and the actions of the ISAs. Secondly, ideological hegemony is brought about by the ISAs, and makes possible the most essential precondition of the reproduction of labor power – the "submission of the labour to the rules of the labour order," which, in technical terms, is "the ruling ideology of the workers." Althusser further points out that it was the "intermediation of the ruling ideology that ensures a (sometimes teeth-gritting) harmony between the RSAs and the ISAs and between the different State Ideological Apparatuses (Althusser, 2001, pp. 100-102).

One of the consequences of such a theory of ideology is the radical break from the often taken for granted distinction between the public and the private. While Repressive State Apparatuses are unified and belong entirely to the public domain, the Ideological State Apparatuses are divided into categories that belong to either the public or the private domain. In this aspect, Althusser echoes Gramsci in that State inevitably includes part of the civil society, such as churches, schools, labor unions, families, cultural ventures, etc. However, the distinction between the public and the private is of little relevance since the very distinction is preconditioned by the State, which is above the law and by the same token above the distinction between the public and private.

Therefore, Althusser concludes, for institutions that belong to the Ideological State Apparatuses, what matters is not whether they are public or private, but how they function. "Private institutions can perfectly function as Ideological State Apparatuses" (p. 144). This notion will be crucial for later analysis in this study for the clarification it provides within the Chinese context in terms of the unity between the private and the public, the corporate and the state, the market and the government.

(2) Determination and Overdetermination: The Structuralist Turn

That being said, let us move on to the role of ideology in relation to the social totality. In Althusser, any social formation is complex and cannot be reduced to the simple correspondence between base and superstructure. It is certainly not a simple multiplicity of causalities either. Here Marx becomes a structuralist in Althusser through a "basic rupture" with a "radical beginning" and "actual end" to any real history. This is possible, Althusser suggests, only because Marxist dialectic is not a simple reversion of Hegelian dialectic (from standing on one's head to standing on one's feet), which is based on a simple determination that is the very foundation of vulgar economism. To set us free from the Hegelian ideology, i.e., a simple internal principle which is the "essence of any historical period," there has to be a restructuration of the dialectic of contradiction within the framework of determination.

According to Althusser (1970), the distinction between Marx's dialectic and the Hegelian one is structural. First, Marx uses the terms of civil society and state in a completely different way from Hegel. In Marx's civil society, individual economic activities are contextualized by the mode of production. This is the moment when the concept of social formation enters the terrain of determinacy (pp. 109-110). State, too, assumes different meaning in Marx in that it is no longer the reality/phenomenon of ideas, but the instrument of enforcing the ruling ideas of the ruling class, which is directly related to the relations of production. Secondly, the connections between these terms are different. This is the place where Althusser spends much effort to argue against the Hegelian formula of "phenomenon-essence-truth of" as an internal principle. The relation between civil society and state, and similarly, between the economic and the political, is not that between essence and phenomenon, but between "determinant instances in the structure-superstructure complex which constitutes the essence of any social formation" (p. 111). Here, determination assumes different dimensions of meaning.

Althusser (1970) believes that Marx has given us two ends of the chain, i.e., the mode of production and the superstructures, and we need to find out what goes on in between (Althusser, p. 111). Using Lenin's analysis of the Russian revolution as an example, Althusser points out that the general contradiction within the economic (between the forces of production and the relations of production) is sufficient to define the situation when revolution is the task of the day. However, it does not guarantee the coming of the revolution, which presupposes not only the fusion of two "basic conditions," but also the fusion of an accumulation of determinations in each of the antagonistic groups (pp. 97-101). It follows that the basic contradiction dominates in all the contradictions, but different contradictions and instances are not merely its phenomena, but have their relative autonomy, essence, and effectivity. The general contradiction also has to be located within the total structure of social body. The dialectic here is that the general contradiction is determining those concrete determinations, but in the same moment is determined by them – by the "various levels and instances of social formations it animates" (p. 101). It is no longer simple determination, but "overdetermination". And this dialectic assumes a different structure, not in the sense of simple inversion, but an interactive relation between base and superstructure (the real world and the world of ideas) determined at multiple levels and instances.

Furthermore, if overdetermination is about differences in a complex unity, then articulation is about how these different contradictions and determinations are connected and thus fulfill the chain of signification. Here we might as well refer back to Hall's idea of articulation. It is quite clear that the concept of articulation is clearly a political one, and one of praxis. The ideology of a class is "articulated" with its socio-economic position in the complex structure of the unity. But again, there is no natural evolution. Ideology has no necessary belongingness, or generic origin in class. Therefore, various social groups and social movements have to struggle to articulate themselves with effective forms of politics and ideology, so as to achieve social changes in its good sense. In other words, articulation is the fulfillment, or specification of overdetermination, and has to be constructed through struggle (in Morley and Chen, 1996, pp. 131-150).

The concept of differences in a complex unity leads other scholars such as Stuart Hall to think about the social formation from a third perspective, namely, neither "necessary correspondence" nor "necessary no correspondence," but "no necessary correspondence." Since the "lonely hour of last instance never comes," and there is no single internal truth that we could comfortably hang on for either understanding the present or predicting the future, we will have to look at the specific connections between ideology and social forces, and recognize how they are determined at specific historical moments.

Here lies the fundamental stance of the present study. First, the idea that ideology is constitutive of what it seeks to mediate constitutes a truly paradigmatic difference from the omnipresent hypodermic model, which has been critiqued in the entire literature of media studies yet somehow was implicitly dominating the vast majority of such literature. Secondly, this project is a practice of cultural intervention on the basis of theorizing advertising and ideology. In Gramsci's term, an "organic intellectual" is one of practice. The notion of "no necessary correspondence" and the essential role of practice in articulation lead us to Hall's idea of "double articulation," i.e., the dialectic relationship between structure and practice, that previous practices result in the present structure, which sets limits to the present practices, but is in turn subject to potential changes by the present practices which are effectively articulated to new elements of ideology.

One last note in the end of this chapter is that whatever advertising is trying to do, it will be completed on the part of individual audience in their everyday life. For a comprehensive study on Chinese television advertising, it is worthwhile to follow with a discussion on the relations between commercial messages and their target audience, especially when audience research rarely deals with the audience of television advertising. However, having no intention to focus primarily on the audience in the present study, I will deal with literature on audience during the discussion of audience when necessary. Also, with the scarcity of sources on this topic, I will relate literature on audience research in general to my previous study of audience perception of television commercials and their consumption behavior, so as to shed light on the identity of the audience and relations between advertising and the new social order in China.

In the following chapters, I will, on the basis of the theoretical framework formulated in this chapter, present a thorough examination of Chinese television as a whole, with careful analysis of its media environment, institutions and policies, contents, audience, and political economy, respectively, with a political reading of these aspects as a conclusion.

Chapter 3. Media Environment of Advertising: The Structural Transformation of Chinese Television

The most noticeable thing regarding the Chinese television broadcasting system in the short history of the past four decades or so is the decline of public service broadcasting and the dramatic growth of commercialization (note: the distinction needs to be clear – the decline has happened to public service broadcasting, though not necessarily to those for Party propaganda). Not surprisingly, this coincides with the overall pattern of development that China has been undergoing, namely, the emergence of the so called "socialist politics" and "capitalist economy." Such a dichotomization, however, may not lead to an accurate understanding of contemporary Chinese society. In the case of Chinese TV broadcasting, from the very beginning of its short history since the 1950s (or 1980s, when it really started to flourish), it has been undergoing constant changes in a complex, often self contradictory system, with its structure reshaped and its functions redefined.

In this chapter, I will document the changes in the Chinese television industry, which has coincided with the (re)emergence and rapid growth of advertising. Such changes will be examined in the context of domestic social economic changes as well as global media expansion. This part will lead to an understanding of the structure of Chinese television today, and why it has been shaped this way, thus providing contextual information for the understanding of advertising in general and television advertising in particular.

3.1 Television in China

China's first television station was launched in 1958 as China Central Television, known as CCTV. The development up to the early 1990's brought about a three-tier structure in Chinese television broadcasting. At the top is CCTV, the national broadcaster. It is under the direct administration of the Ministry of Radio, Film and Television, which later evolved into the State Administration of Radio, Film, and Television, or SARFT in short (see State Council of People's Republic of China, 1997, Regulations on Radio and Television Broadcasting), and then State Administration of Press, Publication, Radio, Film and Television. By the turn of the century, or twenty years into the Reform and Opening-up, CCTV was seen to grow rapidly from two channels to a national network of 12 channels, and 15 channels by 2004,[1] all centrally administered, with production separated so that programs are now coming from more and more dispersed and non-centralized sources. The 32 provincial channels, including those from the 5 autonomous regions and 4 municipalities directly under the central government, form the second tier in the system with similar structure to CCTV. They are subject to both regulations of the SAPPRFT[2] and supervision of local authority of propaganda. In the third tier are the local broadcasting stations within provinces.

Traditionally, there are terrestrial stations which transmit broadcasting signals through microwave relays. Since the acceleration of commercialization in the early 1990s, the basic three-tier structure has remained intact in TV broadcasting, but dramatic changes have taken place in the old way of direct microwave transmitting. Beginning in 1985, the initial microwave transmission was gradually replaced by satellite transmission, which was then distributed through cable system in urban areas (first appeared in 1976 and was fully developed in 1990s) and through traditional microwave transmission in rural areas (see Zhao, 1998, p. 173; Hao, 2000), thus forming a national TV system transmitted by satellite and distributed through cable and microwave stations.

The development of satellite (and later cable) in China can be attributed to the speeding up of economic reform and of commercialization. Examination of the television system in China should be illustrative of the state intervention in shaping the commercial broadcasting structure as well as commercialization in general.

Two major reasons pushed the Chinese government to turn to satellite as its primary way of organizing television broadcasting. Geographically, China's formidable terrain and the fact that around 70% of the country is mountainous have made terrestrial transmission of television signals quite uneconomic. For each percentage point increase in television coverage through terrestrial transmission, the cost doubled since the remaining area tended to have more rugged

---

1   In 2013, a high definition channel that focuses exclusively on sports, CCTV 5+, was added to the network.

2   State Administration of Press, Publication, Radio, Film and Television.

terrain (Hao, 2000). By mid 1990s, although China's television audience had grown to 900 million, there were yet about 146 million Chinese living in areas inaccessible to television broadcast (Wang, 1997). Therefore, to overcome the obstacle in linking the country in a more economic and effective way, and to achieve the goal of building up a national communication network for distributing the Party propaganda and unifying leadership, satellite transmitting becomes a more economic and efficient choice.

Another reason for China to switch from microwave to satellite is its great potential to expand the coverage of China's international broadcasts (Hao, 2000). It enables China to publicize itself to a worldwide audience, and serves as a counter measure to the flood-in of global media products. If globalization could be understood as a kind of unequal flow of information, then to some extent, the satellite television broadcasting of China might constitute an effort to break that corporate monopoly of information, with the hope of joining the homogenizing power as an information producer. As a result, by 1993, China had built 54,084 satellite ground reception stations, and by May 1999, all the CCTV and provincial channels were transmitted through satellite, capable of being received and retransmitted by local cable stations. One thing that should be noted is that back in the 1990s, not all those provincial programs were actually getting carried by local cable or microwave channels due to the struggle for advertising revenue. It was not until mid-2000s that all provincial channels were accessed nationwide, even followed by satellite transmission of smaller city channels.

41

While having obvious advantages over exclusive microwave transmission, this new way of organizing broadcasting, however, is not risk free for the state. Primarily, it is because that while enhancing China's ability to reach out to both nationwide and worldwide audience, it also opened, or at least cracked the door open, to global media broadcasting which also transmitted through satellites. For example, in order to have his channels on China's booming television channel listing, in July 1993, Murdoch spent $25 million for a controlling interest of Hong Kong-based STAR TV (Cook, 1994), which was originally controlled by Hong Kong tycoon Li Ka-shing, and was then the largest commercial pan-Asian television system. The Hong Kong based Star TV had a total of five channels, including MTV, sports, news from BBC World Service Television (partially translated into Chinese), family entertainment, and a channel of mandarin programs. Among the 11 million Chinese households that owned satellite dishes at the time being, 45 percent, i.e., 4.8 million households, were capable of receiving STAR TV broadcasting, which transmits from the satellite AsiaSat1, the same satellite which carried three domestic television channels, CCTV-4, Guizhou (provincial) TV, and Yunan (provincial) TV (Zhao, 1998, p. 173).

Almost immediately after the purchase of STAR TV, Murdoch proclaimed in a London speech that "advances in technology of telecommunications have proved an unambiguous threat to totalitarian regimes everywhere" (Zhao,

1998, p. 173). Indeed, STAR TV's Chinese language news program provided by BBC World Services Television constituted a major threat to the Party's control of information. To quote Liu Xiliang, deputy minister of Radio, Film and Television, this news program "contains a lot of distorted reports about China, and it frequently attacks China's domestic and foreign affairs" (in Zhao, 1998, p. 173). The Chinese government was particularly disturbed by the BBC's documentary (aired in Britain) about Mao Zedong on the 100th anniversary of his birth, which included a section on his alleged sexual proclivities. Charging they exert "subtle influence" on viewers, "especially our youth," a widely published government commentary declared that controlling foreign television "is an important measure to exercise and safe guard our national sovereignty" (Cook, 1994).

The threat of direct-to-home satellite broadcasting of transnational media corporations is actually three fold. First, direct satellite broadcasting, which avoids the filtering process by Chinese government gatekeepers, poses a direct challenge to the information control by Chinese authorities (Hao, 2000). Second, as Herman and McChesney (1997) point out, the impact of global media lies to a great extent in the ideology attached to their programming. It is not surprising that there is concern about the educational function of television, and that the values of the Chinese audience may be altered under constant exposure to western programs. As for the Chinese television industry, the threat is fundamentally economic in terms of the impact upon their advertising revenue, especially for CCTV, who has enjoyed so many years of monopoly as the only national broadcasting network.

The impact of the "Murdoch effect" was far more consequential than Murdoch himself had expected. It also had a quite different effect than what Herman and McChesney predicted about global media (See Herman & McChesney, 1996, p.8). Instead of spelling the end of a totalitarian regime through successful penetration of satellite television, it led to a series of subsequent regulations on television broadcasting, which, to a great extent, have shaped the structure of the national television broadcasting system in China today. The first of such regulations came in 1993, shortly after Murdoch's London speech. The Chinese government passed the "State Council Proclamation No. 109," which makes private ownership or installation of a television satellite dish illegal. In a similar way, "Proclamation No. 10" of the Ministry of Radio, Film and Television (SARFT) placed censorship on programs from foreign countries, which could not be aired unless sanctioned by the central or provincial propaganda administration. Satellite programs from outside the country were prohibited to air on television. The law did not ban the satellite dishes owned by organizations, but stated that they must apply for a license. The regulations on cable television in "Proclamation No. 12" (1994) also laid restrictions on broadcasting foreign programs, as well as re-transmitting satellite programs from outside of the country.

In the early 1990s, besides regulations on satellite broadcasting, the Chinese government also looked for other ways to consolidate its control over the newly established national communication network.

Cable originated in Urban China as a closed circuit network within communities to broadcast self-made video programs, and in some cases, pirate Western video movies (Hao, 2000). The Chinese government quickly saw the potential threat of cable stations to its control of information flow in terms of its capability of broadcasting uncensored foreign programs, receiving and directly broadcasting foreign satellite programs, and consequently, competing for advertising revenue with central broadcasting operations (Hao, 2000). This initial recognition led to a reserved attitude to cable television in the beginning. For many years, cable was regarded as the extension of wireless broadcasting which expands wireless broadcasting and ensured the control over the content of national and local broadcasting (see SARFT proclamation, No. 5, 1991). In the 1990 regulation, cable television was defined primarily as a medium of transmitting national and local programs. Self-made programs by private sectors were not allowed.

Similar to the development in satellite broadcasting, the government also looked at cable as both a potential threat and a great opportunity to consolidate its control over the information flow. As Zhou Caifu, cable director of SARFT, said to the press, "cable television is important to the country's radio and television programming, and should be the party's and government's propaganda tool, while entertaining viewers" (Ubios, 1994). And much to its joy, this time the control would be more efficient through cable, for the reason that, unlike foreign satellite transmitting, cable programming could be censored before broadcasting, and more importantly, cable operators are under the jurisdiction of the Chinese government (Hao 2000).

Eventually, the advantages of cable TV have led the Chinese government to speed up the development of cable stations and make the whole country wired up, particularly in urban areas. First, in 1996, SARFT ordered three domestic satellite television broadcasters to switch from AsiaSat 1 to AsiaSat2, from the latter of which foreign companies could transmit only encrypted channels (source: http://www.cctv.net.cn). By 1999, all the CCTV channels and provincial channels were transmitted through AsiaSat 2, which effectively shut off foreign satellite beaming from outside of the border. Then, cable merged with terrestrial TV stations at the local level and thus become the most important means of distribution in the new broadcasting system (see *Variety*, April 3, 2000). Cable subscriptions rose by 10 million annually, and reached 80 million homes by the end of 1999. Total revenue for the entire network reached $2.5 billion in 1999, according to government estimates. The plan of SARFT was to create a Cable Television Network in conjunction with the existing local cable stations, with the goal of eventually reaching all Chinese television households (Liu, 2000).

Finally, the government reaffirmed its ownership of broadcasting industry. Foreign ownership of broadcasting stations, joint ventures and cooperation in broadcasting are all prohibited. Besides, a specific quota was set up for foreign programming on television. The proportion and broadcast time of imported drama is strictly controlled below 15% during the prime time (6:00pm – 10:00pm). In each channel, imported animated programs cannot exceed 25% of all the children's programs, and 40% of all animated programs (The State Council of People's Republic of China, 1997).

Thus a relatively "safe" communication network was established with specific boundaries within which cable stations are allowed to grow to meet the demand of the newly established "socialist market economy," as well as the demand of the new consumer culture.

The economic reform and the rapid commercialization in the late 1990s brought about a decentralization of the economic structure, greater reliance on market forces to guide production, fast growth of joint ventures, foreign companies and imports of consumer products and services, as well as the change in consumption habits and goals (Hong, 1994). Although the above mentioned structural changes in the television industry came as an essential part of the control over the flow of information within the country, they are by no means incompatible with the process of marketization. In fact, the market is the major justification for the development of the present system. Hand in hand, the policies of control and the discourses of the marketplace led to the dramatic expansion of channels at the national, provincial, and municipal level, and the essential role that advertising started to play in the whole structure of television broadcasting.

Up until the first decade of the new millennium, television had been the single most important medium in China in terms of its unprecedented capability of penetration, which is especially true when the rural population (about 858 million out of 1.2 billion) jumped directly into the TV age without experiencing the stage of the popular press due to the lack of access and high rate of illiteracy (see Ubios, 1994). With TV households more than tripling from 1994 (100 million) to 1999 (314 million), television could reach more than 87 percent of the Chinese population and the television audience was as large as 900 million in 1997 (see Wang, 1997). According to the data from the National Bureau of Statistics, up to 2007, television could reach 96.508% of the population (*National Bureau of Statistics*, 1999-2017), namely, an audience of 1.2 billion people. By 2015, television coverage reached 98.77%, with an audience of 1.36 billion.

During the process of commercialization from 1978 to the mid-2000s, CCTV rapidly grew from two channels to a national network of 15 channels. The four decades also witnessed an explosion in the number of stations in all three tiers of TV networks. The total number of television stations nationwide grew from 31 in 1985 to 347 in 1998 (though slightly decreased to 302 in

2005 and 287 in 2007). There were 41252 television transmission stations and relaying stations in 1998, and 47501 in 2005, which was reduced, due to improved efficiency brought about by technological advance, to 27,163 in 2006, 18,249 in 2007, and 14,900 in 2015. The number of employers in broadcasting industry[3] grew to 459,700 in 1998, 671,700 in 2008, and 919,300 in 2016. The number of channels, with the growth of CCTV, provincial and municipal networks, grew from 1,065 in 1998 to 3,198 in 2008, and 3,360 in 2016, with the programming time week growing from 38,065 hours in 1985 to 66,959.6 hours in 1998, 1,495,340 hours in 2008, and 1,792,000 hours in 2016 (*National Bureau of Statistics*, 1999-2017).

During the process of this development, CCTV was the only network that could reach a nationwide audience until the late 1990s when municipal and provincial channels could be transmitted nationwide via satellite. But CCTV has largely maintained that monopoly in most of the country even today due to the viewing habit formed in the past two decades, and consequently, a huge advantage in attracting advertisers. The mandatory carriage of CCTV news program on all local networks, and its access to much more abundant resources for producing programs of higher quality, has enabled it to maintain the highest rating in most of the country (Broadcasting & Cable's TV International, 1999).

The dramatic changes in the Chinese television broadcasting did not take place in a vacuum. They echo other changes at the global level, which are summarized by Harvey (1990) as the conditions (or perhaps we should call them the "symptom") of postmodernity, i.e., the shift of accumulation, intensified commodification, new division of labor, the compression of time and space, etc. Though this is not a discussion of postmodernity, these characteristics will inevitably express themselves in the examination of the socio-economic changes in China.

The development of Chinese television has to great extent been based on its reaction to and interaction with the "global media." Likewise, Chinese television advertising has developed in the context of the entry of global advertising into China. This is inevitable given the inseparable relationship between the Chinese reform and its opening to the outside world. Therefore, rather than an isolated case of local development, it has to be kept in mind that changes in the Chinese media, especially policies regarding the establishment of a national satellite-cable system, the content of TV programs, and in for the present study, the burgeoning of advertising on Chinese television after the mid-1980s, have taken place within the context of the global media expansion as a result of the neoliberal policies of the Western countries like the US and the UK.

---

3   This includes both radio and television broadcasting, and there is no separate data available in this respect.

3.2 Neoliberalism

In *The Global Media*, Herman and McChesney (1997) point out that Western politics in the 1980s moved toward "aggressive global pro-market policies, personified by Thatcher and Reagan and often referred to as neoliberalism." They believe that the Anglo-American "neoliberalism" since the 1980's at least partially resulted in the process of what is called "globalization" and the formation of "global media" (p. 25).

It is worth noting that neoliberalism is not a continuation of the "second stage liberalism" (See Raskin, 2004) as seen in the New Deal, but looks more like the first stage, classical liberalism, in terms of its emphasis on the market. This, however, is only the appearance. Rather than an ideal associated with a particular social and economic philosophy, neoliberalism is first and foremost an economic practice, characterized by extremely intensified expansion of time and space of the market. The ideal neoliberal market is the 24 hour economy with non-stop transactions throughout the year around the world. The contract is emphasized more than the property (which is central in classical liberalism), in the sense that transnational corporations do not own any production facilities, but buy them from subcontractors who produce but do not own their products.

46 The neoliberal world view evolves around the market. It is ready to answer any philosophical questions such as why we are here, or what should we do – we are here for the market, and we should compete. Every human being is an entrepreneur managing his or her own life, and should act as such. Consequently, it is a moral duty of human beings to arrange their lives to maximize their advantage on the labor market (paying for plastic surgery to improve employability by women, for example). For the neoliberal, there must be nothing which is not market (Raskin, 2004).

Neoliberalism primarily sees nations as business firms, therefore, a neoliberal government will pursue policies designed to make the nation more attractive as an investment location. This is reflected by the fact that one specific culture (American culture) and one specific language (English) have been promoted around the world, as a result of the dominance of Anglo-American corporatism, as well as a necessity of promoting global free trade.

That being said, the consequence of neoliberalism in the global media system is quite predictable. In *The Global Media*, Herman and McChesney depict a "dramatic restructuring of national media industries," and the emerging of a global commercial-media market in the 1990s. The deregulation of media ownership, privatization of television in lucrative European, Latin American and Asian markets, and new communication technologies have made it possible for media giants to establish powerful distribution and production networks within and among nations (see Herman and McChesney, 1997). In short order, the global media have come to be dominated by the ten or so transnational corporations, or TNCs, that rule US media: News Corporation, Time Warner, Disney, Bertelsmann, Viacom, TCI, PolyGram (Philips), General Electric, Seagram, and Sony (and the list is still getting shorter). Most of these TNCs are both horizontally and vertically integrated, controlling significant slices in the sector of production and distribution of specific media. With the aid of the IMF, the World Bank, and WTO, they have opened up ownership of stations as well as cable and satellite TV systems at a global level, especially in most Third World countries.

The impact of this global media structure is far-reaching. As "the new missionaries of the corporate capitalism" (Herman & McChesney, 1997), the media TNCs not only dominate the media market around the world, but they have also accelerated the process of commercialization and privatization in third world countries through the ideology which identifies freedom with the mere absence of constraints on business. More importantly, as Herman and McChesney argue, the global media have an "anti-democratic edge," and "the implantation of the commercial model of communication" and "its extension to broadcasting" as well as the 'new media' tend to erode the public sphere and to create a 'culture of entertainment' that is incompatible with a democratic order" (p9).

As a "necessary component of global capitalism and one of its defining features," the case of global media monopoly reveals the (post)colonial orientation of neoliberalism, which is just like its predecessor, classical liberalism. Realizing the threat of global media to both the national economy and the existing ideology, many countries have demonstrated a resistance to the entry of the global media giants into their domestic markets. For example, in the summer of 1998, culture ministers from 20 nations, including Brazil, Mexico, Sweden, Italy and the Ivory Coast, met in Ottawa to discuss how they could build some ground rules to protect their cultural fare form the Hollywood juggernaut (Herman and McChesney, 1997). In the meantime, foreign broadcasting is restricted in Singapore and Malaysia. In China, the restrictions over foreign ownership, programming and advertising as were mentioned in this chapter precisely reflect such concern about national and ideological security.

3.3 A Peripheral Vision

There are certain limitations within the critique of global media as reflected in the above discussion. Perhaps inevitably, there is the risk of oversimplification and economic determinism. Herman and McChensney (1997) tried to keep a balanced critique by acknowledging the "positive effect" of global media, such as its competitive pressure on, and threat to, the state-controlled broadcasting systems that provide poor services, meeting the world wide demand for products of popular culture, the emergence of global culture and greater sense of connectedness and linkage among peoples, and carrying across boarders some of the fundamental values of the West (individualism, skepticism of authority, women's rights, etc.). They even mentioned the flow towards the cultural centers and horizontal flows within regions (p. 8). In so doing they actually are looking at the local variations and nuances. None of these, however, is their major concern. Once put in a concrete local context, they are at best an inaccurate description of something at a far distance. For example, in the case of China, while there has indeed been a tremendous influence from the West, it has never taken place in a simple, direct way, since the majority of the imported media content came from Taiwan and Hong Kong, and the latest development is that the national network of 15 channels of China Central Television (CCTV) is having little or no foreign content, first due to government intervention, but in the past decade largely due to the abundance and in some cases the popularity of local production.[4]

In the meantime, while the distributors of foreign television programs have been negotiating strenuously to get into the Chinese market, it is transnational advertising that has played a more important role that Herman and McChesney attribute to global media content, as could be seen in the case of Japanese advertising, which entered the Chinese market first in the form of barter trade – free programming in exchange for advertising slots.

The case of China reveals at least two basic assumptions regarding cultural/media imperialism. The first is that the high level of US program importation was a permanent condition rather than a transitional stage in the development of television in other regions. The second one is that not only the US media constitute the primary source of content for third world countries, but the influence of US media takes place in a direct, unmediated way. As Sinclair, Jacka, and Cunningham (1996) point out in their study of Latin American media, both assumptions are problematic in that they tend to overlook the existence of local interest groups and the internal sociological factors within third world countries.

Instead of the image of "the West" at the center, dominating the peripheral "Third World" with an outward flow of cultural products, Sinclair et al. (1996) look at the world as divided into a number of "geolinguistic regions," each of them having particular "internal dynamics" as well as "global ties" (p. 5). "Although primarily based on geographic realities, these regions are also defined by common cultural, linguistic, and historical connections which transcend physical space. Such a dynamic, regionalist view of the world helps us analyze in a more nuanced way the intricate and multi-directional flows of television across the globe." As a critical reflection on cultural imperialism and "media imperialism" (p. 5), this notion of geolinguistic region liberates us from the simple, economically determined pattern of cultural imperialism, and leads us to understand the complex reality of globalization with an analysis of corresponding complexity.

48

---

4   This situation is further complicated by the fact that those, particularly the youth, who have less interest in domestic TV programs actually are able to access form programs through the internet.

For example, Chinese satellite-cable television and television advertising illustrate how neoliberal ideology works in the Chinese context, not in a way contradictory to the Chinese nationalism, but rather in constant negotiation and compromising with it; not as a direct influence through media content, but more as a mediated process in which the environment, policies and premises for the very existence of media have gradually changed, with structural consequences for the Chinese television industry.

With that in mind, it can be understood that the situation in China is not a simple replacement of the traditional political propaganda by the new discourses of market and consumerism. Nor is it a simple struggle between the two forces for control. In contemporary China, it is important to make the distinction between the dominant discourse, i.e., the political propaganda or the "Party line", and the mainstream ideology, which include the discourses about the market, global economy, consumerism, etc., and has become the prevalent belief of the Chinese public, in the past decades. It is more important to understand that the two types of discourses may appear contradictory in nature yet more often than not they are seen to be complementary to each other. Analysis of this particular situation will undoubtedly shed light on the social transformation of China, the complex structure of the newly emerging ideology, and the role of state as "civil society" in its non-coercive sense. This should be elaborated in the following chapters.

With the ground cleared, we can now move on to advertising – the most prominent factor that has jointly (with the state, or, as part of the state) shaped the structure of not only the television industry, but also the social structure in many ways.

Chapter 4. Television Advertising in China: Institution and Policy

Television can be regarded as a social institution which contributes to the (symbolic) environment in which we live and make sense of the world (see Gerbner, 1972). As part of this influential story telling institution, advertising also contributes to the construction of a value system that tells us not only what to believe, but also what to do. But advertising is more than just part of television. With the dominance of the capitalist modes of production at the global level, advertising constitutes the backbone of television and provides the underlying logic of its operation in most countries in the world. In China, which is often hailed as the "largest market of television broadcasting in the world" (Ubios, 1994), the history of the commercialization of television – the process in which advertising has become the major source of revenue for television – has demonstrated a trajectory that is very similar to what have been much theorized by media scholars in America. It is a very short history indeed, yet the speed of commercialization is unprecedented and the consequences are far-reaching. Anyway, duration has never been (and should never be) the criterion to judge the impact of a genuine historical event.

51

4.1 History of Advertising

While nationalist pride may lead some Chinese researchers to the idea that somehow advertising in China can be traced back to the Zhou Dynasty around 3,000 years ago (Cheng, in Frith, 1996, pp. 74-75), advertising that is the concern of this study has to be based on such concepts as "commodity" and "mass media," which designate advertising as a necessary product of industrialization and modern communication technology. Advertising can be "objectively" described as the "paid nonpersonal communication from an identified sponsor using mass media to persuade or influence an audience" (West, et al. 1992, in

Cheng, 1996). In China, it is defined along the same line as an "act of promoting commodities, services, information, or opinions, through mass media, towards a target audience, and paid by advertisers" (Wang, D., 1996, p. 2). These definitions, however, say nothing about advertising as a "privileged form of discourse" and as an "integral part of modern culture" (Leiss et al., 1997, pp. 1-5). Even less do they tell about the social, economic, and most importantly, political conditions of advertising as an institution.

Advertising in China began as a foreign idea which is closely related to the history of colonialism and the expansion of global capitalism. It was introduced into China and first practiced in Hong Kong and Shanghai by British newspapers after the door of the country was forced open as a result of the defeat in the first Opium War with Britain in 1840 (Cheng, in Frith, 1996, pp. 75-76). As a direct consequence of the war, China changed from a country of exports to a country of imports in its foreign trade relations. The flood-in of foreign goods and investment was accompanied by the introduction of modern mass media into China, which was "naturally" followed by the employment of advertising to promote foreign goods in the "untapped Chinese market" (Wang, 2000, p. 26). In the 50 years after the Opium War,[1] more than 300 foreign newspapers and magazines were launched in China (Cheng, in Frith, 1996, p. 75), some of them were in foreign languages, serving foreign residents in the colonial Shanghai and Hong Kong, others were in Chinese, and both carried advertising mainly for foreign products (Wang, 2000, p. 27). During this process, advertising as a foreign – which in the colonial period was often synonymous to modern – idea and practice was well received in China and was followed up by Chinese newspapers and magazines in the first two decades of the 20th century (Cheng, in Frith, 1996, p. 76).

The emergence of a new form of mass media, i.e., radio in the 1920s, brought about the "golden age" of advertising in the semi-colonial China. The new technology enabled advertising to reach a larger population in a more efficient way. With more diversified medium forms, advertising agencies started to emerge. The first modern advertising agency in China, China Commercial Advertising Agency (CCAA), was founded in 1926 by C. P. Ling, the U.S.-educated "father of Chinese advertising" (Cheng, in Frith, 1996, p. 76). Among the four biggest advertising agencies in Shanghai, two were Chinese owned (CCAA and Consolidated National Advertising Company), one was from the UK (Millington Ltd.), and the other from the U.S. (Carl Crow, Inc). In less than 15 years, there appeared 100 advertising agencies in Shanghai, and a few in Beijing, Chongqing, and Guangzhou, which remained part of the economic life even during the Japanese invasion (1937-1945) and the civil war (1946-1949) (Wang, 2000, pp. 27-34).

---

1   The (first) Opium War (1840-1842) between the United Kingdom and the Qing Dynasty ended with the ceding of the Hong Kong Island to the British Empire and the opening of five treaty ports including Shanghai. The war is considered as the beginning of the modern Chinese history.

Much like the mass media at the turn of the new millennium, the clients of these big advertising agencies, particularly those based in Shanghai, the commercial center of China at the time, were mostly foreign. One cannot help feeling the irony about the similarity between Shanghai in the 1930's and Shanghai today. Foreign goods gained acceptance through constant advertising in the modern media, and were changing the way that Chinese people dressed, ate, medicated, and took care of their skin, though not without resistance from both habits and nationalist campaign for "national goods." A look at the list of clients of the above mentioned CCAA shows such brand names as Heinz, Parker Pen, Gillette, and Quaker Oats. Advertising concentrated on consumer goods and "predominantly targeted the affluent Chinese" (See Wang, 2000, pp. 28-32).

These developments of Chinese advertising had been characterized by its confinement within a few big cities, the limited range of outreach through print media and radio due to the lack of accessibility by the generally poor population at the time, and the concentration on the promotion of foreign products. However, they did succeed in bringing about changes in the values of the elite among the Chinese people, and demonstrated a clear connection between advertising and the process of urbanization, commercialization, modernization, and the global flow of capital. All of these have re-appeared around the turn of the 21st century.

The years after the establishment of the People's Republic of China in 1949 did not see a complete disappearance of advertising, though it became "increasingly irrelevant as a marketing tool" (Wang, 2000, p. 34). After January 1956, the time when the socialist transformation was completed, all remaining agencies became state owned. The 108 agencies in Shanghai were merged into the state-run Shanghai Advertising Corporation, which became Shanghai Advertising and Packaging Corporation in 1962, promoting national products and advertising on the packaging of products for exports (Hawkins, 1982, p. 107). All foreign advertising was ended. Changes in the mode of production restricted advertising to an informative tool in newspapers till the Cultural Revolution, during which it was completely eliminated.

I personally find it very interesting that narratives about advertising during the Cultural Revolution are quite unanimous. They all follow the same line that media during the Cultural Revolution all served political purposes and advertising was considered to be useless. All communication media, including neon signs, billboards, newspapers, radio, etc., only function to display political content, or they would not be allowed to exist. Advertising agencies only worked to produce political posters and then were completely closed (e.g., Bishop, 1989, p. 140; Wang, 2000, p. 35; Zhao, in Wasko, 2005).

The political transformation of advertising into a propaganda tool in the 1950's and its total elimination during the Cultural Revolution are always considered to be "ideological," a "fact" which has been universally agreed. While the socialist government was quite explicit in defining advertising as a tool of political propaganda, "objective" historical account and critics of the "authoritarian" state are also complacent with the label (e.g., Cheng 1996; Zhao, 1998, Chapter 1 and Chapter 3; Wang, 2000, p. 35). On the other hand, in both China and the West, the return of advertising after 1978 was always considered without hesitation a purely "economic" act. The conceptualization of ideology, propaganda, and the political in these studies is absolutely fascinating.

The end of the Cultural Revolution and the beginning of the reform and opening to the outside world in the late 1970s were accompanied by the return of advertising (both domestic and foreign) and advertising agencies. Shanghai Advertising Corporation reopened in late 1978, and ten agencies were operating in 1979. On January 14, 1979, an editorial of *Wenhui Daily*, a Shanghai newspaper, encouraged China's newspapers to carry domestic and foreign advertisements and called for "restoring the good name of advertising" and taking advertising as a "means of promoting trade, earning foreign exchange, and broadening the mass' horizons" (Ding, 1979, in Cheng, 1996). On the same day, the first advertisement (by Tianjin Toothpaste Factory) after the Cultural Revolution appeared on the *Tianjin Daily*. On, Jan. 28, 1979, the *Liberation Daily* in Shanghai carried advertisements for several domestic products. On March 15, 1979, "*Wenhui Daily* carried an advertisement for the Swiss-made Rado watches, as the first foreign advertisement in China after the Cultural Revolution" (Cheng, in Frith, 1996, p. 78).

Since the 1970s, advertising in China has experienced a development from a secondary institution with no power of its own, to a primary sponsor of and active participant in the grand socio-economic transformation, though it is still subject to both administrative supervision and ideological constraints. It has been the fastest growing industry of the country since the reform and opening-up. From 1981 to 1992, annual business volumes rose at an average rate of over 40 percent. In 1993, the "Advertising Year of China," the turnover of Chinese advertising soared to $1.9 billion, with 31,770 advertising units, which nearly doubled that of the previous year (Cheng, in Frith, 1996, p. 80). According to a report by the *China Business Review* (1999), "companies in China spent nearly $4.9 billion on advertising in 1998, which is nearly 20 times higher than a decade before," and "the number of firms providing advertising services increased nearly sevenfold between 1991 and 1997 from 13,000 to 86,000 (Prendergast and Shi, 2001). "The total Chinese ad spending reached $30.12 billion in 2005, with toiletries, pharmaceuticals, business/services, food, and real estate as the top categories" (Gao, 2008). Also in 2005, the number of registered advertising agencies reached 84,272 (China Advertising Association). Recent statistics shows that the total advertising spending reached RMB 560.6 billion Yuan, the number of advertising units amounted to 543,690, and more than 2.7 million people are employed in the advertising industry in 2014.[2] It is worth noting that almost all the biggest advertisers are the transnational corporations.

---

2 "Analysis of the development and trend of the Chinese advertising industry in 2016" (2016年中国广告行业发展概况及发展趋势分析),http://www.chyxx.com/industry/201607/429365.html.

4.2 Advertising Media: the Age of Television

The dramatic changes in Chinese advertising industry is closely related to the development in advertising media. The beginning of the reform and opening up also marked the dramatic development of the Chinese television industry. For advertising, this means a whole new world with more efficient communication and more powerful penetration. The opportunity was picked up immediately. On January 28, 1979, Shanghai Television Station aired the first television commercial in China – a commercial for a wine of domestic brand (Wang, 2000, p. 42). Such an act signaled the arrival of a completely different system, in both material and symbolic senses. Again, Shanghai, as the city which once had the most intimate interaction with global capital and colonial powers, now led China in its march towards a re-born commercial culture.

Not surprisingly, with its incredible capacity to reach over a billion people, television soon became the fastest growing advertising medium in China, with its revenue increasing at an annual rate of over 45 percent. Its percentage share in the total business volume of all advertising media in China increased from about 10 percent in the early 1980s to 40 percent in the early 1990s. In 1991-1992, television surpassed newspapers in advertising business volume for the first time and became the largest advertising medium in China, with a national audience of over 800 million at the time (Cheng, in Frith, 1996, p. 86).

At the same time, during the surge of provincial and city networks, conflicts arose between the limited revenue the government had been able to invest in the media, and the demand for more media services in terms of both quantity and quality. Now that the practice of television advertising itself is no longer something prohibited for its alleged capitalist nature, television naturally turned to advertising, which immediately became the essential factor and defining element in the television industry: to be able to attract advertising, especially foreign advertising, is now a symbol of business success (Zhao, 1998).

As was already mentioned, in the decade of 1980s and early 1990s, overall advertising spending was up by more than 40 percent each year. In spite of the already dramatic growth of television industry, the growth in media outlets could not possibly match that in advertising. As the result of recruiting foreign investment with favorable policies, the flood of advertising by joint-venture companies helped push the increase of media rates on advertising. Demand simply outstripped supply. It was undoubtedly a seller's market.

Because of its once monopolistic access to a national audience, the network of CCTV became the hottest advertising medium in the country (Zhao, 1998, p. 58). The total advertising time during the prime time (19:00-22:00) each day on CCTV1 amounted to as much as 32 minutes during prime time in 2000, which increased to 42 minutes in 2005. It is also the one that sets the tone for the hike of advertising rates. In 1993, CCTV raised its average 30-second prime time slot for joint venture advertisers from 16,900 Yuan (US $2112) to 35,200 Yuan (US $4,400, at the exchange rate of 8:1 at the time). Similar increases were slated for stations in major cities like Beijing, Shanghai, and Guangzhou. The rate hikes become the biggest hurdle to local advertisers, but foreign advertisers still see the rate on CCTV as a tremendous bargain compared with other markets such as the United States. For example, in 1996, a 30 second spot on the Super Bowl, which could reach 400 million viewers, is $10,000 in China, as compared with half a million dollars in the U.S. (Cheng, in Frith, 1996, p. 88) which was $3 million in 2008 and $5 million in 2016.

This largely determines the type of commercials on CCTV, which has gradually become the arena for gigantic domestic and transnational corporations. Local advertisers who cannot afford to appear on national TV have to squeeze their low budget and often low quality advertisements into the even more limited space of local channels.

Television is certainly not the only form of medium for advertising. With the explosion of consumer goods and advertising as a legitimate source of revenue for Chinese media, it didn't take long for advertising to take over every form of communication medium, including radio, billboards, neon signs, newspapers, magazines, and recently, the internet. Television, however, remains dominant quite recently with its uncontested number of audience nationwide.

4.3 Policies and Regulations

Under the oxymoronic term of "socialist market economy," the practice of advertising in China can be observed to take place with a gradual decline of the "socialist rhetoric" and growing strength of the "market" discourse. This can be seen in the changes in regulations over advertising.

(1) Advertising agencies

Professional advertising agencies re-appeared and flourished in China's economic life during the 1980s. They are responsible for designing and manufacturing catalogs, media buying, advertisement design, decorating, etc. in the early 1980s, and for advertisement creation, media planning, market research, consulting, etc., in the late 1980s (see Cheng, in Frith, 1996). Within the first 15 years of the reform, advertising agencies in China were affiliated with different government departments, and were subject to both national regulations on advertising and the management of the specific governmental departments with which they were affiliated (Cheng, in Frith, 1996, p. 81). Those affiliated with the Ministry of Foreign Economic Relations and Trade (MOFERT) handled national and local foreign advertising within China as well as Chinese advertising for export products. Domestic advertising was undertaken by non-MOFERT affiliated agencies. In the second half of the 1990s, with the end of MOFERT's monopoly over foreign trade, the increase of foreign advertising agencies, and the business expansion of each type of advertising agencies, such division gradually faded away between agencies that handle foreign advertising and those that handle domestic advertising.

Wang (2000) noticed an "unbalanced agency-media relationship" in Chinese advertising, with "overpowered media and weak agencies" due to the capability of media organizations to set up their own shops to compete with other agencies (p. 43). This was partly changed in 1993, when the State Administration of Industry and Commerce (SAIC) decided to adopt the Western advertising agency system by setting up a clear boundary between media and advertising agency (Prendergast and Shi, 2001). Advertisers must be represented by advertising agencies rather than directly by media for their ads to be released on media outlets (Wang, D., 1996, p. 323).

Foreign advertising has been limited but continued to grow nonetheless. The billing for foreign advertising agencies increased from $15 million in 1986 to $75 million in 1992, both about 6 percent of the total advertising spending in China in the two respective years. In 1993, it accounted for $133 million, 7 percent of the total advertising spending in the Chinese market (Cheng, in Frith, 1996, p. 82). Since foreign ownership is highly restricted, foreign advertising agencies choose to operate with either "representative outposts for their base in Hong Kong," or in joint ventures with local Chinese partners as a more efficient way to enter the Chinese market, the latter of which has continued to be favored even after this restriction was lifted in 2006 upon China's entry into WTO (Sinclair, J. 2008).

(2) Changes in Advertising Laws and Regulations

Between 1949 and 1982, no national regulations on commercial advertising existed due to the public ownership of production under a planned economy. When necessary, regulations over advertising activities were made at the local level according to specific situations.

The first national regulation for advertising came in February, 1982. Promulgated by the State Council, the *Interim Regulations for Advertising Management* (广告管理暂行条例) aimed to "overcome the chaotic situation in advertising, stick to the socialist orientation in advertising practice, and better serve the masses of consumers and users." It also stipulated that advertising should "effectively serve the needs of socialist construction and promote socialist moral standards." Article 8 listed six advertising activities that were forbidden: (1) advertisements that violate state policies and regulations; (2) advertisements that were detrimental to national dignity; (3) advertisements that contained reactionary, obscene, and superstitious contents; (4) advertisements with libelous propaganda; and (5) advertisements related to state secrets. Self employed individuals were not allowed to be involved in advertising, and pricing rates were set by local industry and commerce administrations.[3] The whole document was only two pages long, and there were no elaborated articles on such nuanced issues as deceptive advertising.

---

3   But advertising agencies could set their own rates in places where local governments had not set up standards that could be referred to by the agencies.

In 1987, the State Administration of Industry and Commerce (SAIC) was authorized by the state council to supervise and provide guidance to all advertisers, advertising agencies, and advertising media in China. There are also advertising departments or sections within local the administration for industry and commerce, which are responsible for registration, license, supervision, solving disputes, handling cases of deception and illegal behavior, giving guidance, and so on. In the meantime, there are other government departments such as the Ministry of Culture, the State Administration of Radio, Film, and Television, the General Administration of Press and Publication, the Ministry of Health, the State Drug and Food Administration, the Ministry of Education, which supervise either specific advertising media or products being advertised. They "actively participate in advertising regulation" by issuing media or product oriented rules and regulations or enforcing censorship over specific categories of advertising, such as advertisements for pharmaceuticals or food with health benefit claims (Gao, 2008).

Also in 1987, the interim regulations were superseded by the *Regulations for Advertising Management* (广告管理条例). This newer version removed articles about libelous propaganda and state secrets, and listed 6 types of advertising that were prohibited: (1) advertisements that violate state laws and regulations; (2) advertisements that are detrimental to national dignity; (3) advertisements that contained signs of the national flag, emblem, anthem, as well as the sound track of the national anthem; (4) advertisements that contained reactionary, obscene, superstitious and absurd contents; (5) advertisements with deceptive contents; and (6) advertisements that disparaged other products of the same category. Other two important changes were that self-employed individuals were allowed to apply for a license to engage in advertising, and advertising rates were now to be decided by those who were engaged in the advertising business.

These were the early efforts to regulate a "brand new" industry within an economic and political environment that was still "socialist" – at least at the discursive level. They were experimental and therefore inevitably suffered from its simplicity. It was often questioned whether a "rudimentary regulation less than two pages in length" (Gao, 2008) was capable of governing such an enormous and complex industry within such a huge country. Loopholes caused by vagueness were not scarce. For example, Cheng (in Frith, 1996) points out that initially regulations on tobacco advertisements only prohibited their appearance on radio, television, and newspaper, but not on other forms of media such as billboards, magazines, movies, and sports sponsorship; and that permission of liquor advertisements are based on a confusing identification of "famous and high-quality" liquors (p. 92), which clearly lacked referable operational definition.

Two groups of people were most obviously affected by these unsophisticated regulations. One was the foreigner advertisers. Relying too heavily on individual interpretations, the spirit and application of the law were far from self evident in the eyes of foreigners (Baudot, 1989, p. 198). The other was the Chinese consumers. The inevitable weak enforcement of vague regulations could not possibly solve the problem of deceptive advertising. The decade of the 1980s could be considered as a period of extremely low credibility for advertising, particularly domestic advertising, with "no specific measures for deception control in existing regulations except for emphasizing that advertising should be clear, truthful, and informative" (Gao, 2008). Undoubtedly, regulations on advertising require changes in a much broader social context, which involves all levels of the government and legal system.

Some regulatory actions were undertaken before a more comprehensive law came into being. For example, some new rules were made in 1993 to conform to international practices. For one thing, the requirement was removed (at least in some major cities where international advertising was concentrated) that ads must be sanctioned by media before being displayed, though such a requirement still exists for TV and radio in certain categories that represent the lion's share of the products advertised in China – household appliances, drugs, foods, alcoholic beverages, and cosmetics (Miao, 1993d, in Cheng, 1996). Besides, as was already mentioned, rather than having media institutions produce advertisements for their clients as they used to do, the State Administration of Industry and Commerce (SAIC) banned media from acting as agencies for advertisers and shifted such responsibility to advertising agencies, giving advertising agencies more leverage in setting rates and buying media time.

59

In 1994, the *Advertising Law of the People's Republic of China* (中华人民共和国广告法) was promulgated by the People's National Congress, and came into effect on Febuary 1, 1995 to replace the 1987 regulation. It incorporated many of the previous rules that were made to supplement the 1982 and 1987 regulations and constitutes the one that has continue to be used until 2015. The most noticeable characteristic about this advertising law is that political terms such as "reactionary" and "Chinese nation" are completely absent, and the term "socialism" is rarely mentioned (twice, in Article 1 and 3 respectively). It is now more specific in such regulations as the ban on tobacco advertising, which was extended from radio, TV and newspaper to magazines and public arenas such as waiting rooms in airports and railway stations, cinemas and theaters, and sports venues (Article 18). New articles were added regarding medicine and medical equipment (Article 14 and 15), pesticides (Article 17), foods, alcohol and cosmetics (Article 19), with contents about health and safety standards. Besides, more severe punishments were stipulated to hinder malpractice.

After the 1995 law on advertising, the SARTF has also placed, in the past two decades, a series of restrictions over the broadcasting of advertisements on television. For example, in 2003, the *Provisional Regulations for the Administration of the Broadcasting of Radio and Television Advertisements* (广播电视广告播放暂行管理办法) stipulated in Article 17 that the total advertising time each day should not exceed 20% of the total broadcasting time of the day, and between 19:00 and 21:00, the time that each television channel set aside for advertising should not exceed 15% or 9 minutes of each broadcasting hour. In Article 18, it further stated that television stations should maintain the entirety and continuity of its programs, and no advertisements should be inserted except at the natural breaks of programming. Specifically, during the period other than 19:00 – 21:00, one commercial break was allowed for each TV drama episode for no longer than 2.5 minutes. Interestingly, there was no clear statement in the 2003 regulation about whether or not advertising is allowed within TV drama episodes between 19:00 and 21:00. Definite statement did not come until 2009 in the *Administrative Measures for the Broadcasting of Radio and Television Advertisements*, (广播电视广告播放管理办法), which completely removed commercial slots from TV drama episodes. In Article 17, it was stated that no advertising in any form whatsoever was allowed in an episode of TV drama. In Article 15, it was reiterated that total advertising time shall not exceed 12 minutes in each broadcasting hour, while total commercial time between 19:00 and 21:00 should not exceed 18 minutes, i.e., no more than 9 minutes per hour.

Despite the existence of these clear and strict regulations on the length of commercial time on television, they had by no means been effectively executed by local television stations, and had little practical significance to the television audience. As was mentioned earlier, the total advertising time during the prime time (19:00-22:00) each day on CCTV1 increased from 32 minutes in 2000 to 42 minutes in 2005, two years after the 2003 regulation that placed the 9 minutes restriction on prime time commercial time. Their lack of effective implementation could be seen from people's reaction towards the *Notification on Further Strengthening the Administration of the Broadcasting of Radio and Television Advertisements* (关于进一步加强广播电视广告播出管理的通知) promulgated in October 11, 2011 and the *Additional Stipulations to the "Administrative Measures for the Broadcasting of Radio and Television Advertisements"*, ((广播电视广告播出管理办法)的补充规定) in November 28, 2011, which stated that "beginning on January 1, 2012, no advertising in any form whatsoever is allowed within an episode of TV drama, which applies to all television stations around the country." Ironically, as a clear repetition of the 2009 regulation, the 2011 regulations were greeted with much complaints from TV stations across the country as a "new" restriction that was too strict to the extent that it was named the "ban on advertising" in 2011.

Other than the advertising law and regulations, there are also rules attached to them for their implementation and enactment. More time and effort could certainly be spent on more detailed discussion of these rules, regulations, and laws regarding advertising in China, but for me, the social context in which they were made and the underlying assumptions that other researchers hold about them are far more interesting than the rules, regulations, and laws themselves. A few words are deemed necessary in this respect before we move on to the next chapter.

4.4 Advertising and Its Social Context

Discursively, the economic reform in China since 1978 began as a "social-ist" practice with a clear emphasis on public ownership. Before 1992, adver-tising burgeoned in a controversial social and political environment when the discourse of public ownership and socialist modes of production still laid some material constraint on the act of advertising. By 1992, as many as 12,181 out of 16,683 advertising agencies were state owned. The belief was rather strong regarding the difference between "socialist" advertising and capitalist advertis-ing based on the inherent difference between "socialist commodity economy" and capitalist commodity economy. At the discursive level, it is still a popular phrase that advertising should introduce commodities to consumers and dis-play political ideology.

However, it did not take very long before the Chinese people saw the offi-cial endorsement of the market: a socialist economy is a commodity economy planned on public ownership, and a commodity economy is an unavoidable stage in the development of a socialist economy. As former President Deng Xiaoping put it, we need both a planned economy and a market economy. Such a "combination" of planned economy and market mechanisms would gradually fade out in the official discourse in regard to the Chinese economy. Today, the dominant discourse is that market shall play a "decisive" role in resource allo-cation, while the once important "planning" is substituted by the "more effec-tive role of the government." During such a transformation, advertising is no longer a capitalist tool, but rather an accelerator for the economic development.

In retrospect, the history of Chinese television advertising is at the same time the history of the development towards a state controlled market economy and the history of China's interaction with transnational corporations and the global flow of capital. The economic reform, the development of a national television network, and the burgeoning of advertising are closely related and mutually constitutive. The triangle relationship among the three provides an opportunity to understand the social structure of contemporary China, but in actual research, the outcome is often confusing at its best.

One of the most interesting perceptions of the policy changes regarding ad-vertising in China is that regulations on advertising tend to be "less ideology oriented," or "less ideological," since the 1982 interim regulation. Such a de-cline of ideology in regulatory content is believed to be reflected in the shift from a state monopoly in advertising to the incorporation of self-employed individuals into the newly emerged yet fast growing industry. To put it another way, the "less ideological" regulations are often conceived as more "consumer oriented" (Cheng, in Frith, 1996) in that they have taken into account the rights, health and safety of consumers. All these changes in advertising unequivocal-ly reflect comprehensive social changes, i.e., the legally acceptable status of private business, decentralized supervision over commercial activities, and the highlight of "consumer" rights, should reveal more fundamental restructuring

61

of the Chinese society. The very idea that regulations over advertising have been less "ideological" presupposes many unexamined concepts such as ideology, politics, consumer, (legal) rights, etc. None of them have been clearly defined in studies of television advertising in China.

Chapter 5. The Content of Chinese Television Advertising

Now, advertising not only constitutes the essential lifeline of television broadcasting industry, but also has a direct impact upon the everyday life of audiences in terms of their daily experience of consumption. In China, people are quite ready to acknowledge that they are undoubtedly influenced by advertising in their consumption.

Among both consumers and government officials, advertising is "hailed as an efficient form of communication, a means to improve the quality of both production and life, and an important link between production and consumption" (Hong, 1994). In the meantime, the entry of foreign advertising has changed both production and audiences' conception of television advertising in China. Styles of foreign advertisements are widely imitated with the perception that "modernity, quality and technology" are the most important elements for successful advertising (Wang, 1992; Hong, 1994).

All these developments in television broadcasting and advertising have contributed to the production of a commercial environment in which audiences have to deal with advertising in both their viewing experiences and their everyday life consumption. For the audience of television, the first encounter begins with the messages of commercials that they see on the screen. So let us take a look at what exactly are the messages that the audience are actually receiving when they turn on their television every day and night.

5.1 Descriptive Data: Commercials and Characters

According to the *Interim Regulations on the Administration of Advertising Companies and the Interim Regulations on the Criteria of Advertising Censorship* promulgated in 1993,[1] products advertised on television mainly include the following 13 categories: 1. Major household appliances, e.g., refrigerators, TV sets; 2. Small electronic consumer goods, such as cell phone, MP3/4/5 players; 3. Food and non-alcoholic beverages; 4. Health products like vitamin, melatonin; 5. Clothing, shoes, and caps; 6. Cosmetics and beauty products; 7. Medicine, medical apparatus and services; 8. Cigarettes; 9. Liquor; 10. Education; 11. Agriculture related products, e.g., pesticides; 12. Automobiles; and 13. Financial services. Among these products, we could make further classification based on their production place, target audience, etc. For the sake of convenience, this study picks the prime time commercials on CCTV1 for investigation.

Although commercials on local channels have adopted the format of magazine programming, i.e., inserting commercial slots within programs at regular intervals, the CCTV network has largely maintained the old format with commercials primarily between programs. In the first decade of the new millennium, there are 7 types of programs on CCTV1 during the prime time between 7:00 pm and 10:00 pm, which are evening news, weather cast, Focus (investigation of a particular social issue), drama episode 1, drama episode 2, 10 minute social hotspot or comic show that alternates through the week, concluding with late night news at 10:00 pm. This produces 6 commercial slots, with an average of 92.4 commercials (across all 6 slots) plus program promotions and public interest advertisements, or 34 minutes of prime time advertising per day. Besides, there is a large variation among commercial slots in term of their length, ranging from 1 minute between Evening News and Weather Cast to 12 minutes between the two drama episodes.[2]

Commercials on CCTV1 in a whole week are coded for analysis. Other than the basic information on the time of broadcasting, programs by genres, name, type and source place of product, product user and target audience, the coding concerns three most important aspects: (1) primary character, i.e., the user of a product, subject of narration, or the person who affirms the effect of the use of

64

---

1   See Ha, L. (1996). "Concerns about advertising practices in a developing country: an examination of China's new advertising regulations". *International Journal of Advertising*, pp. 15, 91-102.

2   The sample used for analysis in this study was taken from 2006. With time passing, this basic program structure has experienced some changes, which might be imperceptible by the majority of the audience but nonetheless of tremendous significance in various senses. Specifically, if we look at the evening program of CCTV1 today, we will only find 5 types of programs, i.e., evening news, weather cast, Focus (investigation of a particular social issue), drama episode 1, drama episode 2, and the late night news. This produces 5 commercial slots between different types of programs. With the total program time remaining the same, the removal of the short social report/comic show means a net increase of 10 minutes for commercials during the prime time. A longitudinal study on this respect would be quire revealing about Chinese television and advertising.

the product being advertised; (2) the main theme, which is the narrative thread that is explicitly expressed in linguistic or visual forms, such as personal care, social status, domestic chores, interpersonal relations, education and career development; (3) outcome, namely, the award for the use of a particular product as explicitly expressed in linguistic or visual forms, such as personal happiness, social recognition, more friends, romance, good performance, and success.

The actual data set used for analysis here excludes trailers, program promotions, public interest advertisements, corporate logo displays during the weather cast, and 5 second commercials that are broadcast during the first commercial slots between the Evening News and the Weathercast, for the reason that they are mostly a display of product logos without showing any characters or narratives. Thus the average number of commercials each day drops to 80.4, resulting in a total of 563 for analysis. Five second commercials in other commercial slots after the Weathercast are included within the data set because of their portrayal of characters' relationship with advertised products.

In terms of the length of individual commercials, the majority (67 percent, N=377) are 15 seconds long, 18.5 percent (N=104) are 30 seconds long, and 14.4 percent (N=81) are commercials that last 5 seconds. There is only one commercial that lasts 60 seconds or longer, which is the Coca Cola sweepstake described in Chapter 1, which occupies a whole 5 minute commercial slot.

The number of commercials during a slot is clearly related to the genre of programs. Television drama is the most popular audiovisual narrative form (Yin, 2002, p. 30, in Zhao and Guo, p. 524), and consequently the most attractive to advertisers. Over half (52.6 percent, N=296) of the commercials are shown during the two slots after the two drama episodes, and the commercial slot between the two episodes of prime time drama can be as long as 12 minutes.

Seven product categories dominate the prime time television commercial breaks, i.e., consumer electronics, food and non-alcoholic beverage, pharmaceutical products, alcohol, automobiles, health products, and beauty products. Commercials of these 7 categories amount to 81.3 percent of all prime time commercials. Other categories, including major household appliances, clothing, tobacco, education, agriculture related products, financial services, and other (unspecified) categories, amount to 18.7 percent of all prime time commercials. As shown in the following table:

Product categories	Consumer electronics	Food & beverage	Pharmaceutical products	Alcohol	Auto	Health	Beauty
Percentage	22.6	22.4	9.6	8.2	7.5	6.0	5.2
Frequency	N=127	N=126	N=54	N=46	N=42	N=34	N=29

Table 1: Percentage and Frequency of the Commercials by Product Category

None of the minor categories has a percentage higher than 2.5 percent, except the unspecified category, which takes 12 percent of prime time commercials.

Among all advertised products, 85 percent (N=477) are represented as domestic brands, and 15 percent (N=86) as foreign brands. One thing that stands out about these commercials is that the vast majority of them (83 percent, N=467) were primarily aiming at the high income group.

Most commercials (65 percent, N=368) target both male and female audiences, while a few more target primarily a male audience (19 percent, N=104) than primarily a female audiences (16 percent, N=89).

Not surprisingly, nearly half (42.5 percent, N=239) of the commercials target young and settled adults as a social group. About the same amount of commercials (43 percent, N=242) are age neutral. Children and elderly people are rarely the target of prime time commercials.

Characters portrayed in Chinese television advertising deserve special attention. Two hundred, or 35.5 percent of the commercials, do not have characters, and many have only one character. About equal number of commercials have female characters (42.5 percent, N=239) and male characters (42.1 percent, N=237), with 22.4 percent (N=126) commercials having female characters only, 22 percent (N=124) commercials having male characters only, and 20.2 percent (N=114) having both. However, looking at all characters that appear in TV commercials, there is a visible discrepancy between the number of male and female characters. Altogether, there are 621 characters in the 563 sample commercials, with 54.3 percent (N=337) males and 43 percent (N=267) females (there are 17 characters whose gender are not identifiable).

In terms of the ethnicity/race of characters, 55 percent (N=307) of commercials have Han Chinese characters only,[3] and 6 percent (N=33) have foreign characters. Four percent (N=23) commercials have both characters of Han Chinese (including those from Hong Kong and Taiwan of China) and Foreign characters. Thirty five (N=200) percent of commercials do not have human or animated characters. Among all 621 characters in the sample, 87.9 percent (N=546) are Han Chinese characters,[4] and 12 percent (N=74) foreign characters. No ethnic minorities are noted in the sample.

Young and settled adults are the dominant age groups in television commercials. 63 percent (N=356) of the commercials have young adults or settled adults as their primary characters, while children, teenagers, and elderly adults together appear in only 17 percent (N= 96) of all commercials. Out of the 621 characters, young adults are by far the most popular group, constituting

---

3   This number includes 54 characters, about 10 percent of the total, which are from Hong Kong or Taiwan of China.

4   This number includes 75 characters, about 12.1 percent of the total, which are Hong Kong or Taiwan of China. Theoretically, these characters may include non-Han Chinese, but are coded as so given the explicit national appearance in their representation.

over half (53 percent, N=330) of the total characters, followed by settled adults (29.6 percent, N=184).

In terms of employment status, 13 percent of the commercials have characters who are explicitly represented as not being employed (e.g., children and seniors), 20 percent have characters who are represented explicitly as being employed (e.g., appearing to be in a business meeting), and in the rest of the commercials characters are not identifiable regarding their employment status. Among characters, the employment status cannot be recognized at all for most of them (62 percent, N=386). Twenty five percent (N=152) of the characters are represented as being employed and 13.4 percent (N= 83) are not employed (children or elderly people).

The number of characters with observable family roles is low and widely spread out across all categories. One thing noticeable is that even though characters who are represented as fathers and mothers are both low in number, the number of mother characters (N=38) doubles that of father characters (N=19). In the meantime, characters who are represented as wife (N=26) and husband characters (N=23) are about the same.

The income status of characters was not coded, but the overall appearance is that of high income group. Except for very rare occasions, characters are presented as upper middle class, designated by their living environment (e.g., large house), professional look (e.g., high end business meeting), and activities engaged (e.g., golf, tennis, driving luxury cars).

5.2 Value System in Television Advertising

Now let us look at the explicit values that the commercial on Chinese television convey through visual and verbal narratives. Specifically, these values are measured by the themes of commercials and rewards presented as the end results of consuming the advertised products. This section will deal only with the unambiguous and overt themes that can be directly observed and explicitly stated. Interpretive and critical engagement will follow in both the discussion part of this chapter and later chapters.

Themes	Social Status	Personal care	Relationship	Household chore	Education	Career
Percentage	39.6	32.0	25.6	14.3	11.2	2.8
	(N=223)	(N=180)	(N=144)	(N=81)	(N=63)	(N=16)

Rewards	Personal Happiness	Social recognition	Performance	Love	Success	Friends
Percentage	49.6	41.6	29.1	24.3	4.4	2.5
	(N=279)	(N=234)	(N=264)	(N=137)	(N=25)	(N=14)

Table 2: Percentage of Themes and Rewards

Table 2 shows the percentage of themes (both minor and primary) that appear in prime time commercials on CCTV1. Social status (39.6 percent, N=223), personal care (32.0 percent, N=180), and relations – romantic, family, social, etc., are the three most prevalent themes (25.6 percent, N=144). The table also reveals that individual happiness (49.6 percent, N=279), social recognition (41.6 percent, N=234), performance at school or at work (29.1 percent, N=264), and love (24.3 percent, N=137) are most frequently end results in the form of rewards for those characters who consume the advertised products.

A strong correlation exists between certain themes and rewards, though causal relationship may or may not be obvious, as can be seen from the following table.

Rewards \ Themes	Personal happiness	Social recognition	Friends	Love	Performance	Success
Personal care	.46**	-.33**	.07	-.030	-.09*	.18*
Social status	-.36**	.88**	.02	-.17**	-.25*	-.05
Household chore	.22**	-12**	-.02	-.32**	.56**	-.08
Relation-ship	.43**	-.16**	.24**	.81**	-.07	-.12**
Education	-.28**	-.20**	-.06	-.20**	.59**	-.04
Career	.06	.01	-.03	-.09**	.12**	.55**

Table 3: Correlations between Themes and Rewards

**. p<0.01

*. p<0.05

The theme of personal care is closely related to the end result of individual happiness, but is most unlikely to be connected with that of social recognition. Not surprisingly, when social status is presented as the theme of a commercial, social recognition is the primary form of reward. Personal happiness or performance is the least concerns in commercials that underscore social status. In commercials which feature products related to household chores such as cooking or cleaning, better performance and personal happiness are most likely to be the end results, but social recognition tends to be excluded. Love also tends to be excluded from the possible end results in narratives about household chores, which is somewhat surprising given the supposedly love-giving-family-environment within which stories unfold. In line with conventional wisdom, commercial narratives that evolve around relationships end with love, personal happiness, and friends, but are not likely to depict social recognition or success in one's career. Also quite easily observable, when education is the center of a story, better performance is rewarded, while when career is the theme, success is naturally the end result. In both of the last two cases, it is more striking if we move our attention away from what is presented as the rewards of consumption towards what are excluded, namely, personal happiness, social recognition, love, friends, etc.

Closer examination of the themes and rewards in relation to character related categories reveals more about values that are clearly presented by Chinese television advertising today. The themes and rewards of a commercial are clearly related to the gender of the primary characters in that commercial. A simple correlation test shows the connection between the presence of male or female characters and the presence of each theme/reward commercials:

Themes \ Gender	Personal care	Social status	Household chore	Relationship	Education	Career
Male	-.18**	.03	.15**	.29**	.01	.09*
Female	-.01	-.29**	.07	.24**	.19**	.00

Reward \ Gender	Personal happiness	Social recognition	Friends	Love	Performance	Success
Male	.20**	.03	-.03	.28**	.10*	.04
Female	.26**	-.29**	-.13**	.28**	.26**	.12**

Table 4: Correlation Coefficient for Gender with Themes and Rewards

**. $p < 0.01$

*. $p < 0.05$

Table 4 shows the overall patterns of correlation between gender and themes/rewards. The presence of male characters is negatively correlated with the chance that the theme of personal care will be seen and positively correlated with the theme of household chores and relations. The presence of female characters is negatively correlated with the theme of social status and positively correlated with the theme of relations and education. In terms of the rewards that characters receive in the portrayals of the commercials, both males and females are positively correlated with the rewards of personal happiness, love, and better performance. Besides, females stand out as negatively correlated with the rewards of social recognition and friends. Females also have a much stronger positive correlation with better performance and success in their work.

Themes / Gender	Personal care	Social status	Household chore	Relationship	Education	Career
No male or female	0.73	0.91	0.19	0.33	0.02	0.00
Female only	0.82	0.50	0.16	0.21	0.54	0.07
Male only	0.48	1.19	0.27	0.30	0.29	0.13
Both	0.39	0.39	0.48	Oca.33	0.16	0.03

Rewards / Gender	Personal happiness	Social recognition	Friends	Love	Performance	Success
No M or F	0.64	0.89	0.09	0.30	0.18	0.00
Female only	1.07	0.61	0.00	0.21	0.92	0.22
Male only	0.94	1.30	0.06	0.22	0.63	0.10
Both	1.50	0.35	0.00	1.35	0.66	0.01

Table 5: Mean Score for Themes and Rewards by the Gender of Characters

**. $p < 0.01$

*. $p < 0.05$

Table 5 shows the mean scores for the presence of themes and rewards (0 not present; 1 = present as minor focus; 2 = present as primary focus) in relation to the presence of different characters in commercials. They further demonstrate the role of gender of characters in determining the themes and rewards of commercials.

When commercials feature only female characters, they are more likely to have narratives that focus on personal care and education. When male characters appear, either alone or in combination with females, themes of personal care and education dramatically decline. What makes male characters distinctive is their role in commercials with the themes of social status and career. Commercials with male characters alone consistently present narratives about social status. In the same token, when female characters appear in commercials, either alone or in combination with male characters, the frequency of the themes of social status visibly decline. Besides, commercials with no characters often verbally emphasize personal care and social status over other themes. In commercials that have both male and female characters, household chores and especially relationships tend to be the most prominent themes.

The relation between gender and rewards as the end results of consumption presented by commercials is also easily noticed. Better performance at work (or housework) is the most visible reward in commercials that feature female characters only. When there are male characters, either alone or in combination with females, this theme becomes significantly less frequent. Success in career is not as prominent a reward as better performance at work, yet commercials with female characters are much more likely to present this reward compared with commercials with male characters. In the meantime, social recognition constitutes the dominant form of reward in male only commercials, and shows a dramatic decline whenever female characters appear in commercials. When commercials have both male and female characters, personal happiness and love are the more likely to be the primary rewards. Finally, when there are no characters, social recognition, more than anything else, is verbally communicated as the primary rewards.

The most prominent fact about gender roles in Chinese television advertising can be better illustrated in the following table with the frequency of characters involved in different themes and rewards:

Gender	Themes			Rewards		
	Personal care	Social status	Education	Social recognition	Performance	Success
Female	52	32	34	40	63	18
Male	31	75	18	83	40	6

Table 6: Frequency of Themes and Rewards by the Gender of Characters

Most prominently, males are less likely to be portrayed in commercials that depict personal care, and females are less likely to appear in commercials that talk about social status and social recognition. In the meantime, education appears to be a female related theme, with better performance and success at work being more likely the rewards for female characters.

Now let us move on to the categories of race and ethnicity. The percentage of foreign advertising is low, as already shown before. Characters are predominantly Han Chinese. The percentage for characters other than Han Chinese is also low. Ethnic minorities are not shown at all. Residents of Hong Kong and Taiwan combined only occupy a small percentage of all characters in Chinese television advertising. Even less shown are characters that appear to be foreign.

Theme / Race	Personal care	Social status	Household chore	Relationship	Education	Career
Han	-.04	-.07	-.24**	.46**	-.15**	.03
Others	-.08	-.08	.02	-.17**	.32**	.04

Rewards / Race	Personal happiness	Social recognition	Friends	Love	Performance	Success
Han	.36**	-.07	-.08	.47**	.09	.06
Others	-.10*	-.09*	-.08	-.15**	.25**	-.06

Table 7: Correlations between Race/Ethnicity and Themes/Rewards

**. $p<0.01$

*. $p<0.05$

As table 7 shows, Han Chinese are much more than any other ethnic groups[5] to be portrayed in relationships but not in household chores or educational settings, while other ethnic groups are not usually depicted in relationships but play a predominant role in education. In terms of rewards, Han Chinese characters are more likely to be connected with personal happiness and love, while better performance is more likely to be the reward in commercials with characters from Hong Kong and Taiwan of China, and foreign countries.

Table 8 in the following page shows the mean scores for the frequency of themes and rewards in relation to the racial and ethnic identities of characters in the commercials. Commercials that feature Han Chinese characters are much more likely to depict social status and relationships than those with characters from Hong Kong and Taiwan of China, and foreign countries, while the latter are more likely to appear in narratives with the themes of household chores, education and career. Characters from Hong Kong and Taiwan of China and foreign countries are not very likely to be represented in relationship alone, and is completely absent in any relationship with Han Chinese. Besides, they

5 Given the complete absence of national minorities in Chinese television advertising, "other ethnic groups" here refer to characters that are identified as coming from Hong Kong and Taiwan of China, and foreign countries. Conceptually, grouping Hong Kong and Taiwan residents—who could be easily identified as Han Chinese—with foreigners may appears odd at the first sight. The reason for such coding choice is two-fold: (1) residents of the Chinese mainland must apply for a special pass in order to travel to Hong Kong or Taiwan, which creates a sense of geographical separation; and (2) in terms of the development of popular culture, Hong Kong and Taiwan have, historically, had much closer affinity to the West (and Japan), to the extent that these two regions have functioned as ports of cultural import for the mainland of China. It is only in recent years, with the expansion of commercial culture in China as a whole, has the sense of distance, in both geographical and cultural terms, been significantly reduced, and even reversed in some cases of cultural exchanges.

are never related to the representation of social status. When both Han Chinese characters and non-Han Chinese characters are present, personal care becomes the predominant theme, much more likely than when either Hans or non-Hans alone are present. Also, commercials with the combination of Han Chinese and characters from Hong Kong and Taiwan of China or foreign countries tend to see the theme of social status more prevalent than when there is only Han Chinese, and the theme of career more prevalent than when there are either Han or non-Hans alone.

Themes / Race	Personal care	Social status	Household chore	Relationship	Education	Career
None	.82	.76	.15	.26	.21	.01
Hans only	.74	.58	.32	.76	.19	.07
Non-Han Chinese	.67	.00	.67	.18	.61	.12
Both	2.00	.67	.00	.00	.00	.33

Rewards / Race	Personal happiness	Social recognition	Friends	Love	Performance	Success
None	.69	.80	.07	.24	.35	.01
Hans only	1.28	.81	.03	.73	.63	.14
Non-Han Chinese	.61	.73	.00	.18	1.36	.00
Both	1.33	2.00	.00	.00	.00	.33

Table 8: Mean Score for Themes and Rewards by the Race/Ethnicity of Characters

In terms of rewards, Han Chinese characters alone are more likely to be related with the reward of love, while characters from Hong Kong and Taiwan of China and foreign countries alone predominate in commercials that present better performance as a reward. The combination of Han Chinese characters and non-Han Chinese characters plays a prominent role in commercials with the rewards of personal happiness, social recognition, and success in career. That is to say, although Han Chinese are observed to appear in these commercials more frequently compared with other groups, such a correlation is the strongest when there are both Han and non-Han Chinese characters.

It is worth noting that the race/ethnicity of a character by no means dictates the origin of the advertised product. Foreigners only appear in commercials for domestic products, while foreign advertising only employs Han Chinese characters. Product origin has its unique relationship with the kind of images and narratives of television commercials. The following table shows the mean scores for each theme and reward by product origin.

Theme\Origin	Personal care	Social status	Household chore	Relationship	Education	Career
Han	.56**	.79	.28	.54**	.26**	.05
Others	1.01**	.72	.14	.28**	.02**	.06

Rewards\Origin	Personal happiness	Social recognition	Friends	Love	Performance	Success
Han	.91**	.82	.05	.49	.60**	.07
Others	1.33**	.71	.02	.37	.22**	.09

Table 9: Mean Score for Themes and Rewards by the Origin of Products

**. $p<0.01$

*. $p<0.05$

As shown in Table 9, domestic commercials are much more likely to talk about things like relations and education, while commercials for foreign products predominate in depictions related to personal care. Personal happiness is often presented as a reward for consuming both domestic and foreign products, though the latter is far more frequently awarding consumers in this way. Finally, commercials of domestic products are much more likely than foreign advertising to present better performance at work or school as the end result of their narratives.

The income of the target audience is another variable that is closely related to the themes and rewards of commercials.

Theme	Personal care	Social status	Household chore	Relationship	Education	Career
Correlation Coefficient	-.05	-.03	.09*	.07	.15**	.06

Rewards	Personal happiness	Social recognition	Friends	Love	Performance	Success
Correlation Coefficient	.18**	-.05	.07	.13**	.22**	.06

Table 10: Correlations between Target Audience Income and Themes/Rewards

**. $p<0.01$

*. $p<0.05$

The above table shows that income is significantly correlated with themes like education – a connection that deserves much attention – and such rewards as personal happiness, love, and performance at work. This could be further illustrated by the mean scores of the presence of each theme/reward (0 = not present, 1 = present as minor theme, 2 = present as primary theme) in relation to income:

Theme Income	Personal care	Social status	Household chore	Relationship	Education	Career
Han	.73	.83	.15	.37	.00	.01
Others	.61	.77	.28	.52	.27	.06

Rewards Income	Personal happiness	Social recognition	Friends	Love	Performance	Success
Han	.56	.90	.00	.24	.13	.02
Others	1.06	.79	.05	.52	.62	.08

Table 11: Mean score for Themes and Rewards by the Income of Target Audience

**. $p<0.01$

*. $p<0.05$

High income audience alone is connected with the education as the theme of the commercials, as well as household chores and relations. Low income audience are a little more likely to be correlated with the themes of personal care and social status, even though it appears to be not significant given the fact that only a very small number of commercials within the sample target the low income audience. In terms of rewards, commercials that target high income audience are more likely to present such rewards as personal happiness, love, and better performance at work. As was seen in the relation between income and the theme of social status, low income audience is more likely to be correlated to the reward of social recognition, but again, such correlation is contingent given the small number of commercials that target low income audience.

5.3 Discussion: Some Other Issues

As was mentioned earlier, this section is not a hypothesis driven content analysis, but rather an effort to provide some concrete evidence for (a) the transformation of television advertising in China; and (b) the most prominent values conveyed through television advertising as a departure point for further discussion of the social transformation of contemporary Chinese society.

That is to say, what concerns me is not just the content, but the driving force behind such content and its social, cultural, and political consequences. The significance therefore lies not only in what those commercials tell people to buy, but also what to believe, in a rather unconventional way to Chinese audiences. The explicit, unequivocal values conveyed through television advertising, regardless of the self-claimed ways of reception by the audience, constitute an undeniable part of the symbolic environment of contemporary Chinese society, with its influence reaching beyond the domain of television, which is considered to be transforming from a mouth piece of propaganda towards a commercial system primarily aiming at entertainment.

The above descriptive data, quantitative as it is, has tremendous qualitative implications, as will be elaborated in the following discussions. The explicit patterns described above in regard to the content of Chinese television advertising foreground some interesting issues which are worth our attention. Among them, there are gendered advertising, race and cross cultural branding, product origin in the context of local advertising vs. global advertising, age as a cultural indicator, class culture in China, and the blind spot of urbanization.

Gender – Chinese television advertising unequivocally presents images of a gender divide, albeit with subtlety and nuance on such occasions.

Given the conventional discourses which have the agricultural China and the socialist China as two prominent traditions, gender images in Chinese television advertising presents a rather inevitable return only to the more traditional gender relations of agricultural (Confucius) China, which places women in a subordinate position, constantly seeking approval from men. This could be clearly seen in the correlation between the characters' gender and the themes and rewards of commercials. Females, when they are alone, are often related to themes that are personal, especially those depicting the care of their bodies (hair, skin, shape, etc.), while social occasions are unambiguously dominated by male characters.

Besides, the exposition of female bodies is a prominent factor in Chinese television advertising. In fact, it has always been a controversial issue regarding television advertising in China. Up to 1999, the exposure of female body was still considered excessive and obscene, which provoked public complaint, especially against local shopping networks (Zhao, 1999).

On a side note, female characters are by no means rare in working environments. They often enjoy better performance and success as the reward for their use of certain products. These seemingly positive portrayals, however, should not be looked at in isolation. They are never just about the success of women, but almost always presented in gender relations, i.e., women are working hard as subordinates waiting for approval from their male superiors. Besides, women are observed to be constantly in need of education or help in education, while men are always already successful and need only to be entertained.

Depictions of household chores, though not statistically significant in the content analysis, can be observed as a theme often correlated to male characters and the reward of love. Apparently, it is a quite "progressive" picture in which men are doing household chores and are working hard to "earn" love from other family members. Yet careful examination of individual commercials shows that men were in the pictures entirely to be served rather than serving people. The reason why male (rather than female characters) are significantly correlated to the theme of household chore is simply because in such commercials, male characters, including husbands and sons, always outnumber female characters who are alone and performing as both wife and mom at the same time. The reward of love is therefore the satisfactory result of the female character's domestic labor that wins the approval of the male characters who are the majority within the family. In other words, males are only correlated with household chores as the ones who provide the reward of love to the female character, who successfully performs her gender role within the family.

That being said, it must be pointed out that the match between gender image in television advertising and some cultural "tradition" must not be taken for granted. Tradition and cultural norms regarding gender roles here must be understood as both real and imaginary. The focus should not be how well the depiction of female characters fit (or do not fit) Chinese cultural traditions, but rather which tradition (or which particular elements of a tradition) is/are constructed and utilized to join the grand project of formulating the great Chinese tradition.

Race and ethnicity – race and ethnicity are often used interchangeably in Anglo-American contexts, as a result of either theoretical confusion or a deliberate effort to maintain a broad applicability of critique (see Chow, 2002, chapter 1). In the Chinese context, however, race and ethnicity must be treated separately for the sake of descriptive clarity, with race denoting the concept of being "foreign," while ethnicity refers to minority nationalities within the geopolitical boundaries of China.

The first thing that can be seen is the complete absence of Chinese ethnic minorities in television advertising. The reasons for such an absence are both cultural and economic. In cultural terms, it illustrates the result of "assimilation," of ethnic minorities into the all embracing "Chinese ethnicity," or the cultural tradition of the "greater China." Such a process of civilization, in Benjamin's term, could be quite "barbaric" (Benjamin, 1968, p. 256). Economically, ethnic minorities mostly live in underdeveloped regions, and thus belong to low income groups, which fall out of the range of the target audience of most television advertising. This is all that can be said about ethnicity here.

Race per se is not a prominent category either, but nonetheless is worth noting for it draws attention to the issues of cross cultural branding. Only 6 percent of commercials feature foreigners, who are mostly Caucasians and Africans. What is really revealing is the very presence or non-presence of race as expressed in the use of foreign characters as a means to achieve persuasiveness of the commercial.

It was mentioned in the descriptive data that the race/ethnicity of a character is not necessarily denoting the origin of the advertised product. Foreign characters appear exclusively in commercials of domestic products, and foreign advertising uses Han Chinese characters only. Apparently, there is the direct opposition between domestic commercials that use images of foreign characters and discourses about globalization on the one hand, and transnational advertising that tries all means to localize with Chinese characters and local cultural references on the other. A perfect pair of examples would be Haier electronics and McDonald's fast food. Haier, as a Chinese brand name, creates a sense of sharing the global development of technology through images of world cities and business people who are constrained by neither their physical location nor the perspectives of any given culture. McDonald's, on the other hand, resorts to the emotional details of an ordinary Chinese man in his late 30s through a nostalgic memory of McDonald's in relation to the shared happiness within his family in the past two decades.

Both transnational advertisers and cultural critics have recognized the localizing strategy as the only effective means for global advertising. However, the underlying principle of seemingly antithetical advertising practices has been largely ignored. I call it the principle of reciprocity between the global and the local. McDonald's, or any other established transnational brand, is able to attract a Chinese audience particularly with a staged sincerity towards details of local life precisely because it is already a transnational brand name. In the meantime, like Chinese film directors who won international awards to make their movies hits at home, Haier must rely on its global success to be able to persuade domestic consumers that it is a (global) brand. In some sense, the distinction between global and local is not an informative categorization at all. There is only one advertising strategy – to fill the void of meaning. The void could be either local (for global advertising) or global (for local brands), contingent upon the actual context in which advertising is presented. That is why Haier is all about American life when it is on cable television in the United States (e.g., as the sponsor of NBA games). In spite of the appearance of their contradiction, domestic and transnational advertising share the same pattern and logic.

That being said, it would be no longer surprising to find that brand names or popular perception of the origin of a product by no means guarantees its actual origin. Through joint ventures, transnational capital has turned many local brands into international brands while still maintaining their appeal within the domestic market through keeping the same old brand name. What the above examples of Haier and McDonald demonstrated is not any exceptional phenomenon, but the norm in the current world.

Therefore, I would insist on treating foreign advertising and domestic advertising in the same way, and treating foreign characters and Chinese characters in the same way. That is to say, the concern should not be the Chinese or non-Chinese cultural values they symbolize, but their roles in the story telling process of advertising – narratives about social values and rewards presented to those who are portrayed as consumers of these products in the commercials.

Descriptive data show some different focus between commercials for domestic products and those for foreign products. Apparently, it fits with the stereotypical understanding of a collective Chinese culture (advertising focusing on relationship, education, and better performance) and an individualistic Western culture (advertising focusing on personal care and individual happiness).

In the complacency with such stereotypical dichotomy about cultures, the real issue could be easily overlooked and missed. Comparison of the correlations between themes and product origin with the correlations between themes and race/ethnicity of characters in commercials shows that Han Chinese, i.e., the majority of Chinese population, has a much stronger correlation with the theme of personal care than any other group, including foreigners who are predominantly Caucasians. Such a discrepancy reveals more about marketing strategies than the fixation of infinitely heterogeneous cultures in two totalizing categories.

This caution against hasty generalization about different cultures is further supported by the presentation of the theme of education and the reward of better performance at school or work. The contradiction between the two is much more than the consistency. If we may for a second assume that Chinese culture is indeed a collective one which is reflected in commercials of domestic products, such a confident conclusion is immediately cancelled out by the emphasis on outperforming others at school or at work, which, in the imaginary collectivistic Chinese culture, can never be publicly announced.

One thing for sure is that the localized transnational advertising and the globalized Chinese advertising diverge only in a superficial way. Gender, race of characters, and product origin are the most visible aspects of Chinese television advertising demonstrated by quantitative data. Now I would like to draw attention to a few other things which are an important part of the content of Chinese television advertising. They are factors that may not be best illuminated with quantitative data, but their existence must be highlighted in order to understand the nature of advertising and contemporary Chinese culture.

Age – in Chinese television advertising age is closely related to a concept that previous studies put forward in regard to Chinese culture: the separation of the purchaser and user through a gifting culture (Lu Taihong, 2005 in Wang 2008, p. 16). Gifting is a form of face consumption in that those who buy a product do not use it while those who use do not buy. For example, during the mid-autumn festival, moon cakes of luxury styles are purchased as gifts even though what every family really needs have nothing to do with that style. Such practice is based on the consciousness of the central importance of maintaining positive relationships with relatives, friends, peers, and people of seniority in terms of age, rank, or social status.

According to Wang (2008) face consumption is one of the major forms of contemporary Chinese consumer behavior, which complicates marketing theories by an act of purchasing that does not lead to direct consumption and brand ownership. It would be both redundant and absurd to emphasize the cultural uniqueness of the gifting practices of Chinese people, given the singularity of style of gifting practices in any culture. It suffices here to say that in the Chinese context, a gift is valued more for its function of sending a message of respect/love than on its actual quality or usefulness.

How does age plays a role in this "face" consumption? A particular aspect of this gifting culture involves a social hierarchy in relation to age, and the sense of moral obligation to express respect and piety (or love, in the new petty bourgeois vocabulary) for senior members of a family.

Advertising that involves such a form of face consumption is highly concentrated in three specific categories of products, i.e., festival gifts, tonic products and liquor. The first category may or may not be event driven. For example, in the mid-autumn festival, moon cakes are the primary form of gift that is more appropriate for the occasion than any other items, but for other festivals or holidays such as the Spring Festival or the National Day, the gifts may as well be anything, including the other two categories listed above.

The other two categories are interesting. For example, *nao bai jin* (脑白金, literarily translated as "brain platinum," also known as Melatonin in the West), a health tonic, is advertised and purchased solely as a gift to senior family members, or people in senior positions in one's working environment. Within the samples of this study, there are also commercials for the product of *nao ba jin*, in which the oldest member of a family happily breaks his words of no gift this year. In fact, the very catch line of this commercial is "no gift this year except *nao bai jin*."

Nao bai jin is a perfect example of the semiotics of advertising. The whole relationship of demand and supply is established entirely on the basis of the symbolic meaning of a product. In such a situation, to believe would mean to follow the ritual. Everyone knows about *nao bai jin*'s lack of substantiality, yet one purchases it anyway and delivers it as a gift regardless of its material uselessness.

Other than the example of *nao bai jin* as a new health products, the tradition of liquor as a gift illustrates in a much more eloquent way the integration of the hierarchical tradition of the Chinese culture into the newly emerging consumer culture. When a liquor of a particular brand is presented to the elderly male member of a family, the combination of the two – the patriarchal senior and the gift – constitute an element that unites the whole family on a festival occasion.

The two-fold cultural meaning is quite obvious: that the male elderly is at the center of the happiness of the family, and that the center of his happiness is the reception and consumption of a bottle of liquor.

Class is a visible yet unspoken factor in television advertising, which is mainly expressed through the emphasis on social status as the most prevalent theme of television commercials. It is safe to say that Chinese television commercials, even those targeting low income groups, rely exclusively on images that depict a life style of the upper middle class. Take for example the commercial for one of the popular brands of cooking oil, *Jin Long Yu* (Golden Dragon Fish). What is seen is a nuclear family in a large house, with the wife cooking in a spacious, clean and comfortable kitchen. Clothing is leisure style. Food appears to be fresh, colorful and appealing. The husband, in white shirt and looking professional, is waiting with the son at the table. The catch line is aiming at the housewife: *Jin Long Yu* cooking oil, for the health and happiness of your family.

Other than the effort to construct a causal relation between consumption and happiness, such depiction has two more implications, neither of them hard to notice. One is a (mis)conception that such is the life style of most of the "people" out there. The other one, consequently, is a hike in prices for goods of daily necessities because it is now perceived as part of a higher living standard. For consumers, this is an unnecessary extra cost that they have to pay for something with exaggerated use value. On the side of the advertisers, both foreign and domestic, this very strategy partly stems from a popular assumption that overestimates the purchasing power of the general population. Miscalculation takes place at two levels. Advertisers and advertising professionals are too optimistic with the market of luxury products when they inadvertently conflate the newly emerging "white-collar" consumers with "those who are genuinely at the gold-collar level," i.e., businessmen and top tier of joint venture companies' employees (Wang, 2008, p. 12). At the same time, the effort to gain volume from the low end market relies heavily on the appeal of the upper middle class life style.

This strategic mistake is further complemented by the fact that "statistics about the exact size of the blue-collar segment in China are unavailable" (Wang, 2008, p. 14). The very absence of data about blue collar consumers illustrates an actual indifference towards the low-income group and poor. For scholars who study Chinese advertising to make it more effective, this is an obvious difficulty that needs to be overcome. For those who seek to understand the political aspect of advertising, this is the expression of ideological inevitability, or a necessary stage that must be experienced by transnational marketers in China.

Rural China, as the last category of this discussion, is in fact completely missing in Chinese television advertising, despite the vast majority of the population are rural. While the blue-collar consumers, i.e., low income, working class people, are still largely talked about within urban confinement, the only phrase to describe rural China would be total absence. Such absence is not an omission just in television advertising, it is an omission in scholarly works about China too. To be fair, this does not mean that rural markets have been ignored by marketers, both domestic and transnational ones, who are actually quite fast in recognizing their mistakes. For example, Motorola and Nokia once rolled out under $60 cell phones for rural users, even though this was by no means reflected in their advertising campaigns. It would be interesting to speculate whether or not their slow reaction in this respect to some xtent contributed to their extinction in the Chinese market today.

A major sign of the intensity of urbanization and the consequent exclusion of rural markets is the disappearance in television advertising of such agricultural categories as fertilizer and pesticide, which was very popular in the first 10 years of the economic reform, the beginning stage of commercial Chinese television. To be sure, this is by no means a lamentation of a missing category of television advertising. Rather, it is a reminder of a serious consequence during the whole process of commercialization which is in the same time intense urbanization: the unequal development of different sectors, and consequently of different social strata in contemporary China.

In this chapter, I have presented an overview of what the commercials look like on China Central Television. Through the descriptions of the product categories, characters, narrative themes and end results of the commercials on CCTV1, I have tried to present a list of the most explicitly expressed values in Chinese television advertising. Given the enormous spending on advertising, these are probably the most strenuously propagated values in contemporary Chinese society, more so than the popularly resisted Party propaganda. They are both constituted and constitutive of the perception of social reality of ordinary citizens in their everyday experiences. This newly emerging value system as demonstrated by television advertising – we might as well call it commercial values – obviously has been educating the Chinese people in every aspect of their life, from what to eat to what to believe. The significance of television advertising, however, goes far beyond individual life style. This may be illustrated first and foremost by the collective behavior of the audience of television advertising, who are the primary concern of advertisers and advertising professionals.

Chapter 6. I Love What I Hate:
The Audience of Chinese Television Advertising

Revealing as it is, content analysis leaves many questions unanswered about the Chinese television advertising and its implications. The relation between cultural tradition and values prevalent in contemporary Chinese society must be further explored: how does the Chinese culture/tradition respond to advertising as something new and antithetical to the cultural tradition(s), and vice versa? Given its once contradictory nature, what are the (political, economic, ideological) conditions for the return and rapid development of advertising in China? What are the consequences of this seemingly neutral, purely economic, apolitical institution when it comes to shape the structure of everyday life in China, culturally, economically, and politically?

I will investigate these questions in two steps. This chapter will utilize interview data on the audience of Chinese television advertising that I have collected in the span of 15 years so to explore the audience perceptions of television advertising, which is the reflection of broader social changes at a micro level of everyday experience. Together with the empirical data of content analysis, it will pave the way towards the analysis of a new social order in China of which the new commercial ideology is of central importance.

Back in the year 2000, I had a series of interviews with a few groups of people in my hometown in Northern China. The topic was the advertisements that they saw on television. One of the conversations was with a senior college professor, in which he told me a story about his experience with advertising. It goes as follows:

*I used to subscribe to the **Guangming Daily** (a supposedly mouthpiece newspaper of the Communist Party of China) since the 1960s. Sometime during the 1990s, I forgot which year, probably in the middle of the 90s, one day, I got the paper of the day. There was a whole page just for a single commercial. It was a blank page, with only one word: Pooh! It was a commercial for mosquito repellant. It was all blank! There was only one word! I wrote a letter to the editor. I said I was a long time subscriber, and was really upset about it. I stopped subscription ever since. But it doesn't matter if one individual stops subscribing. They still exist. At that time, advertising was just starting to grow, and it was getting overwhelming. I didn't understand, and I got very angry. I'll never subscribe. I hate it (advertising) from the bottom of my heart. It's better not to have it. Now I still subscribe to three newspapers, which still have a lot of advertising. But now I understand, there is no use to be angry. You don't subscribe, and then you don't have anything to read. I still have to subscribe. It is like when you buy pork, you have to have some fat attached. If you want to read, there is some blank space, some commercials attached. It's the same for TV, if you want to watch, you've got to watch what is attached. As for my opinion, I don't want any single one commercial.*

The story stunned me with the sharp contrast between the not so distant past when advertising was hated and its legitimacy questioned, and the current era when advertising prevails to such an extent that no one seems to bother to complain. For quite a while I kept asking myself: how do we come to terms with what we hate? For the present study, the question becomes: how have we come to accept a whole enterprise as the defining element in our value system when such an element is in every sense contradictory to the so called cultural tradition(s) and our own sense of decency? For me this question contains the whole secret of contemporary Chinese culture and society. Its answer lies in the core of the logic of the China-in-transition ideology and provides an ideal cutting point for genuine critique. This important question has led to a series of focus group interviews that I conducted since the year 2000 up to 2015. The data collected from these interviews constitute the departure point in three investigations: (1) the way that the audience in general cope with advertising in their daily viewing experience; (2) the form of production that advertising involves and the creation of value in such production process, based on the pivotal role of the audience within the media industry—be it "old" or "new" media; and (3) the ideological transformation that both reflects and is constitutive of the social transformation in China. I will elaborate on these three points in this chapter (point #1) and the next chapter (point #2 and 3). Before that, a few words would be necessary with regard to the research on the audience in general and audience of advertising in particular.

6.1 The Issue of Audience (Research)

Speaking of people's perception of advertising, while studies of television audiences and of advertising are countless, studies of the audience of advertising are relatively scarce. The present study is certainly not concentrating solely on the audience of Chinese television advertising, but reference to the literature in this aspect will be highly valuable in shedding light on the actual process of the ideological transformation of China.

In early effects study (up to the 1950s), the study of audience began as part of the "science" of the effects of the mass media. At this stage, "all of communications research aims at the study of effect" (Katz, 1995. p. 18). In fact, this comment strikes even for the present study. In the area of mass communication, popular belief is that the initial effort of paradigm building was made by Laswell, whose model is represented as one of "sender-medium-receiver," which answers the question of "who-says what-in which channel-to whom-with what effects." According to its critique, effects in this model are determined and predictable. The audience under this model are a passive, anonymous, homogeneous "mass" who demonstrate point to point correspondence between components of a message and specific forms of response.

Apparently, this model has received criticism from the first day it was publicized in the history of media studies. For example, Katz and Lazarsfeld (1995), Radway (1983), Jenkins (1988), to name just a few, all take as their departure point the critique of the so called hypodermic "tradition" since Lasswell, explicitly or implicitly.

We should avoid the tedious review of effects study. It suffices here to say that these examples illustrate the major effort in conceptualizing "the audience" up to the present time in the realm of media studies. What strikes me most is a contradiction between the unanimous critique of the early (hypodermic) model and the implicit compliance with it. The supposed shift of perspective turned out to be its variation rather than its annihilation. According to Lazarsfeld, for example, the sender becomes what he calls the "primary group," which is a different entity than media, but still a sender itself, while in the meantime, the receiver, i.e., audience, remains passive, anonymous, and homogeneous, waiting to be informed and enlightened by social elites around them. This is especially true when it comes to the study of a non-Western society such as China.

Critiques of the effects study in its variations are in fact quite precise. Through time, effects studies have been criticized for their "market orientations" in that "the audience choice is limited to buying and not buying" (McDonald, 1957) or, in political campaigns, "sale and purchase" of the election candidates (Rossi, 1959). Williams (1980) finds that "nearly all forms of contemporary critical theories are theories of consumption" (p. 45-46). Audience research from that perspective is mostly concerned with the understanding of media content "in a way that it can be profitable or correctly consumed" (Williams, 1980, p. 46). Indeed, scholars such as Michel De Certeau (1984) picks up this vision and argues that the notion of consumption is inherent in, or even functions as the conceptual basis of all effects studies. In other words, the way researchers conceive cultural consumption predetermines their perspective on the effects of mass media upon the audience.

Critique and theory fail when they lead to the same old practices in disguise as something new. This happens to the understanding of the audience (in the name of effects) in two ways.

First, later studies have not deviated from the early "theories of consumption" (or from the hypodermic model) in the understanding of audience. What is changed is the definition of consumption. In this sense, Radway, Jenkins, Michel de Certeau, people of cultural resistance, etc., still have their works grounded in the realm of consumption, alternative ways of consumption, or non-consumption.

Secondly, subtlety gets lost when talking about Third World countries or ideological dissidents. For example, Nazi and Communist propaganda have always been considered to be the most effective by advocates of the liberal democracies (Arendt, 1951). This is also true in critiques within liberal democracies as could be seen in the critique of the Western consumer culture by the scholars like Adorno (Adorno, 1954), who has argued that "the majority of television shows today aim at producing or reproducing the very smugness, intellectual passivity, and gullibility that seem to fit in with totalitarian creeds

even if the explicit surface message of the shows may be anti-totalitarian" (Ibid, p. 222).

The most important thing to note is perhaps the fact that despite all the effort of critique and search for alternative paradigms, the bullet (hypodermic) model is still bullet proof and remains the dominant one today in actual social, economic, and political practice, with advertising and political campaigns in countries of liberal democracies being the most prominent examples.

In a sense, the sender-media-receiver model, in its apparent absurdity and effective persistency, presents us with the most difficult task of media studies: if, after being critiqued and even ridiculed for half a century, it is still the dominant paradigm of practical thinking—explicitly in the corporate world and implicitly in the academia—how do we come to terms with the categories that simply would not go away: sender, media, and receiver?

I have no intention to fully answer this question here, but by talking about the audience of Chinese television advertising, I am hoping to start thinking about these categories as part of a whole ideological configuration. As was elaborated by S. Zizek (1989), ideology here does not imply false representations that mask the hidden truth, but a construct that has no deeper meaning except its surface representation. I will come back to this point in later chapter.

That being said, let us move on to the audience of Chinese television advertising, which must be looked at as a concept with multiple levels of internal splits.

The concept of audience has already been a highly problematic one. It is principally a split of a subject into an arbitrary relation with something external. The notion of the audience of Chinese television advertising, with its further contextualized splits in genre and nationality, is constructed solely for analytical necessity at the risk of isolating a social entity into the confines of an extremely narrow dimension of the social. Such consciousness would be present throughout this section.

Now back to the example that I mentioned in the beginning of this chapter. Quite obviously, the emotion and action of this elderly man cannot be accounted for within the existing framework of audience research. Categorizing them as active, passive, or some combination of the two by no means provides adequate understanding of either advertising or its audience. In order to account for these emotions and actions, two things must be clear. One is the unique characteristic of television (advertising) as a visual medium that lies at the core of all submissions to its power. The other is that a different split of subjectivity must be recognized—not the one based on genre and nationality, but on the fact that audience perception of advertising is not just an act of a subject as a television audience member (as a matter of getting used to a consumption style), but an existential position within a whole new social formation as "always already a subject," who is constitutive and in the same time constituted by ideology. (see Althusser, 1971, pp. 170-177). The central idea is that at certain moment the identity of the audience appears to be missing, and it is this moment that the meaning of the three subjective categories—Chinese, television, and audience—get revealed. Furthermore, only when we recognize this temporary absence of audience identity can we truly understand the ideology of the marketplace and subjectivity during television viewing. What follows will be an elaboration of this point based on a discussion of the perception of the audience in regard to television advertising.

6.2 Good Commercials Are Not "Commercial"

In order to obtain an accurate understanding of the audience of television advertising, we must first and foremost get a clear idea about what exactly the audience are doing at the commercial time. At the surface level, the viewing patterns of commercials on CCTV1 are quite complex and diverse among the respondents. Table 12 shows the distribution of viewing patterns, i.e., what the respondents do at the time of advertising if they are watching the CCTV.

Fifty two interviewees[1] were asked about their viewing habits and 46 of them gave clear and definite answers to the question concerning their activities during the commercial time. As the table shows, attitudes towards advertising vary from like to dislike very much, with various options in between. Despite the apparent diversity, only three respondents among the 52 interviewees rarely watch commercials, and only six of them expressed any negative opinion

---

1 The interviews were conducted in the form of focus groups, with random selection of interviewees from different gender, age and income groups.

towards advertising. What the table reveals is a general tendency of constant viewing and positive perception of commercials on the television.

Viewing Pattern	No. of Respondents	Percentage (%)
Like commercials and keep watching at the time of advertising	7	13.46
Switch channel or do something else, but would watch commercials if they are interesting, or watch commercials on particular channels such as the CCTV1	23	44.23
Do not switch channel and pick some commercials to watch	3	5.77
Do not switch channel due to inertia	1	1.92
Do not switch channel and pay no attention	1	1.92
Watch commercials right before or after the show they watch (no negative opinions)	4	7.69
Do not like commercials but feel they are forced to watch	4	7.69
Do not like commercials, never or rarely watch	2	3.85
Rarely watch commercials due to rarely watching TV	1	1.92
Not applicable	6	11.54
Total	52	100

Table 12: Audience Viewing Patterns of Commercials on CCTV1

The majority (33 out of 52, i.e., the first three rows combined) of the respondents explicitly express that they would watch commercials if they are interesting. The follow up conversations show that those members of the audience who would stay with advertising due to inertia, those who claim that they stay with the same channel but pay no attention to commercials, and those who watch commercials because they don't want to miss the beginning of a program, actually watch commercials in the same way as the first three groups, which means 75 percent of the respondents constantly "pick" "interesting" commercials to watch. This of course, does not mean that they would concentrate on every single commercial on TV. Rather, it displays a general positive attitude towards advertising, which keeps them watching and expecting what they think as interesting and attractive in commercials. What we can see from this data is that advertising does constitute a very important part, favorable or otherwise, of the viewing experience of television audience. No matter they like it or not, the audience have to recognize its omnipresence and find their idiosyncratic way of dealing with it in their everyday viewing.

Quite obviously, the emotion against advertising as demonstrated by the example that was cited at the beginning of this chapter should not be understood as representative among the Chinese television audience. In fact, as we have already seen from the above table, most of the audience would watch commercials if they are interesting and there is little negative opinion against advertising as such. In everyday life, the majority of the audience watch commercials constantly, either intentionally or unintentionally, and we could assume that in some sense, they all watch commercials selectively. That is to say, all of the audience, including those who really hate advertising and rarely watch commercials (further conversations show that they watch no less than others based on the examples they give of their favorable ads), like some commercials and dislike others. Given the fact that they are obviously making distinctions (possibly unconsciously) between "good" and "bad", "enjoyable" and "unenjoyable" commercials, it would be interesting to see what it is that they like and dislike about the commercials on television, which may serve as a revealing departure point for understanding how audience make sense of television advertising as an important part of their daily viewing and possibly, of their daily life.

While talking about what they like about commercials in general, the following comments could be seen in their different versions:

Excerpt 1

Liu: I like to watch commercials mainly because of their exquisite pictures, especially the colors. They produce a comfortable feeling, particularly in those cleaning stuff.

Except 2

Lee: I think I like those which could tell a story. For example, the one with Chou Run-fat, the one for the Aoni shampoo. I think I like those which are realistic, those which touch your feeling.

89

Excerpt 3

Wei: Well, on the one hand, I feel there are so many commercials which take so much time and space, and most of the times you are watching commercials. On the other hand, I feel commercials are quite watchable. In a way, we enjoy them, like watching soap operas, you could appreciate. There are good and bad ones.

These first two excerpts are representative of those who like to watch commercials. The first demonstrates an important feature of television advertising, i.e., high visual quality, which is explicitly or implicitly expressed as one of the reasons for their like of television commercials by almost all respondents. The second reveals a tendency to talk about advertising at a more abstract level, with clear demands for narrative, authenticity, and emotional engagement—things that are not normally connected with advertising.

The third excerpt, however, is revealing in a different way. While leaving the annoying aspect of television advertising to later discussion, I wish to draw special attention to the fact that this is the most critical person within her group. This means that even those who feel "commercials force people to watch" in fact have a lot in common with those who claim that they like commercials. To some extent, those who like commercials and those who don't come to an agreement that commercials can be good and can be appreciated. This tendency is consistently found in each group that the most critical person within the group enjoy commercials on no less occasions in their viewing experiences. Given the possibility that the interviewing environment and peer pressure might have an influence on respondents who would be more likely to give positive and agreeable answers, this phenomenon at least reminds us that the attitude towards television advertising is not at all a simple like or dislike. More complex relations between messages/images and the profiles of the audience need to be carefully examined, which will be done in later sections.

Having said that, let us take a look at how respondents talk about some specific commercials they like in order to gain a better understanding of the audience's encounter with television advertising.

Excerpt 4

*Qi: There was an old Ericsson commercial. It is about a secret agent with a **James Bond element**. The **camera moves and cuts** fast. The most important shots like information collection at a particular spot, or murder, are edited together. Cell phone is used to contact or provide data and information. It plays a very important role. It demonstrates implicitly the functions of the cell phone....*

Excerpt 5

*Cheng: for example there is one that old people like to watch. The one in which a kid squeezed all tooth paste out and collect the covers to exchange for candies. It is a bit stupid, but shows the **innocent heart of children**. You hear the peddler's cry and you remember your own childhood... Another example has **cultural content** too. There is a kid wearing traditional clothes and hat, and a typical woman of the 1920s. The woman is making black sesame paste. The kid was looking at it with eagerness. He licked his bowl after he finishes. This one is full of the **spirit of children** and it is fun. It has its cultural content....*

Excerpt 6

*Wei: For example, the one for the cooking oil, it's quite **comfortable**... As for Rejoice shampoo, it makes you feel that if you use it, it does give you a kind of confidence. It's very comfortable...Probably people would rather believe the one like Rejoice, feeling that it's more meaningful. I mean there is something in it. It's not emphasizing hair. It gives priority to human being and hair should give such a feeling too.*

I put an emphasis on all the keywords in these comments. The first impression is that they are not talking about TV commercials, but rather about a prime time drama or a feature film. Excerpt 4 talks about the James Bond elements, camera movement, cuts and editing, etc.; excerpt 5 highlights the cultural content, childhood memory, and the spirit of children; excerpt 6 concerns feeling, being comfortable, confident, or meaningful. It is interesting to see that at certain moments of television viewing, commercials are not quite distinguishable from television programs in the experience of the audiences, and that they pick commercials in very much the same way that they pick programs.

Here the audience obviously steer away from the material side of advertising (i.e., the products) and deal with it at the abstract level of signification. The direction of these comments is consistent with that in their statements about advertising in general, except that it is much more specific here. Apart from pure visual aesthetics of television commercials, one thing is particularly prominent in their assessment of "good" commercials. First, a "good" commercial tells a story. The narrative should be interesting, the plot well designed, and the general mood compliant to what people feel in other forms of popular culture such as film or TV drama. Indeed, audience do watch commercials with similar expectations as when they watch television dramas or feature films. For example:

Excerpt 7

Song: yeah, these commercials should have revisions now and then. Have different versions all the times. I mean, it should make something beyond your expectation, gives you a sense of novelty. When it comes out, you would say yeah this one is good, really cool, it's attractive, feelings like that...

It is acknowledged by the audience that to achieve this in such a condensed form would be very hard, but it is firmly believed that this is what advertising has to do in order to make people accept the commercial, and consequently, persuade people to buy those products which are being advertised. 91

Another impression from these comments is that "good" commercials should be "meaningful", and the meaning of commercials goes beyond the products being advertised. It is not the meaning of the products, but the meaning of the images and the narratives, which becomes a medium connecting a product with some meanings that the product does not originally have. Thus, through talking about beauty, success, confidence, childhood memory, cool guys, and so on, good "commercials" please the audience and make them feel "comfortable".

The absence of the "real" signifier, i.e., the products, in audience's discourse demonstrates the arbitrariness of the connection between the signifier (the products) and the signified (the "James Bond element", the "spirit" of Children", the "confidence", and the "feeling" or "meaning" in general), since all these abstract properties originate entirely from the images rather than the products, and the connection between these properties and the products is everything but natural. It is assumed here that the preferred meanings of these commercials are: first, to make the products distinguishable from others of the same kind; and second, to express a meaning, or value, which draws upon their cultural context and the most prevalent beliefs of their social environment. In decoding the actual commercials, the audience do recognize the deferential function of these commercials and the meanings conveyed by those images or narratives.

As one of the audience states: "advertising does not advertise quality (of products), it only advertise a brand name." Here, the audience make a leap from the material level of the product to the discursive level of brand names, which is connected to the meanings of those images and narratives. Consequently, consumption is not only a material process concerning the need for everyday life, but becomes a discursive process that contributes to a meaning system that is equally important to humans as social beings.

It should be added that both excerpt 5 and 6 are comments from those who appear to be the most critical audience. As mentioned before, their critical perspective does not prevent them from identifying the positive aspect of advertising. Besides, excerpt 4 is by someone from the seniors' group, while excerpt 3 and 5 are comments from younger audience. Apparently, there is a difference between the old and the young in the sense that older people are more consciously concerned with the "cultural content", even though all the three conversations are about culture, or different dimensions of culture, and that the older people seem to be more articulate than the young. Besides, the audience in all these three groups are the more affluent ones. A look at the comments made by the working class audience reveal some further difference based on social economic status. For example:

Excerpt 8

* Which one impressed you most?

Liu: Those that are related to our everyday life. The one like Nokia,[2] it has nothing to do with us.

Fu: Cell phone is too far away from us. Working class still has the problem of food and clothing, what do we have to do with cell phones? We don't even have [landline] telephones.

....

Fu: The actors or actresses in commercials should be good looking. Don't make it too ugly....

* So it's a matter of looking?

Fu: yeah, a matter of looking. If it is a good looking one, people will feel (good). If you are not good looking, well, at least it shouldn't be bad looking. The ugly ones are disgusting.

Two things are worth noting in the comments made by the working class audience. First, they are particularly concerned with things that they could afford, or that are "related" to their everyday life. Second, and more importantly, this difference is in fact shadowed by a strong consistency among audience from different socio-economic background: while talking about what they like, both

---

2   This interview was conducted in 2000, when Nokia cell phones still existed in the Chinese market as a well-recognized brand name, and when cell phones were not as widely used as they are today.

the poor and the rich show clear preference over the more "meaningful", "cultural" and "comfortable" commercials, and criticize the aesthetically and narratively bad ones. That is to say, while socio-economic status does lead to difference in the audience's perception of television advertising, such difference only concerns the commercials that they do not like. Low income audience, as those from any other groups, prefer the image centered commercials to the product centered ones. Compare the groups of different age and social economic status and we could see that while preferences do exist over commercials of different categories of products, there is no direct identification between class and/or age and attitudes towards advertising as a whole.

Furthermore, even those who do not like commercials acknowledge that they too find commercials "watchable" sometimes and could enjoy something delivered by television advert. It is true that no one would concentrate on every single commercial on television even they generally appreciate it greatly, and that this positive attitude does not simply dominate among all audience all the time. However, this ability of identifying something positive aesthetically about television commercials is of tremendous significance in their daily television viewing.

Positive descriptions of commercials perfectly demonstrate the semiotics of advertising as Barthes (1973) and Williamson (1978) theorized, or the branding process that Klein (1999) described. Even though the ultimate goal of advertising is to sell products, audience are now neglecting products and focus exclusively on the entertaining aspect of commercials. The term "realistic" is used to describe the most "non-realistic" aspect of television commercials, such as a story of James Bond style. For audience, what they like and think as "realistic" about advertising actually has nothing to do with the product being advertised. As a matter of fact, while talking positively about television advertising, the products being advertised are completely absent. The persuasion of purchase is achieved through something that is not in the product itself.

What *is* mentioned is something other than the product. The audience never just talk about a commercial as such. A good commercial is always about something else, for example, a soap opera, or a James Bond film. It is about things they hold dear in life: culture, childhood memory, feelings, comfort, confidence, beauty, success, in short, meaningful things of life. In this sense, the audience expectations for commercials are not quite distinguishable from expectations for television programs. While talking about their favorite commercials, the audience always leave the material dimension of advertising, i.e., the products, and instead deal with it at the level of signification. Apart from the pure visual aesthetics of television commercials, the narrative should be interesting, the plot well designed, and the general mood compliant to what people feel in other forms of popular culture such as film or TV drama. Indeed, audience do watch television commercials the way they watch television dramas or feature films.

This reveals the pervertibility of the audience of television advertising. The audience, in their interaction with images in television advertising, reverses the definition of the realistic: the objective, external existence of an object is turned inward to provoke some internal sentiment that is considered to be concrete, real, and for that reason, objective. At this moment, life becomes meaningful through images in a commercial that has nothing to do with the advertised product yet has everything to do with real life. "Good" commercials thus become a relevant part of life, for they are attractive, meaningful, and memorable. They are part of the culture. In some sense, commercial culture is *the* culture.

This reversed perspective of understanding reality, this relevance of advertising in the experience of everyday life can be further illustrated by the existence of another category with an opposite meaning: bad commercials.

While taking about commercials that they do not like, the focus of the audience completely shifts. For example:

Excerpt 9

LY: The profit making is too obvious (in this commercial), it's not good. There should be something more, some more beautiful images. There was one for Dove Chocolate. It was very beautiful, which isn't so "commercial", not directly asking you to buy or promoting sales.

Excerpt 10

ZH: I feel among domestic commercials, the bad ones are those that just introduce products. The commercials are solely based on products. It is rather a menu of the product, but not a commercial. These give an impression of being too rigid, people don't like that. In fact, foreign commercials, while introducing a product, connect the product with life, and make prominent the function of the product in life. For example, the series of Pepsi Cola, the soccer series, are all very original. It connects Pepsi Cola with soccer matches. It's creative.

The interesting thing about these comments is that the audience expect that advertising, while being a means of promoting sale, should do this in a subtle and non-commercial way. To put it in a rather self-contradictory way: good commercials are not "commercial", only bad ones are. Without being aware of it, the audience criticize the first stage of advertising, namely, the "menu" type, product centered commercials which only introduce products and makes no (arbitrary) connections with abstract meanings or values. Furthermore, this obsession with images and stories has led the audience to request for the meaning and feelings that are not part of the products being advertised. While recognizing that advertising is actually a kind of "seduction", the audience are actually telling the advertisers: if seduction is what you are doing, you've got to do it in a skillful way!

It is not surprising that great majority of the audience consider "bad" commercials as everything opposite to the "good" ones, i.e., no comfortable feeling, no pleasing effect, no cultural content, no stories, etc. But what is really interesting is a different and rather contradictory tendency when the audience talk about what they dislike in advertising: products, which completely disappear in the discourse about good commercials, return in the conversations about bad commercials. This could be seen from the following comments from the audience:

Excerpt 11

Wang: These commercials we saw, I have an impression that they are not concrete and honest. All of them, no matter what it is about, there are no concrete content in it. What I mean is, if a product is introduced, there should be information about its functions, properties, effects, and even the price. There is no such information. Everything is exaggeration, including images. Besides, some commercials have their own special targets, such as lip sticks, facial care stuff. But others are universal, like toothpaste, which is not just for female. Everyone uses it, and you've got to tell us in a concrete way the functions of the toothpaste you advertise.

Excerpt 12

Liu: -Commercials should be close to our life. Those cell phones, and many other things, I never use them and I'm not interested. Those we watched, it seems that none of them has anything to do with my life, except the toothpaste....

Excerpt 13

Li: The problem is that it (the commercial for cell phone) doesn't let people know what the functions are of the cell phone.

Han: it doesn't say anything about the functions. It just tells you that there are many different models for this brand.

The discussion here mainly focuses on the "real" content of the commercials, i.e., the products themselves, which were rarely found in the comments on "good" commercials. Functions of a product—the absent center of all consuming behaviors yet excluded when the audience talks about good commercials—now become the pivotal point of evaluation. Complaints about (bad) commercials are all related to the product. Some, or most commercials, are bad because they either present false information about a product, or they provide no information about its functions at all.

What accounts for "bad" commercials then, is that they either say something false about the products, or they say nothing about the function of the product, or that they say nothing about things that are relevant in one's life. While good commercials are all about feeling (they "have to make you feel comfortable"), only in bad commercials do products and their functions matter.

Precisely due to the presence of the product, bad commercials, as everyone recognizes, are low in aesthetic quality. They are not interesting. They are repetitive and over-exaggerating. They directly ask the audience to buy. Their intention is too obvious. Bad commercials are naturally the embodiment of contradictions. They are both honest ("like a product menu") and dishonest (always claiming things they can't do) at the same time; talking too much about the product and not talking about the product at all. They are simultaneously too commercial and not "commercial." In a sense, it appears to the audience that they do not qualify as commercials.

At the first glance, comments made by the audience so obviously contradict each other that they become nonsensical. To be able to make sense again, they must be placed side by side with the above mentioned positive comments. As mentioned above, the audience are requesting advertising, explicitly or implicitly, to do their business in a "non-commercial" way. The implication of such perception is that for the audience, good commercials are not just a part of commercials, they are commercials as such. Being interesting is not just a criterion of good commercials alone, it is *the* criterion of *all* commercials. In this symbolic assertiveness, the audience complete the branding process by themselves and in turn require all advertisers to advertise brands, rather than products. I will elaborate on the issue of branding in the next chapter.

In relation to the audience, this is certainly not all.

On many occasions, the audience would often go beyond the products themselves, or even the commercials themselves, to talk about their resentment against commercials as a whole in relation to their viewing experience. For example:

Excerpt 14

Zang: You know sometimes I can't stand the terrible length of commercials before a program. It's too long. Then I'll do something else while waiting. If it's not too long, like shorter period of commercials between programs, I might just keep watching...

Excerpt 15

Pang: Why have commercials become a problem? The problem in our country now is that there is no fixed time for it. As I said, in other countries, the commercials can only have 3 minutes within half an hour. That means you could work it out when you should be back for the program. While what we have here is that sometimes it's long, and other times it's short. You can't figure it out. Sometimes you miss the beginning of a show. Thus you have to wait there to avoid this. ...Another thing is that good commercials are indeed worth watching. However, usually a good one will be repeated over 100 times a day, which makes you tired of it. It's like however good a food is, you can't have it every day.

In these conversations, again, the audience acknowledge that "commercials" could be "good" under certain circumstances. But this time it is not their focal point. These comments concern primarily the length of the commercial slots, which is a slight change of focus from specific advertisements to advertising in general. It means that the context of discourse shifts from the commercial time to overall television programming. Once being positioned among the general television programs, several things about advertising on television are identified as quite annoying, sometimes even unbearable, e.g., the extreme length of commercial slots, the unpredictability of the length of each commercial slot, and the high repetition rate of each commercial including those "good" ones. Here, advertising is obviously regarded as a problem which must be solved for the sake of pleasure in television viewing.

One thing which is of particular significance is that these problems are mostly related with local channels. In other words, while talking about the problems of advertising, the audience seem to make a comparison between CCTV network and the local ones, with the two at the good and bad side of the spectrum, respectively. The following conversation includes a typical attitude towards CCTV and local channels:

Excerpt 16

* Let's put it this way, the clips I showed is about 8 minutes long [about the average length of commercial breaks on CCTV1]. When you watched it, did you feel that it was too long?

97

Wu: I didn't feel it was long, since CCTV's commercials, its commercials are very expensive, therefore these commercials on CCTV are made short and concise, and the content is rich. It's not like the commercials on local channels, like on ITV, or HTV, all commercials are like...

Han: repeat the words for three times, and that's all for one commercial.

Wu: yeah, three times, and it's fairly long. Give you every detail, address to contact, etc. That you will feel...

Han: especially when two or three commercial periods are inserted within a TV [drama] series.

Wu: yeah, that really makes you feel long, but CCTV, like when I watched it just now, I didn't feel it was long. It was over soon.

* So what is your impression about the commercials on TV in general, are there too many, or just OK?

Li: it depends on the channel.

Han: CCTV has just the right amount.

Liang: yeah, CCTV has good setting. The audience don't feel it's redundant. On local channels, commercials are really long.

Han: especially those commercials are too blank, tasteless, not interesting.

But for those like the ones we watched, you won't feel uncomfortable.

Liang: those are local channels anyway. They are not like CCTV, which has all the big enterprises as advertisers. They invite celebrities. CCTV commercials make you feel comfortable.

In this conversation, respondents have repeated the problems that were already identified above. They also express a negative opinion towards the practice of inserting commercials within a program. CCTV is "superior" to local channels because it not only has "better" commercials, but it does not have commercials within its programs. Overall, in comparing local channels with CCTV, the respondents are not comparing two types of television channels, but two types of advertising, namely, the product centered advertising and the image centered one. An advertising slot with good commercials is not considered to be long even though it may be exactly the opposite in reality. The 5 minute Coca Cola commercial on the CCTV is only the most extreme example, but is by no means an exceptional case for the audience.

It should be noted that the above negative perception of television advertising is highly consistent across different age and income groups. It is true that overall, older people and working class people are more critical than the youth and the affluent. Older people are more likely to talk about advertising in a negative way, and older working class people are least interested in advertising. However, all the differences are quantitative rather than qualitative. In spite of the more frequent criticism from the older people than from the young over the unbearable characteristics of television commercials, no significant difference could be found in the way advertising is disliked. In other words, when the audience talk negatively about advertising, older people and young people express dislike about the same things. If we compare the comments in the excerpts from 11 to 16, which were arranged in a way that alternate between the older and younger audiences, it is amazing to see that the old and the young are so much alike in their criticism in every negative aspect of advertising from the function of the products to the length and timing of advertising on television. As for the variable of social economic status as specified by family income, hardly any evidence can be found in terms of its influence upon what the audience dislike about advertising.

If advertising is a problem that needs to be solved for the sake of pleasant experience of television viewing, what could be possible solutions for the audience? For such a persistent negative existence in television viewing, the audience are in fact quite explicit about how advertising could become bearable in their daily viewing:

Excerpt 17

Wang: the problem today is that advertising is too low in quality and too much in quantity. If there are reasonable amount, like what we said, three minutes every half an hour, it would be all right. Reasonably, people won't feel bad about it.

Excerpt 18

*Then do you think in general the advertising on television is too much, just OK, or perhaps, not enough?

Liu: can't say there are too much. As long as commercials are not inserted into programs, it's OK.

* But they are within programs, aren't they?

Yan: some channels are good, just two or three minutes, but others, like the M Economic Channel, and HTV, those commercials! They come just at the part of the show that interest you, they will insert commercials there, and it never ends. That is too much.

Liu: Commercials on CCTV1 and 2 are quite interesting. But on ITV and HTV, the commercials are all texts on the screen. That is not interesting at all.

* If we only talk about CCTV1 here, do you think there are too many commercials on it?

Liu: I think it's OK. CCTV is quite standard. It's punctual, the shows start at the time they are supposed to. So I think it's acceptable.

Apparently, the audience has found a simple solution to the problem of unbearable advertising: to identify good commercials (in good channels) and enjoy them. To put it in concrete language, their requirement for television commercials (mainly for local channels) is: be like those on CCTV1!

This certainly does not mean that the audience really love CCTV programs more than those broadcasted on the local channels, or that they watch CCTV more than the local channels. The point here is that in some sense, they are reaffirming the fundamental principle of advertising, that good commercials are never "commercial."

And in some sense only, because this is not just a simple return to what has already been said. Something else is at stake here. Identifying good commercials, as a particular way of coping with the problem of advertising, is not fundamentally different form the acts of switching channels or going to the toilet. What we must understand, is the conditions of these conscious choices by the audience.

As the audience explicitly expresses, if commercials and commercial slots are not that long, and if the quality of commercials are improved, they are actually quite OK with their existence, even will happily live with it, enjoying both programs and commercials. And right in front of our eyes there is a model to follow—the CCTV network is good in that their commercials are interesting, comforting, entertaining, short (as in the audience's feeling), less repetitive, and are placed between, rather than within programs. Such a negotiating position on the audience side is worth contemplating. First, for the audience the problems of advertising as were mentioned above are by no means inherent in advertising as such, but rather the matter of design and presentation. Second, all the comments from the audience on television advertising are of an ahistorical nature. The very (historical) existence of advertising, as a rather new socio-economic phenomenon, is never a question. Now we have come closer to the answer to the leading question of this chapter. To understand how the audience come to love something that they used to hate or actually are hating every day, something that is still annoying to the extent of being unbearable no matter how one looks at it, we have to go beyond advertising and television to see how the audience understand advertising as part of a bigger context of the economic.

The discussion so far presents a rather complex combination of love and hate of commercials on television, as well as a high consistency across diverse audience groups concerning what is liked and disliked about advertising respectively. These contradictions and consistencies lead to an obvious question: how does the audience maintain equilibrium between the programs that are supposedly the focus of their television viewing experience on the one hand, and advertising that is essentially an interruption of the viewing. In other words, in spite of the existence of "good" commercials, why do they have to cope with something other than the programs they watch, something that could be unbearably annoying most of the time? To shed light on these questions, we need to further explore the perception of the audience in regard to the social function of advertising.

6.3 Advertising and Consumption

It is widely acknowledged that television advertising has a great influence upon people's purchasing decisions, and it is so despite the vigorous growth of the social network.[3] In North America, for example, "a report from the Television Bureau of Advertising and Knowledge Networks Inc. reveals that

---

3   It must be acknowledged that after the turn of the century, particularly into the second decade of the new millennium, the dramatic development of new information communication technologies, third party payment, and logistics have led to a much more diverse influence upon people's purchase decisions. Advertising as a tool of marketing and persuasion is no longer limited to printing and broadcasting media. This means that instead of seeing less advertising, we are getting even more advertising given its omnipresence now with the ever growing presence of cellphones, mobile internet, and social network in our everyday life. When the television audience switch to their mobile phones for entertainment that they used to get from television, they are exposed to, and rely more heavily upon, advertising either in a subtle manner such as ad placement, micro-bloggers' recommendation, We-chat friends, etc., or in a rude and annoying way of being imposed upon them in online games and videos that they watch. This topic deserves a separate work for a more detailed discussion.

37 percent of television viewers make purchase decisions after watching advertisements on television compared to 7 percent for social networks."[4] In China, some previous study shows that 60% of the audience admit that they are influenced by adverts in their consumption. While empirical surveys cannot give any definite explanation to such extensive influence, the interview data of the present study may shed light on two important aspects concerning the influence of television advertising upon the audience: the degree of awareness on the effect of television advertising, and how the audience themselves make sense of its relationship with their consumption behavior.

At the surface level, the present study provides similar data with those obtained in large-scale surveys. Out of the 33 respondents who are asked whether advertising has an effect on them, 17 explicitly expressed that advertising has a direct effect on their consumption choices. For example:

Excerpt 19

Wu: well, for me, I learnt about Rejoice and Head & Shoulders from commercials. I feel that in the commercials their hair is very good after using the products. Of course, they pick good hair for advertising. Then I buy it and use it. Before I had a lot of dandruff, and now I almost have no dandruff. Later on I keep using it. It's good for me.

* Do you think that commercials have an effect on your consumption?

Li: It certainly has an effect!

Han: a great impact, indeed.

Wu: I think when people learn something new, they learn it from commercials on TV or radio, but not learn it when you go shopping and see them. You see it first on TV.

Han: Usually it's not you feel like buying something when you are in the store, but you go to the store with something in your mind, and compare different products before you buy. Usually you learn it from commercials. That's why I said we must have commercials.

Excerpt 20

Liu: if you ask me, when I buy something, I pay special attention to those advertised products. For example, shampoos. The assistants in stores would introduce to you this or that, but I was thinking, well, I never heard about them. I would buy Rejoice. This is the psychology when I buy something.

This is quite representative for both young (excerpt 19) and the old (excerpt 20) audience who think advertising is influential in their consumption. It also tells us that most of them are clearly aware of the role of advertising in terms of informing them about what is available and what is good in the market.

---

4   "The Influence of Television Advertising," by Gary White, in *Chron*, http://smallbusiness.chron.com/influence-television-advertising-64010.html. Accessed in January 24, 2018.

Together with survey data in other studies, these examples suggest that advertising indeed has a great influence upon consumption, and the audience are quite explicit on that fact. In the meantime, there are 12 respondents who did not give a direct answer about the role of advertising in their purchase decisions and 4 who state that advertising has no influence on them. It is only when the conversation shifts from television commercials to their everyday consuming behaviors, do these audiences begin to talk about television advertising, and demonstrate equal degree of reliance upon advertising in actual consumption. For example:

Excerpt 21

*Among so many brands, how do you choose the one you buy?

Yan: Me? I first watch advertising, and then take a look at the price, and buy the affordable ones. But often times, I buy those famous brands that have reasonable prices, and also those being advertised. As for those which are never advertised, I can't be quite sure whether they are good or not.

Excerpt 22

Wang: I can't say that I don't believe them (i.e., commercials). I also wish to buy famous brands, because the brand itself has its value, or it is something that has been tested and prove to be good...

102   The two examples come from one younger group (21) and one older group (22), and the latter one is also the one who holds negative attitudes towards advertising at another time. Both of them express that advertising has no effect on them while being asked directly. However, as the conversation goes on, they start to talk in a completely different language, showing a contradictory opinion. In both cases, famous brands are prominent in their choices. For the first one, there is also a more general distinction between those "advertised" and "non-advertised" products. As all the previous examples, what these two excerpts show are exactly two fundamental functions of advertising: to cultivate demand and to differentiate one particular brand name from all others. For the latter function, the excerpts refer back to the previous discussion. It won't be too off the track if it is assumed here that the "famous brands" in these two excerpts are synonymous to those in the "good" commercials as the audience have clearly defined. Since we already know that "good" commercials tell nothing about the products themselves, preferences in consumption are once again based on the ability of "good" commercials to provoke "feeling" of comfort and reliability.

It is quite obvious that the impact of advertising is in the same direction here as was shown by earlier examples. What these audience tell us is that while the degree may vary in terms of the awareness (or unawareness) of the impact of advertising in our everyday life, one thing in common among all the audience is the belief that without advertising, there is no effective way to tell which product is good. Such belief is popular cross the board, and no age or income related differences have been found among the audience.

Specifically, those who are aware of the influence of advertising are those who like advertising or at least do not have much negative opinions about advertising, while those who think advertising have no influence on them tend to be more critical. In either case, however, the audience show the same degree of familiarity with the same commercials, as well as the same tendency in their consumption under the influence of advertising. Such influence is instructional: they tell people what to do when they have dandruff, or when they are happy or sad, or when they need friends, or when they try to express love for their parents. For the audience, being "critical" towards advertising does not lead to any resistance in actual consumption, as could be seen from the following example:

Excerpt 23

Z: I don't think they are that magic. And some products, you use them and they are not magic like that. Tides, we all used, it's not that magic, like it cleaned without any effort, it's not true, you still need to wash it with some effort.

* Then are you going to buy it?

Z: Certainly I still buy it, it's just that I don't believe it as it says. You've got to buy washing powder anyway.

* Then how would you choose when you buy?

Z: When I buy it, maybe, ah, I still think that American products are a little better. Besides, there is a fashion, everyone buys it.

* What do you mean by American products?

Z: P&G products. It's like, I feel that P&G products are a little better than the old Chinese brands. Besides, domestic ones are not well packed, they look bad.

* Do you mean they look good? Or you think they are better because you use them and think they really are better?

Z: look better. In use, I didn't do a lot washing.

The same respondent states at another moment that she "rarely" watches commercials, and there is a strong argument that she does not believe advertising because what it says is not true. However, her comments on specific products demonstrate clear instructional influence from advertising—picking the product that is advertised the most on television. It is a choice based on its frequency of appearance on television rather than quality. More importantly, the audience in general accepts a value judgment that certain kinds of products are better than others, which, in this case, are the American ones. The same value attached to certain brands could be seen more clearly from another example:

Excerpt 24

LN: If prices are close, maybe I'll have my choice among different brands (of cell phones), since it's not a matter of the product itself. It's like, you buy this one and people see well it's Iphone. But if you bring one and it's ah, say, Dongbao, it's different, right?

Everyone in the group laughed at the reference to Dongbao. The respondent did not elaborate on what the difference was. The meaning is obvious in its context to everyone present. "*Dongbao*" is a fake name, indicating a brand that is basically anonymous, undoubtedly made in China. The central idea is that "it is not a matter of the product itself," which implies the connection between a cell phone brand to such things as social status, rank, self-desirability, etc. It is most interesting that the same respondent used to work for Motorola in China and made a clear statement from the perspective of a technician that "all cell phones are the same inside" and "the only difference is the cover."

The above examples have demonstrated a strong correlation between preference for "foreign" commercials and that for foreign products, which could be the US shampoos, Japanese electrical appliances, or Finnish cell phones (around 2000) and Iphones (after 2009). This correlation is quite noticeable throughout the research, and is especially prominent among the younger generation, though not exclusively so. One may argue that it's hard to say whether this preference is because of good advertising or good product. As one of the respondent says:

Excerpt 25

* Can you make a comparison between Coca Cola and "Fei Chang Cola" [a domestic brand that existed in the late 1990s and early 2000s with similar packaging style as Coca Cola]?

Wang: ah, I feel Coca Cola is better. I feel so.

* Better in taste or better in advertising?

Wang: no, absolutely there is no influence from advertising. It's the product that is better. Perhaps there is some influence, but not very important. Whether one buys it or not will ultimately depend on its quality. However, when you know its quality, you already buy it. Given the large market of China, it is marvelous profit even if one buys it only once.

Both the audience own experience (as in the case of former Motorola engineer) and critical advertising research have illustrated that no significant difference exists between different brands, and certain products are connected with certain social status or images. It follows that for an ordinary consumer, trying a product of certain brand is simply a test to see which one is the best, but for its advertiser, this "once" might mean "forever". Therefore, while acknowledging the possible interference of other factors—quality of the product, for example—in determining the preference for foreign brands over domestic ones, it is impossible to eliminate advertising as an important independent variable.

As shown in the above conversation, even though the audience would like to believe that product quality is what leads to their purchase decisions, they do admit that "when you know its quality, you already buy it". Not only does this statement imply how consumers buy a product before knowing anything about its actual quality, but how the audience mean exactly the opposite when they say advertising has no influence on consumption. This discrepancy between the actual influence of advertising and the audience perception of such influence is illustrated in no better case than that with Japanese electronics products. Let us first look at an example of how the Japanese products are represented in the memories of the audiences:

Excerpt 26

Zhao: My family usually would buy quality stuff. When VCR was popular, we bought Toshiba M 747, which was the best model at the time. At that time, there were products of different prices. My mother said, the best one must be the most expensive one. It's still very reliable even today, many years. Our first TV was Toshiba too. It was in 1985, the first imported color TV sets were given to those government officials of the province, and they sold them. We bought one, and used it for more than 15 years; it's still working without any problems.

Excerpt 27

Li: at that time, there was no advertising, but in people's mind, those brands are quite reliable. Although there were no advertising, people thought they were the good ones. Like Philips, Toshiba, Sony, Panasonic, the Japanese brands.

This preference for Japanese electrical appliances is most articulate among the affluent people, but remains consistent in different age groups, and is especially prominent among the middle aged. The above two excerpts demonstrate simultaneously the power of advertising and people's unawareness of it. Both respondents in the above conversations emphasize the fact that those Japanese products relied solely on their quality in occupying the Chinese market. In the meantime, their memory is accompanied by a denial of any influence from advertising, or on certain occasions, of the very existence of advertising of Japanese products on television in the early 1980s. However, research has shown that Japanese companies were actually the most aggressive advertisers in the Chinese market throughout the 1980s, when they established the first foreign advertising agency in China and two thirds of foreign advertising in the 1980s were Japanese. By 1985, most Japanese advertising was conducted in the form of barter programming, which means that CCTV received "free" programs from Japanese programmers, who got the commercial time in exchange (see Hong, 1994; Zhao, 1998). Not surprisingly, those commercial slots were sold to the big transnational companies such as Sony, Panasonic, Toshiba, Hitachi, etc. More interestingly, by 1985, the time mentioned in the above excerpt when the first imported TV sets came, all those Japanese companies had been advertising without their products easily accessible in the market. It is a perfect example about how demand is produced before the actual consumption. In this case, the influence is preparatory in that advertising tells people what (new) things are (going to be) available in the market and inform the potential buyers. The impact on consumption is indirect. It prepares consumers and cultivates demand and brand loyalty.

6.4 The Social Function of Advertising

As shown in the above sections, the viewing patterns of and attitudes towards television advertising are quite complex, at least at the surface level. The attitudes cannot be simplified as watching or not watching, like or dislike, and contradictions and inconsistencies are frequent. The audience as much as pleased by the "interesting" commercials as they are annoyed by the poor quality, the length, and timing of advertising on television. Despite all apparent variations in viewing patterns of and attitudes towards advertising, it is quite interesting to see how unanimous people are in their perception of the influence of advertising in their life, and how positively this influence is conceived. Although on many occasions the audience may feel disturbed by "bad" commercials and bad timing in the broadcasting of them, the general attitude is that advertising has a positive effect. The following excerpts might be illuminating as of why there is such a unanimous agreement about the positive effect of advertising:

Excerpt 29

Han: Advertising is certainly good. It has good effect, very good. Otherwise, why do they bid for the five second golden time after the evening news every year? It surely is good. It lets you know about more products. Without media like advertising, it's quite, ah, primitive, right? You don't know about things and can't recognize what it is (without advertising).

Excerpt 30

W: I think they are very useful, especially when you have so many things, and you enter a department store and you see immediately what you want...

Excerpt 31

X: Advertising is indeed useful. For example, Head & Shoulders, it tends to emphasize its anti-dandruff function, which distinguishes itself; while Rejoice tells you about soft hair. I feel I had dandruff before, so I used the shampoo Head & Shoulders.

What these examples suggest is that the overall positive and affirmative attitude towards the existence of advertising is determined and conditioned by the perception of the audiences in regard to the social function of advertising. The apparent divergence in their perception of "good" and "bad" aspects of advertising conflates in the perception of the positive existence of advertising as such, whose informative function is unanimously acknowledged and applauded. The consensus is striking across all age, gender and income groups that without advertising, there is no effective way to inform people of what is available out in the market, and as a result, fewer choices will be available. Not a single member in the 14 groups by any means deny the positive effect and importance of advertising in their life.

The most significant fact her is the identity shift while talking about their opinions about the function of television advertising: the respondents are actually unexceptionally assuming the position of consumers rather than that of the television audience. The primary concern here is no longer television programs and television viewing, but that aspect of advertising which is considered to be directly related to their everyday life. As have been repeatedly demonstrated, the audience regard advertising as a useful source of information, and often times as a way of problem solving. In a modern society, it is something that makes life not "primitive" and more prosperous materially.

Among the audience, the perceptions on the social function of advertising are multi-dimensional. As an important component part of the commercial system, advertising involves manufacturers, media institutions such as television, and audiences as consumers. The first thing to be noticed is that taking the position of consumers, people tend to feel that it is quite natural for manufacturers (or to be exact, the branding companies) to have advertising, regardless of its annoying amount and interruption of the programs they watch. For example:

107

Excerpt 32

ZG: Now you must advertise, otherwise who would buy your products? It's hard to imagine that people would buy a new brand. Who dares to? Unless they are things like what you said, things which are necessary but have not been available. Otherwise, who dares to buy it?

Excerpt 33

Zhi: You can't live without it. You've got to tell people what products there are. That's the means of informing. Otherwise how could I know what brands are there? Right? You've got to inform me of the manufacturers, quality, prices, and so on. All these need to go to people through the media. It's a means of propaganda.

It is consistently recognized that as a means of opening the market for particular products, advertising is essential for corporations. In fact, as is shown in the above two excerpts, advertising is required to be there by the audience. They may like or dislike the commercials on TV, but advertising is necessary, helpful, and therefore indispensable in our society. And this fact should not be challenged. As one of the respondents points out, yes, it is "a means of propaganda", but this propaganda must not be confused with the political one that has been losing credibility and popularity. For this new propaganda, no one feels that it brings negative influence, since it is the propaganda that the audience/consumers want and that the society demands.

Besides the consideration for manufacturers—that they must have advertising in order to sell/inform of their products—there is also an understanding of advertising for the sake of the TV networks:

Excerpt 34

*Liu: ...the commercial itself is very entertaining, but I don't want to buy it. I'm not going to buy it because the commercial is well made. It depends on whether the product is useful to me. Therefore, I think advertising is not of much use. **But if you remove it, it is too costly to fund a TV station. If the TV stations don't provide programs to us, we'll really have nothing to do.** I don't do anything except watching TV after I retired. My two sons said I'm sufferring snile dementia, and only watch TV on weekend. Some people play chess every day, but what good does that do? At least you learn something from TV every day.*

Excerpt 35

Pang: that has to do with a country's economic situation. For example, Britain is rich, and they can rely on the national financial budget to fund their broadcasting stations. The state could support TV stations with money. While in our country, TV stations are all self-supported. They all depend on advertising revenues. So, it's understandable. There is too much advertising, we could understand that, since TV stations are going to buy or produce diverse entertaining programs, they have to have the money. Like if you are going to investigate the origin of the Yangtz River, it all needs money. Where does the money come from? We can say that most of it comes from advertising.

* So we still have to have advertising?

Pang: yeah, we must have it. This is inevitable.

In addition to the already discussed function of advertising, these conversations reveal two other popular beliefs among the Chinese audience. First, it is the audience who are dependent on the media institution instead of the other way around. Television broadcasting does not rely on its audience, but on advertisers who provide the major part of its funding. The audience are at the mercy of television stations and government policies to lay restrictions over the timing and amount of commercials on television. These restrictions, ironically, are not likely to take place (and should not take place) according to the above logic, since there is something objective in all these commercial activities, something that should not be subject to any deliberate control. Second, the commercial broadcasting system supported by advertising revenues is a natural system, which is inevitable and perhaps the best possible system we could ever have. Therefore, if this system needs advertising, the audience certainly have no reason to oppose. The obvious misunderstanding of both the current Chinese system (as entirely supported by advertising) and the British system (as entirely relying on state budget) is by no means insignificant in that it reveals what is inaccurate but preferred by a newly emerging commercial system in the context of China in a transitional period.

It must be admitted this is the ideal type of audience that advertisers and media industry could ever wish for. There is a strong argument for the cause of advertising, in the shoes of both advertisers and TV networks, that advertising exist because there are too many commodities and too many brands, and we must have advertising so that television may have programs to show us and we have someone to inform us which product is the best choice. The ideal audience is the one who look at themselves not as viewers but as consumers.

This argument among the audience is based on the assumption that more commodities and more brands are good for individuals as consumers. For example, some respondents have argued for the materialistic prosperity:

Excerpt 36

WS: and the thing is that more brands is a good thing for consumers. If there is only one or two brands, it must be bad for consumers. I have more choices, and there is the competition in both price and quality. There will be monopoly, if there is only one brand. There will be no choice for consumers.

One thing seems to be self-evident for the audience: since everyone loves to have more consumer products, there is no reason why we should not have advertising, which is an intrinsic part of the materialistic prosperity. This perception of being materially better off and the inevitability of advertising are so strong that it holds even among those who did recognize that there is little difference among different brands, and advertising is simply making connections between totally unrelated things. For example, respondents would talk about Rejoice shampoo (which has the narrative about the confidence of a female student who chooses space aeronautics as her major in college) in the following way:

Excerpt 37

LY: Too artificial. How could they be connected?

CA: What does aeronautics engineering has to do with Rejoice?

Q: What does it have to do with bright hair?

C: Buy a dozen Rejoice shampoo for her, and she could go for aeronautics engineering.

LY: Then Ph.D. students get a bunch of Rejoice shampoo when they graduate.

Q: See how many Rejoice you use for your degree. It's ridiculous. Neither female nor male can identify with it. It doesn't flatter anyone.

LY: Well, usually when you get used to one brand, you only buy that brand, and rarely change. Since things like shampoo, it's hard to say which one is better, and which one is not as good as others. For shampoos, advertising may be quite necessary.

* Do you think you need so many brands?

Q: well you can have your own choice!

LE: it's good to have many brands.

Q: anyway, consumers won't lose, ah... won't lose much.

While talking about the commercial for the Rejoice shampoo in the beginning of the above excerpts, they are pointing out that it makes a bad connection between a girl's confidence to go for the major of aeronautics engineering and the Rejoice shampoo. Apparently, they are engaging with this commercial in quite a critical way. However, when it is put in the context of their perception of advertising in general and examined in relation to other commercials they mentioned, the finding is just the opposite: the same respondents would emphasize the advantages of the commercial system. Even though there is little difference in quality among various brands, it is still good to have these brands and consequently, necessary to have advertising. The rights of the audience and citizens are never raised, and the question of environmental cost of materialistic proliferation is completely neglected, and the free access to television channels as public properties without having to watch commercials is simply out of the question.

Now we could give a definite answer to the fundamental question: how come the audience loves something they hate?

While the audience may feel negatively about many commercials on TV, they all think positively of the act of advertising as consumers. Behind this apparent contradiction lies a fissure of identity, i.e., the position of consumer vs. the position of the audience. Collectively, the audience gives up their identity, or betrayed their identity as audience. They become consumers, who feel thankful of the availability of choices among many products with advertising ready to help. At the fundamental level concerning the nature and legitimacy of television commercials, all the resentment against advertising has been subdued by the firm belief in the practical function of advertising.

That is to say, the audience solely assume the identity of consumers rather than that of television viewers in their perception of the social functions of advertising, and would assert that advertising is definitely necessary in various dimension—manufacturing, distribution, and consumption.

Thus we can see that the audience willingly gives up their identity of audience because they understand that advertising involves the multi-dimensional relationship in which the various parties involved—the corporate sector, the

110

media, and the public—are not of equal importance and therefore should not enjoy equal rights in determining how television should be operated. The relationship between the media and the corporate sector is far more important than that between the media and the audience.

At a deeper level, the present data show that the perceptions in regard to advertising by the television audience is closely related to the general economic situation (though not economically determined). Earlier in excerpt 35, it was already seen that some respondents were referring to the general economy to explain the legitimacy of advertising. In fact, the tendency to contextualize advertising within a "commercial" system is quite popular among the audience. For example:

Excerpt 38

Cheng: This does not change according to our will. If it is a commercial world, everyone has got to sell, then advertising will never be eliminated. We'll only get more of it. As for whether people believe it or not, it is a natural process. Some do, and some don't. You don't have to believe. The world is... it's hard to say. As far as I see it, celebrities are people who know nothing. If they are to make commercials, I absolutely don't believe. But if it is a member of the Academy of Sciences, or Ph.D. from a medical school, then I will trust him, because scientists are the most honest. They won't say it cures if a medicine doesn't....

Excerpt 39   111

Wei: ... and I think it is an economic phenomenon, I mean advertising. It's like an economic law. I think it should be "capitalistic", as some may call it. Since there is commodity, value, there is money, currency, naturally these things would come into being. It's weird that China has this "socialist market economy". I feel it's very awkward. In fact, this is just like the moving of stars in the natural world. It has its own laws of movement, which ensures its normal movement.

Excerpt 38 reveals two interesting facts. First, one may dislike commercials, but its existence is not questionable since it is part of a system that is assumed as fundamentally good and natural. Not only is change beyond the reach of the audience/consumers, but to talk about such change would be unrealistic and therefore meaningless. Second, this system will always resort to "experts" to increase its credibility. Under the circumstances that audiences assume the position of consumers, there is no need to talk about the legitimacy of advertising (which is always already legitimized by the audiences themselves), and the only thing left is to gain credibility of the advertised products. Since most of consumers know nothing about products, "experts" are the most reliable source of good reference. Not all respondents are conscious of the influence of experts, but experts do constitute an important part of the system and offer valid support that is considered neutral and trustworthy. Excerpt 39 further reinforces the assumption that underlies the legitimacy of advertising—that advertising is something inherent in the economy. In other words, it is not just advertising, but the whole economy, the exchange relationship, the need of selling and profit making, which sets the boundary of any argument concerning the commercial system. In the specific case of television advertising, economy (i.e., the need to sell and consume) and the rules of commercial system undoubtedly have priority over the uninterrupted programs on television, even though the latter is supposedly the content, perhaps the only content of intentional viewing.

This explains why respondents are so obsessed with the practical significance of advertising, and insist on the positive effect and social function of it. The examples we have quoted so far have illustrated that the perception of the audiences in regard to the social function of advertising is based on their understanding of the operational rules of a commercial system in which the most important thing is to sell and profit has unquestionable priority. The legitimacy of advertising is actually the legitimacy of the commercials system of which advertising is a part. Advertising becomes symbolic, and discursive—it represents the whole commodity relationship, and to recognize its legitimacy means to identify oneself as a member of the mainstream.

However, the fact remains that commercials on television cannot be watched unless viewers are attracted to watch by programs, i.e., one has to be a television viewer first in order to be a consumer who watches television commercials. Given this, it is quite surprising to see how difficult it is for respondents to assume the position of television viewers. Even when they are pushed to think of the issue as audience instead of consumers, there still cannot be any challenge to the legitimate existence of advertising. As the following excerpts illustrate:

Excerpt 40

* Would you think it good if we have fewer commercials?

Rong: It depends on when the decrease takes place, if it is the commercials within programs, I'd be happy.

* What about fewer commercials on all slots.

Liu: That is not good.

* Why? You can better enjoy the program.

Liu: Well, it's tiring to watch programs all the time, there should be an adjustment.

* What if there is no commercials but something else, something that gives you a break, such as trailers, but no commercials, what about that?

All: That's not possible.

Liu: it's like there is nothing to watch on television, and it's not bad to have commercials to watch, just as a change of mood.

Excerpt 41

* Aren't people disturbed by advertising?

Wang: Not by its practical functions. Commercials introduce products to consumers. Of course they have their value. They have their influence on us. What disturbs us is its lack of substantial content. We don't like it when it does not give substantial information which we need.

Besides the possible improvement in terms of better commercial slot (between programs instead of within), this conversation demonstrates a reluctance and even resistance on the side of audience to the possibility of removing advertising, or just part of the commercials, from their daily viewing, even though it could be very annoying as they mentioned before. While being forced to make a choice—only in theory—between enduring the annoyance of television advertising and television without advertising, the respondents would rather choose the former and completely disregard any alternative without hesitation.

This resistance further answers the question that was raised in the previous section as of why the audience have to cope with advertising even though they may have very negative opinions that are sometimes so strong among all of them. We already know from various examples that the viewing experience of the audience is conditioned by their recognition of two contradictory facts. As the audience, they see commercials on television as too long, poorly made, deceptive in content, disturbing in the timing broadcasting , which therefore constitutes a problem that has to be solved. As consumers, however, they admit that advertising has a very positive effect as a whole which is helpful in their shopping experiences. The apparent contradiction is resolved when economy enters the picture. It turns out that the very act of taking the consumer's position is predicated by the consensus that economic practice has the absolute priority in the operation of television network and the survival of manufacturers. The economy has its own laws and rules which are objective and have to be respected and observed, sometimes at the cost of the viewing pleasure of the television audience. In the case of television advertising, and advertising in general, it constitutes an indispensable part of the economy in the sense that it links manufacturers with consumers, which are two important sectors in the chain of production. Consequently, advertising is perceived to be inherently positive and all the problems are temporary and can be solved through improvement in technical and management terms.

Now the relationship between the audience and television advertising becomes clear. All the positive perception of "good" commercial is in fact a particular way of coping with advertising in the viewing experiences of the audience. Even under the circumstance that a commercial break within a popular program actually ruins the viewing pleasure, it cannot be possibly removed due to (1) the practical guide it provides for consumption, and (2) the essential financial support it provides for the TV networks to broadcast programs. Both excuses that the audience find to legitimize the existence of advertisements on television are conditioned by the economic law, objective, neutral, and untransformable in comparison to any individual will. This "objective" law—the natural relations of exchange, the fundamental pursuit of profit-making—sets the boundaries of peoples' imagination. To reject advertising is to reject the very logic of the economy. The audience not only welcomes advertising, but also insists that there must be advertising. It is an obligation to love advertising if one is not so insane as to reject the commodity proliferation and return to the extreme poverty the past, i.e, 40 years ago. Everyone understands, and must understand, the importance of the economic, as well as the role of advertising in the economic. It is mandatory for corporations to advertise for the sake of opening up the market for a product. It is mandatory for media to advertise in order to be able to fund their programming. This new, commercial "propaganda", it is said, is what the people need. After all, how could we possibly be an informed consumer in front of a hundred brands of shampoos and know which one suits us the best?

The legitimacy of advertising is therefore the legitimacy of the whole commercial system and the whole commodity relationship. Advertising is but a part of this relationship. It has presented the image of commodity proliferation, demonstrated the self-evidence of exchange relations, and negotiated with the audience through television programs played at the intervals between commercial slots. Yes, I mean it: programs are what the audience get at the intervals between commercials, a reward for watching the commercials.

114

The comments made by the audience quoted in this chapter reveal two major themes concerning how the audience cope with television commercials in their daily viewing and ensure an endurable viewing experience. First, they focus on the entertaining aspect of television commercials, and appreciate its aesthetic quality and narrative structure, as demonstrated in the conversation about their favorite commercials. It is true that commercials can be "false", "too long", and "interrupting programs", but they will be bearable to viewers as long as they are able to find "good" commercials and look at them as another type of entertainment on television, something that is superior in aesthetic quality, more condense in structure, and more exciting in their narrative. The distinction between program and advertising is somewhat blurred in this situation. To push it to the extreme, commercials become a kind of functional program, which may serve as a "break" during the viewing of regular television programs. In prioritizing the aesthetic quality of "good" commercials and the practical function of breaking up programs, the audience persuade themselves about the legitimacy of advertising and live with it as an inherently positive part of television with some flaws that can be overcome.

The second way that the audience cope with commercials on TV is more subtle. Recognizing the status of advertising as a discursive symbol of the economy in general, television viewers can achieve a prompt switch from the identity of audience to that of consumer when they have to face the problems in their daily experience of television viewing. As the interview data expose, there are inevitably moments when commercials are so "badly made", "so long as to be unbearable", or play at such a bad time that is the most exciting part of a program, that nothing can make the audience appreciate them. Yet the boundary set by the unchallengable priority of the economic interests does not provide a space to question the nature of advertising. What the audience do at this moment is to switch their identity from that of television viewers to that of consumers. Commercials, however disgusting they are for the television audience, are important and positive in the eyes of "consumers".

Once one identifies him/herself as a participant of this "objective" and "inevitable" relationship, the identity of the audience can only be temporary and fortuitous at best. Once the identity of consumer is established, even the possibility of talking (hypothetically) about television without advertising would sound absurd. The audience would rather choose to cope with the annoying commercials in a variety of idiosyncratic ways: switching channels, going to the toilet, having some snacks or drinks, taking a nap, stretching, walking around, waiting for the "good" commercials, and so on. But a television without advertising is simply disastrous and therefore unimaginable. It would mean, in the collective consciousness of contemporary China, a system without economy, a return to the horrible poverty of the old days and even to spiritual poverty.

Contextualizing advertising in the broader social economic relations, watching television is no longer merely an individual practice for pleasure, but rather a collective behavior through which each individual identify him/herself with the mainstream of society and catch up with the social advances radically undertaking in contemporary China.

When commercials are good, we love them. When commercials are bad, we love them as consumers. Such is the ideal type of television audience, who look at themselves as not audience but consumers. The implication of the audience of Chinese television advertising cannot be exaggerated since it reveals the direction of a new hegemonic process in contemporary China and the formation of a new mainstream ideology, which will be elaborated in the next chapter.

Chapter 7. Advertising and the New Social Order in China

Let me continue my investigation with the hope that the empirical data in previous sections may provide an opportunity for further theoretical reflections upon the very idea of the political economy of television advertising, which in turn may lead to a different angle for understanding changes in contemporary Chinese society as a whole. To that end, I would like to address in this section one aspect that was mentioned but not fully explored in the previous section, i.e., the issue of class in advertising, in a way that will illustrate the way that the working class has been marginalized, even rendered invisible within the rapidly commercialized society of contemporary China. Television advertising has been both reflective and constitutive of this status of the working class in China today. This discussion will then lead us to an investigation into the social and political conditions within which such marginalization could be possible.

7.1 Watching, Working and Class

Talking about class in China is an awkward attempt. It means to act against both the official discourse and popular sentiment, to insist upon a topic that has been discarded in the Chinese society since 1978 with tremendous effort at the state level and which is greatly celebrated at the private level among intellectuals. A critique based on class distinction is often considered to be the residue of the Cultural Revolution, and dismissed as an obsolete perspective that is too simple and negligent to various other forms of sufferings at the micro level of everyday life experiences.

In this section, the issue of the working class in relation to television advertising will be discussed at two levels. First, I will look at the creation of a new type of "working class" in the act of television viewing, as laid out in the political economy of communication. This involves the idea of the audience as a commodity, watching as labor, and the process of producing surplus value for broadcasting networks through the audience's watching. To such existing critique of advertising, I would add that the creation of a new type of "working class" through watching is in fact the creation of a "watching class" who produce surplus value for advertisers (in addition to the network) through the symbolic production of meaning. Secondly, the present study tries to provide some insight in regard to the exclusion of the working class (as actual factory workers) from the process of such a symbolic production. In this sense, it is in the same time a process in which the working class in the most traditional sense of the phrase retains their status of working class without turning into consumers. In other words, they remain to be audience as they watch television without experiencing the split of identity into one of the audience and the other of the consumer.

7.1.1 The Political Economy of Watching

Now is a good time for us to revisit an old question that was left unanswered while reviewing the literature of political economy of communication. The answer to this question will lead us to a much better understanding of both the political aspect of political economy and the root of social changes in contemporary China.

Do industrial workers indeed produce all surplus values of a commodity, and is there indeed nothing happening and therefore nothing to explain in the watching behavior of the audience? As was mentioned, Jhally (1990) did not offer a direct argumentative response to the critiques of this kind, but rather used them to highlight his own approach (p. 119). He does, however, end with a hint that "human activity (watching) as a power" is missing in the critique of orthodox Marxists. My argument will continue from this point of "valorisable human activity" (p. 120). In order to walk out of this mystery, we have to look at a part of the broadcast media, which has been pushed to a secondary position (if only for analytical reasons) so far, namely, the message. Here I do not mean the content of television programs, but of commercials. This is certainly not to argue for a return to the message centered paradigm, but the investigation of messages as an integral part of the unified process of production.

Despite the insights gained in not focusing on messages, and despite a total lack of attention to commercial messages by orthodox Marxists (even by Jhally, in the sense that their meanings are somewhat irrelevant in the production of value and surplus value), messages remain an important, even indispensable part in the whole process. The fundamental argument I would like to make is that in the objective act of watching (commercials), the audience not only produces the commodity of watching time and consequently surplus value for the network, but also produces—through interaction with the commercial messages—surplus value for advertisers. This is what I mentioned as the significance of Smythe's analysis that he himself failed to recognize—that the audience also labors for advertisers in a way that surplus value is produced and expressed in the increase of the exchange value of a product as an inevitable result.

Jhally makes a very good point in clarifying the true creator of values and profit for commercial media industries. But if one does not believe that watching time is a commodity, then one does not have to accept the value of watching time. For these people, the answer lies in the phenomenon that is unique to late capitalism, i.e., the branding process in which the (exchange) value of a commodity/product increases.

As always, advertisers' self perceptions already revealed the secret, who have made it very clear that it is the audience who completes the branding process (see Wang, 2008, p. 38).

This, of course, may be easily brushed aside as something based on marketers' self conception that is an upside down understanding of reality and therefore should not be taken seriously as a legitimate starting point. Such disregard of advertisers and media institutions, however, is based on the assumption of a total, complete, and uninterrupted process of production of surplus value achieved by, and only by, factory workers. This is hardly tangible today when production has assumed different characters at both quantitative and qualitative levels.

119

The first interruption comes from the advertising agency. It is much harder to deny that people working for an advertising agency—copywriters, graphic designers, photographers, video producers, etc.—are dependent upon the surplus value produced by factory workers. Given that as a significant part of the "production" cost, this part of the expense paid to an advertising agency for promotional materials is evaluated on the basis of the exchange value of the creative work (e.g., the ad) by workers in advertising agencies, can we still assume the total accomplishment of surplus value by factory workers?

The second intervention comes from the mass media, such as television, and its audience. We should take seriously what advertisers say about the branding process. If it cannot take anyone other than the audience to complete the branding process, what do they do to make a brand valuable, that is to say, to assume a higher exchange value?

I might have moved too fast and already bypassed the answer that I tried to get—a commodity as the result of production in the era of "late capitalism" necessarily contains two *indissociable* but heterogeneous parts: (1) the product, i.e., the object with use value, and (2) the brand, as represented by the logo with its particular meaning attached. Both are purchased by consumers, and each presupposes specific conditions for its use value and exchange value.

In the very beginning of her book No Logo, Naomi Klein (1999) points out that ever since the 1980s, corporations have recognized that they must primarily sell brands, as opposed to products. In the era of branding, the production of goods is more and more a foreign concept to a corporation. Consequently, advertising is no longer about the product, but rather the vehicle used to convey the "core meaning" of the corporation to the world. A brand is not just a name, a symbol, an image. It is a "concept," an "experience," a "lifestyle" (Ibid, p. 21), it is the only possible way that one experiences culture. The arrival of the "era of branding" may have arrived even earlier than Naomi Klein has perceived. As early as in the 1970s, advertisers had recognized that their task was no longer to "rob sales from competitors," but to "teach the new consumption behavior," to give people confidence to try "better foods, new ways of keeping clean, use of tools, a raft of objectives and techniques which the village schoolmasters fail to get across" (Stridsberg, 1974, p. 77, in Sinclair, 2008).

The distinction that Klein makes between advertising and branding is conditioned by the distinction between a product and a brand. The latter is of far more significance—it constitutes an act of extreme violence in the era of late capitalism, which completes the fetishism with the exchange level by cutting off, through advertising, the production of goods from not only daily experiences (something that has already been achieved), but from the discursive possibility in regard to the chain of production.

120   This understanding of the separation between product and brand is essential to the present discussion. Let me approach it in a concrete way, as Marx (1912) says, "our investigation therefore must begin with a commodity" (p. 1).

Take Nike as an example. In its early stage, factory workers made Nike shoes which were sold by Nike as just shoes to realize their surplus value. Today, in the era of branding, however, there can be many interruptions between the labor of a factory worker and the final realizations of all the surplus value of a pair of Nike sneakers upon completion of the transaction by an end user. We all know that Nike has long ago stopped producing sneakers itself. It buys from sub-contractors and labels them as "Nike." Then, there is the advertising agency, which produces commercials that promote Nike the brand but not the shoes which happen to be named Nike. Finally, there is television, among other media forms, that draws the audience (through programs) to participate in the branding process by watching, processing, and transforming commercial messages into an integral part of their memory, and then of their lifestyle despite their obvious distrust and disgust of advertising.

Each of these interruptions constitutes a related but independent process of production of value and surplus value. To assume that all the profit made in these intervening sections are but distributions of surplus value produced by the factory workers in the first stage sounds far fetched. Nike makes a lucrative profit, that is much bigger than what is obtained by the manufacturers, advertising agencies, and broadcasting combined. The important fact is that this happens at the remotest time and place away from where manufacturing wage labor takes place and gets compensated.

In theory, a pair of Nike sneakers can be compared with a pair of non-brand name sneakers, both produced by the same worker with the same amount of labor, on the same machine, and in the same factory in Guangdong, China. The former sells at a retail price of $200 in North America, and the latter $20, in the Chinese market. If, according to Marxian analysis, wage is determined by the necessary social labor, while profit is determined by surplus labor, then the discrepancy between the prices of the two pair of sneakers must be caused by something other than the labor of the factory worker, whose wage compensation is the same for producing the two pair of sneakers with different brand names.

The answer lies in the fact that as soon as a pair of shoes, as nothing but shoes (with use value and exchange value) before the labeling, leaves the hands of the sub-contractor, another production begins, the production of making the shoes into Nike or Li Ning (a domestic brand name) sneakers. The effort of branding by both can be easily noticed, as the differences in the frequency and intensity of their advertising on television.

As part of the branding process, the broadcasting of a TV commercial involves two activities: selling the air time to advertisers, and wathcing the commercials by the audience. In this process, the watching behavior of the audience is essential for both the network and the advertiser. It is the condition of selling the air time for the former, while the condition for selling the brand for the latter.

But the act of watching is by no means the end of the story. It has to be the right kind of viewing. As Klein (1999) points out, "within a context of manufactured sameness, image-based difference had to be manufactured along with the product" (p. 8). Such a manufacturing must be completed at both the encoding and decoding ends. That is to say, the meaning of a TV commercial has to be produced, in a structural way, by both the encoder (producing company and its crew) and the decoder (the audience). To that end, it must be an active viewing that constantly engages with the ideas, concepts, values, and lifestyles articulated by the words and images of the commercial. In the case of Nike, the creation of the symbol of sports, athleticism, and a way of healthy, energetic life, must be achieved by an interaction between the audience and the Nike commercial.

It is thus the audience's labor that produces the highest surplus value—in addition to that produced by the factory worker—hence the staggering amount of profit for a pair of sneakers that is called Nike. The condition of it is a necessary separation of Nike the shoes and Nike the brand. That is to say, with the shoes, there is something additional, which is a symbol, a concept, a meaning of life, a spirit, an abstraction that may exists independent of any concrete products.

Ontologically, a product and a brand are not separable, i.e., the concrete, material thing is the necessary condition for the symbolic meaning, while the symbolic meaning, the brand name, must be attached to some concrete, material thing. In the branding process, however, the relation is a perverted one. Instead of being something secondary to the product, the brand name assumes relative autonomy of its own. It still has to be connected with something concrete, but much like the relationship between money and commodity, now the brand name assumes primacy, while the concrete product has to be attached to a brand name in order to assume high exchange value. Though a brand name requires a concrete product, it does not rely on any fixed one. That is to say, for a brand name, the concrete thing can be *anything*—be it a pair of sneakers, a T-shirt, or a book mark. Like Marx (1996) says, "consumption appears as a [conceptual] moment of production" (p. 139).

It has been well recognized by even consumers themselves that consumption is no longer limited to the confines of material goods, even though it by no means lacks materiality. Consumption is now more about image, idea, and concept, than about the mere product of sneakers. What is less visible is the fact that such values, concepts, lifestyle, in short, the brand, is their own creation, albeit a symbolic creation as the result of interaction with the commercial messages.

Therefore, advertising is inherently an exploitative form of mediation. Throughout this symbolic production, the audience is under multiple exploitations. They are poorly compensated by the television network,[1] they are working for advertisers for free, but not just free, they have to pay the advertiser the cost of the production of the commercials and air time when they buy Nike sneakers, a combination of shoes and a brand name. In short, they are paying for the product of their own free labor. This leap from the symbolic to the material, from the abstract to the concrete, constitutes the double exploitation of viewers as workers.

Now we can say that surplus is created by two types of workers, the factory workers who are underpaid for their work, and the living room workers who pay to work.

This, I believe, is to look at capital as a whole, and to look at the chain of production as a whole. It is an expansion of Marxist materialism, one similar to what Raymond Williams tried to achieve by expanding the domain of the "base" (Raymond Williams, 1980, p. 35), to emphasize the "social character of communications" (p. 41), that production of meaning is a concrete process of value (and surplus value) production.

122

---
1   In this respect, the theory of the "least objectionable" program is perhaps having great interpretive power. Given the overall low quality of television programs, what the audience chooses to watch is not something they like the most, but rather something they dislike the least.

In the meantime, we must take a cautious step in getting too excited about the symbolic production of meaning and the surplus value that is produced during this process. As I said, such a process is conditioned by a violent cut that removes the very possibility to talk about "real" production process—the productive labor that increases the material wealth of a society. That is to say, while there is an increase in the exchange value (at the symbolic level) in the branding process, there is no increase of use value at the material level. The increase of capital is achieved mainly through the redistribution of wealth. Despite its existential truth, television viewers as workers are still fundamentally different from factory workers in one thing. That is to say, they largely belong to two different classes in the social reality beyond living room. For this reason, the audience whose labor involves the symbolic production of meaning can be called the "watching class." To name them as "watching class" and maintain the traditional sense for the category of "working class" is of crucial significance in contemporary China. The distinction helps highlight the pervertibility of television advertising: while the only "freedom" of the workers is the freedom to sell their labor, the real working class is deprived of such a "freedom" to sell their "labor" as the audience. This will be elaborated in the following section.

7.1.2 The Watching Class and Working class

In China, the significance of the creation of this "watching class" cannot be grasped on its own terms. It must be put side by side with the real working class, in its most traditional sense, i.e., factory workers. The comparison includes three steps. First, the working class is too poor to be the target audience of advertising and is therefore excluded from the "watching class" who produce surplus value for advertisers through the symbolic production of meaning for brand names. Second, the watching class subsumes the status of "working" class within the domain of television watching, i.e., the symbolic domain. Third, the transformation, or the subsuming of the working class status by the watching class is not only an achievement by the advertisers, but reflective of some bigger changes in a broader context. Let us look into these three aspects in details.

(1) The Working Class and Advertising

In both daily talks and interviews, one repetitive theme is that of affordability. The following are a few examples from my interviews in the early 2000s with a few workers (in their fifties) from former state owned factories (translated from Chinese and edited slightly with repetitions and cross talking cut off and some words of clarification added in parentheses).

Respondent 1: Cell phones are so far away from us. The working class is still struggling for food and clothing, what do cell phones have to do with us? We don't even have (landline) telephones…. I don't buy Head & Shoulders (shampoo). I use soaps, for washing my hair. There are very few things that I can afford among those advertised products. We haven't reached that level. It is impossible to rely on advertising in actual life, because they are too expensive. I don't like advertising, if it is removed, I'm glad to do that. Most people would be happy about it.

Respondent 2: What we ordinary people ask is cheap and substantial stuff. We can barely survive now, not to mention buying things that we see in commercials. It (advertising) is useless, because you still have economic problems. You want to buy it but couldn't afford it. Many families, like mine, don't even have a refrigerator.

Respondent 3: There is no use of it (refrigerator)—there is nothing to be stored, no leftover. Besides, we can't afford electricity. A family that I know goes to bed as soon as it passes 9:00 at night, to save electricity. They use 15 Watt bulbs, and they don't watch TV.

Respondent 4: There are fewer things that I'm able to purchase today than I could in the past. Yeah, salary is higher, but still we couldn't afford as much as before. The price is 20 times as high as before. There are more things today, and larger variety, the market is prosperous. It's all a matter of whether you have the money or not.

The level of their disposable income determines that these members from the working class are primarily excluded from the process of symbolic production of meaning through television viewing. It is quite obvious that these people are not the target audience for advertisers. The striking contrast is their capability to imagine (even just imagine, and temporarily so) the possibility of television without advertising, and their capability to say that advertising is "useless" is shocking enough given what has been heard from the "middle class" audience.

As was mentioned in the previous chapter, audience members would refer to the product itself when they identify a "bad" commercial. The return of product in the conversation has yet another internal distinction: a (not so fine) line between the critiques of "bad" commercials from the middle class and that from the working class. While the middle class audience is unsatisfied with the first stage of advertising—the menu-like introduction of products—and requesting a subtle form of seduction, working class people are yet to be completely assimilated into the commercial culture and its ideology.

Critique of television advertising from the working class primarily focuses on affordability. It is unequivocally situated in, and constantly refers to their living conditions. Such a critique of advertising's relevance (or the lack of it) to their living reality is nothing close to an aesthetic judgment as what was mentioned before. Rather, it is a declaration of their socio-economic status, which is a condition that leads them to a non-fetishistic and non-fantastic perception of social reality.

If, according to advertisers, consumers can be divided into different "collar" groups, then the working class has to be defined as "no-collar" due to their existence outside the category of target consumers defined by advertisers. This is particularly true for former workers in the state owned factories who became unemployed during the process of the reform, or the privatization of what was once public property. They have lost their jobs and have no health insurance, no pensions,[2] and no experience of the positive effect of the reform. They are perfectly aware of the fact that the factory that belonged to them only a few years ago has now become the private property of their former factory leader, while there is nothing they can do but to endure the poverty under the socialist market economy. For them, television commercials are but another reminder of the absolute decrease in both their purchasing power and social status.

In his famous "notes towards an investigation" of ideology, Althusser (2001) points out that ideology is a "representation of the imaginary relationship of individuals to their real conditions of existence" (p. 109). In the above moments when working class members talked about advertising and their lives, they showed no signs of anything imaginary. For the working class audience, the fantastic relationship between advertising and "real" life does not exist, at least not in its complete sense. We need to take into account that these workers are the generation who grew up under the influence of Mao Zedong and the socialist revolution and construction, and their "weapon of critique" therefore differs fundamentally from the mainstream, i.e., the relatively young middle class audience. Their being able to stick to such a weapon of critique, of course, is first and foremost due to the deterioration of their economic conditions and the down shifting of their social status. What is prominent is the consciousness of the absolute lack of connection between television commercials and their life experience, namely, the un-affordability of the vast majority of consumer goods presented on television commercials.

This type of critique is rather unsystematic and often incoherent, but is obviously a different form from what is described in most literature on cultural resistance, which is based on the act of consumption or no consumption (see Duncombe, 2002, pp. 1-15). The much clearer grasp of reality by working class people is conditioned by the specificities of their very existence. Their existence as well as their perceptions of such an existence testify both the totalizing potential of the commercial ideology and the impossibility of ideological totality, which must be kept in mind if one is ever to understand the hegemonic process unfolding in China.

(2) Watching Class Subsumes the Status of "Working Class"

The term "working class" is used by both the working class people themselves, and by the advertiser. The very fact that advertisers are the only group who appear to use this term today in the public sphere is rather ironic. This is certainly nothing coincidental.

---

2   My interviews showed that the former SOE (State Owned Enterprise) workers who became unemployed in the 1990s did not have their social security reinstated until at least 10 years after their layoff, and the monthly payment that they receive (RMB 600 Yuan for one who has 30 years of employment according to the 2016 policy) is too low for them to enjoy the latest high-tech products.

Now we are facing two working classes. The self-evident yet largely invisible working class is old, poor or extremely poor, and resistive to brand names. They rarely contribute the symbolic labor for advertisers, hence producing little to no surplus value for them. They are excluded from the statistics of advertisers. They are, in fact, excluded from the very process of meaning production, for advertisers in particular, and for commercial culture in general.

The "working class" (created through television watching) in advertisers' vocabulary is young, affluent, and active in television watching in terms of their participation in the symbolic production of meaning to complete the branding process. In short, they are the target audience as suggested by the content analysis. As if to reflect what actual happens among the audience during the process of television viewing, advertisers name them the "working class," and in doing so, replace their real-life socio-economic status with their working status in the domain of symbolic production. In a perverted way, advertisers are simply being descriptive.

This can be categorized as a process of valorizing one group while excluding another from the discursive process of constructing a new social structure. Considering what we mentioned before, that commercial culture is *the* culture to be recognized, for those who are unable to participate in such a culture, the valorization/exclusion is necessarily a process to remove them from social life altogether, very much like creating a concentration camp for the (real) working class, so that they will neither be seen nor heard. The transformation of the "watching class" into "working class" therefore functions as a discursive process to replace the real working class with a "better" version, one that looks good, and never complains about either their own socio-economic status or their role in the process of branding. Indeed, if the "working class" is living such a wonderful life, what the factual workers and the unemployed former SOE workers suffer would be a nothing but a painful but necessary sacrifice for the overall progress and development.

Among advertisers, "the working class" is both an accurate term and a misnomer. On the one hand, they are working for advertisers and network television, with the political consequence of making the real working class invisible. On the other hand, they are not the working class in its strict sense, that is to say, factory workers, immigrant workers from rural areas, service labor, etc. Subsuming the position of working class and assigning it to the watching class who are in reality middle class—joint venture employees, college professors, government officials, doctors, lawyers, stock market brokers, etc.—effectively transforms the conditions for the accumulation of social wealth (namely, the labor of the real working class) by fetishizing the element (i.e., middle class consumers) that is most essential for the domain of exchange.

In advertisers' vocabulary, "working class" has a nick name, "the blue collar" consumers. This specification does nothing but add further confusion to the term, as they use an interesting term to describe the "blue-collar"—mainstream consumers, or the perceived majority of the population (Wang, 2008, p. 15). Apparently, it does nothing but repeating what advertisers have already done to the middle class audience, namely, labeling them with something that they are not, first working class and now blue collar.

What is the cause of confusion then? Well, while it tells us again about the above mentioned transformation, the term "blue collar" consumers does include blue collar workers in its real sense. In other words, the use of "blue collar" by advertisers reverses (at certain moment) the process of the infamous transformation of the watching class into the working class. Even though the middle class consumers are the target audience of television advertising and for that reason the real "mainstream" consumer, the idea of blue collar consumers as the mainstream consumers is integrating the real working class into the category of consumers, thus making it assume the *appearance* of being part of the target audience, which ultimately means that they are now part of the same watching class to which the middle class audience belong.

But it is a fake consumer status for the working class. This reversed process can only take place at the discursive level. The real blue collar workers—blue collar without quotation mark and mainstream only in terms of their size—cannot be possibly turned into middle class at the socio-economic level, and therefore cannot be possibly turned into the watching class for the symbolic production of branding. It is obviously so even in the advertisers' own report: the consumption habits of the "mainstream" consumers (i.e., the blue collar workers) appear to be very much like the working class (the proletariat in its exact sense) that I cited earlier, in the sense that they are characteristic of having the urge for saving, caring for prices first, and making purchases based on need rather than desire, and so on (Wang Jing, 2008, p. 16).

This additional "misnomer" is by no means insignificant. It inadvertently brings about the most prevalent misunderstanding about contemporary Chinese society in the most ironic way: that by the sheer size of its population, China constitutes the biggest market in the world. The absurd nature of such a notion can be easily seen in the fact that the center of capital flow is located in the United States, as well as the fact that the most noticeable strategy adopted to attract the so called "mainstream" consumers is the representation of upper-middle class lifestyle.

Such a misconception also echoes the one mentioned in the discussion of the content of Chinese television advertising, i.e., the overestimated purchasing power of the blue-collar—real or otherwise—consumers. It is both strategic (albeit an ill grounded strategy) and an ideological inevitability. Even though transnational marketers have picked up these blue collar consumers and started to gain volume from low end markets through low prices, the creation of desire and a whole set of new value system can not be simply brushed away, just like advertisers' own research has shown that Chinese consumers do not buy out of desire (Wang, 2008). Such strategic and ideological inevitability are based on

127

something undeniable—that class distinction is a simple fact in China today. The working class, as a real social force in global capitalism, must be transformed into the middle class with either real purchasing power or consumer status at the discursive level. If both fail, then they must be pushed into oblivion where they are invisible and what they say will be dismissed as irrelevant.

(3) Working Class in the Reform (Post-Mao) Era in China

The discursive transformation of the role of the working class in television advertising reveals a structural similarity with its role in Chinese society since 1978, when their decreased purchasing power has been accompanied by an increased degree of urbanization, modernization and commercialism.

The idea that advertising reflects an ideological transformation in Chinese society presupposes a chronological order, and social phenomena characteristic of distinctively divisible stages in history. In the dramatic changes in urban China during the past four decades, "working class" as both an economic and political category stands out as a defining (though sometimes invisible) element of the social changes since 1978. In retrospect, even though the reform began in rural China, it has its holistic nature and an eventual urban focus. In any case, discourses about the working class, or the lack of such discourses, may tell a lot about the nature and direction of these changes.

Up to 1978 and well into the first decade of the economic reform, the working class has been unequivocally defined as the leading class of Chinese revolution and socialist construction, as could be seen in public addresses by government officials, newspaper editorials, and textbooks at all levels. The second half of the 1980s witnessed a gradual fading away of the leading role of the working class in the Chinese economy, official discourse and social consciousness, particularly when state owned enterprises started to undergo structural changes that aims to "separate the (political) functions of the state from the management of enterprises," remove party involvement in decision making, and initiate the stock ownership.[3] This process sped up after 1992. Restructuration within the state owned enterprises led to the reduction of public ownership and rapid growth of private enterprises and for the first time since 1949, unemployment became one of the most visible social problems in China. In the meantime, the working class related discourse has continued to fade out. At the turn of the millennium, class was already an obsolete word which was replaced by stratification and is only used when the "middle class" is concerned. This has happened at all levels including civilians, intellectuals, and government officials. In popular discourses, there is now only a "wage

---

3 These goals have been achieved to various degrees, contingent upon struggles among interests groups. For example, the stock ownership has been established with relatively less resistance. As for the state intervention in management, it has never been completely removed, and even strengthened on certain occasions. The problems of state owned enterprises today is that on the one hand, government interventions in various forms do not always result in improved efficiency, and on the other, government functions may not be well performed leading to serious loss of the state owned assets.

earning" strata and the term "working class" no longer resonates with workers. In academic research, workers are no longer a unified entity (if they ever were) but a strata, or interest group, which is deprived of any political implications (e.g., see Duan et al., 2002).

To be cautious, we must not assume that the working class is an indivisible entity that is homogeneous and lacks any internal variations. For example, the blue collar workers in Wang (2008), if they refer to real workers, are in fact a group who is clearly better off than those factory workers of former state-owned enterprises who lost their jobs during the process of SOE related reform. Such internal distinctions, however, become insignificant given the similarity in the consumption habits of the two groups. The blue collar workers documented as mainstream consumers by advertisers (or their research assistants within academia) in the first two decades of the new millennium appear to be very much like the "no collar" (unemployed) workers in the 1990s. But Wang is at least right in one thing: those "blue-collars" are the mainstream in terms of their ideology, which may further help us understand the oxymoronic term of "blue collar" consumers.

The ideological shift in China has many concrete reasons. One of them is that the reform and opening-up policies has made it possible for the Chinese to access images from the West, images of immense accumulation of wealth that look more like the socialist promises than the socialist reality in China during the two decades before 1978, even though such images ultimately led people even farther away from those promises. 129

The working class, namely, the workers from the former state-run enterprises who are now unemployed or the "no collar" workers, continue to live at a low living standard. Some of them may even have experienced a decrease in their absolute purchasing power as was shown in my interviews. At the same time, they have seen little sign of a social transformation that may actually help them regain the status of the master of their country. They have come to accept the reality that some changes are inevitable, such as the existence of advertising on television. Also like the omnipresence of advertising on television, (social) changes can only be quantitative, rather than qualitative for them. The gap between images in television advertising and their living reality is far from encouraging. Popular reaction to social inequality is that it is largely one's own fault if one is poor. The swinging between a leftist position (when facing a corrupt bureaucracy) and a rightist one (when facing a potentially radical alternative) is by no means a mutually exclusive ideology, but has a consistent underlying logic, i.e., the inevitability of the market economy—whether it is called socialist or capitalist—or the end of ideology (ideology as represented by the discursive style of Cultural Revolution). The mechanism and process of this ideological shift deserves careful examination. In the Chinese context, it illustrates in a rather convincing way the relative autonomy of ideology that we dealt with in the section on the theoretical framework.

The widened gap between rich and poor, as well as the fact that the working class is struggling for survival and necessities, has demonstrated a clear homogenizing development in the four decades after 1978. In the 1980s, one felt angry about printing an ad that takes one whole page of a newspaper; in the year 2000, the working class can still talk about the possibility of a different television system; in 2008, "blue collar" workers became the totalizing term used to describe the "mainstream" consumers. During this process, advertising has assumed more and more material as well as discursive power, and constituted part of a mechanism to obscure the (re)appearance of a working class who has not genuinely enjoyed the reward of the reform. To understand such a mechanism, we have to understand the conditions that make advertising possible in the first place.

7.2 State, Civil Society, and the New Social Order

The deliberate effort by advertising agencies to identify blue collars as the mainstream and educate/seduce them with images of upper-middle class life style has been explicated. Needless to say, it would be absurd to attribute the ideological transformation in contemporary China solely to the manipulative and exploitative existence of advertising. In fact, it would be highly problematic to claim that such transformation is mainly caused by changes in the economy and therefore the primary concern should remain in the domain of the economic. To understand the Chinese television advertising, one must grasp the dialectical relation between the economic and the political, and more importantly, the relative autonomy of the ideological superstructure that, in the case of China, had a decisive role in the social development of China.

7.2.1. In the Beginning Was the State

(1) What is Transition?

One popular critique of China by the left in the West is that after over two decades of commercialization under the banner of "socialist market economy," China has developed into a state that combines "political socialism" and "economic capitalism." Correspondingly, there exists another descriptive dichotomy between the political propaganda of the socialist (or "communist" as a term used in the Western context) state and the commercialism that promotes material enrichment or proliferation through a free market economy.

Apparently, China is now in a transitional era in which the political propaganda is no longer producing consensus but is still holding control, and in the meantime the voice for liberal democracy and its consequent privatization and commercialization becomes the mainstream among the people but still cannot be dominant at the level of state power.

Within such a discursive context, some questions are naturally of primary concern, such as, how will the present trend of commercialization end up? Will it take over at the political level, replacing Party control with commercial hegemony as in the United States? Or will it be exploited by the Party as another means of political hegemony? Under this binary perception, advertising would either become a dominant factor that is omnipotent or a functional factor to be utilized by the political power, which would lead to the idea of advertising as an integral part of the ideological state *apparatus*.

Also, two critiques may result from these questions. One looks at China as already too "capitalistic" and the socialist discourse is nothing but an effort to maintain Party control and social stability. The other looks at China as not "capitalistic" enough, and that socialism (or totalitarianism, as a synonymous term for socialism in Hayek and his followers around the world; see Hayek 2007, p. 43) is impeding the development of a truly free market and democratic society.

All these binary understandings are based on a fundamentally flawed assumption that the so called "socialist" discourse and the marketplace discourse are antithetical and mutually exclusive to each other, thus rendering impossible a clear understanding of the very existence of advertising on Chinese television that is still a tightly controlled medium though without the appearance of Party "mouthpiece." This is not to return to the harmony in the official discourse of the "socialist market economy," but rather to point out something that is obvious yet has been constantly ignored: fundamentally, the (re)appearance of advertising is a political act that has been effectively depoliticized.

To truly grasp the reality regarding the Chinese television advertising and the social totality it embodies, we need to focus on the "political" aspect in the "political economy." To do so, the power of the state must be clearly understood for its being the very site of the political (Schmitt, 1976). In China, this can be testified by the discourses that befriend the market economy and distance from the planned economy—a term that has been missing in several consecutive reports of the CPC National Congress—at the state level, which set up the very parameters of what can be said and what cannot. A side note would be that since 1978, *effective* expression of state power was primarily non-violent, relying mainly on what Althusser calls "the ideological state apparatuses," of which advertising is an integral part. This may sound counter intuitive. Human rights advocates may have a problem with the "non-violent" characteristic, but one only need to be reminded about the fact that all alleged violations of human rights are connected with the "communist" China, rather than the "capitalist China," even though criticism of China exists along both lines. This deliberate choice of prefix is sufficient to demonstrate the ideological success by the state power in and outside China, and how badly those critiques miss their target. It is at the very moment when one thinks "freely" that state power expresses its truly hegemonic control. Let me explain in detail by looking at one of the loaded concepts that has become part of common sense (a Gramscian term regarding how hegemony is achieved) in China: transition.

The very concept of "transition" is, according to Wang Hui, "both historical process and historical myth" (Wang, 2003, p. ix). In every historical moment since China's first traumatic encounter with the West in the first Opium War in 1840, the concept and the discourse of transition have functioned to mobilize people for a wide range of specific political causes, although none has gone beyond the parameters of the liberal constitutional state. The narrative and the naturalization of the process of transition since 1978 is in itself part of a new ideological project, which, according to Wang (2003), started with the unraveling and transformation of the traditional socialist regime. Fundamentally, it is a discourse that is to legitimize the "Chinese characteristics" more than the socialist characteristics and the "market" economy more than the planned economy. Despite internal nuances, the narrative of "transition" in contemporary China since the very beginning of the reform and the opening up has always been revolving around the economic development. Behind the breaks and disruptions at the specific historical moments lies a highly consistent line that has guided the social development in China since the reform and opening-up.

The key moments when such discourses function have to include the following ones: 1978, the beginning of the rural reform and the individualization of agricultural production; mid-1980s, the beginning of the urban reform, or the separation of the political and economic function within state owned enterprises, and the fast growth of non-public ownership; and 1992, Deng Xiaoping's talk in his "Inspection Tour in Southern China" which ended the debate over the nature of the reform. I will elaborate on these key moments in the following sections, with a special emphasis on the relative autonomy of ideology.

(2) Rural Reform—the Individualization of Agricultural Production

The 3rd Plenum of the 11th Party Congress in December 1978 marked the official turning point towards a Post-Mao era in China—or what is later called socialism with Chinese characteristics, a term that in the official discourse is an innovation in applying the basic tenets of Marxism to the concrete national conditions of China as had been initiated by Mao Zedong. However, even though at the time there was no explicit criticism of Mao Zedong and the reevaluation of the Cultural Revolution was to be put off till an "appropriate time" in the future (which turned out to be 1981 when it was officially defined as a 10 year unmitigated catastrophe), it was quite clear that Mao and his policies were no longer the guidance in actual political and economic works. The principle of practice as the "sole criterion of truth," adopted from Mao's writing, was used as an implicit criticism of Mao's policies during the Cultural Revolution, and a precursor to the torrents of criticism of Mao's line but a couple years later.

The most publicized decision of the "1978 Plenum" was the shift of focus in the Party's work to "socialist modernization," which, as Maurice J. Meisner (1996) points out, was hardly a new phrase, but has ever since assumed a "new" meaning in Deng Xiaoping's era. It was officially declared that "the aim of our Party in leading the whole nation in making revolution and taking over political power is, in the final analysis, to develop the economy" (Han Gang, "On the Development of Modern Industry," Beijing Review, March 24, 1979, p.9, quoted in Meisner, 1996, p.99). Modernization is no longer the "employment of state power to develop a backward economy to serve ultimate socialist goals," or "a means to achieve a socialist and communist future," but the very end itself, which subordinates "all considerations, social and otherwise, to the task of rapid national economic development, pure and simple" (p. 99). It is no coincidence that the first television commercial since 1949 appeared on the Shanghai TV in January 1979, immediately after the 3rd Plenum of the 11th Party Congress. Both its timing and geographical location is suggestive of the return of a once (shortly) repressed desire for a mode of production that is not based on public ownership or central planning, at both material and symbolic level.

The inversion of the end and means of the socialist state and the representation of "socialist modernization" as a newly discovered task have been accompanied by a discursive process in which every act or decision of the reform could be invariably contextualized by the narrative that attributes the devastated economy (and other social and economic problems) to the Cultural Revolution, and at the fundamental level, to "ultra-leftism." Despite popular indifference to Party propaganda, this official version of a rather recent history has never been seriously questioned up to today.

Indeed, popular perception of social reality often conflates heterogeneous categories into a confusing undistinguishable totality. Mao is considered to be the one who is solely responsible for the mistakes of the Cultural Revolution; the Party is a unanimous bloc under the one man dictatorship of Mao Zedong; and correcting mistakes means correcting mistakes of the idolized patriarch, without any further reflections upon how exactly the mistakes were made, when they were made, and who made them under what conditions. In the meantime, intellectuals' perception of the Cultural Revolution is by no means more reflexive. For example, the following quotes can be easily found from both the left and the right: "the economic reform was launched when the nation was still under the shadow of more than a decade of disastrous destruction of economic and human capital due to ideological radicalism from 1966-1977" (Wang Hui, 1994, p. 7); "this elite recruitment policy was reversed after Deng Xiaoping came to power because the previous policy had brought disasters to the country" (Zheng, 2004, p. 35); and the popular phrase of "the ten years of turmoil and cultural liquidation" (Wang Jing, 2008), to name just a few. In any research about China between 1949 and 1976 that mentions the Cultural Revolution, the same idea is guaranteed to be found which varies in nothing except the wording.

Under close examination, the no-one-should-ever-doubt conclusion about the economic situation during the Cultural Revolution appears to be ill grounded at best. For example, both industrial and agricultural productions were shown to be continuously increasing through the Cultural Revolution. According to the numbers from the National Statistics Bureau, the annual increase of agricultural production was 2.7 percent, as compared with 2.5 percent between 1979 and 1990. Overall, the economy achieved a 6 percent per annum growth rate throughout the Mao's era (Ma, 1990, in Goodman, 2008, p. 25).

Besides, the two years between 1976 and 1978 are rarely talked about, when the Party continued to govern primarily under Mao's line. Rarely have questions been raised concerning these two years: was it a time when the Chinese economy grew in spite of the existence of Mao's line, or a continued chaos and to-be-collapsed economy in spite of the ending of the Cultural Revolution? A careful investigation should yield very informative results.

One may immediately point out the propagandistic nature of any statistics under a "communist" regime (that scientific work has been stamped with the ultra-leftist idea of class struggle during the years of the Cultural Revolution), hence a certain degree of skepticism should be kept in regard to the credibility of statistical reports about that period of time. Powerful as it appears to be, such refutation is completely irrelevant and proves nothing but intellectual inertia.

The intention of this study is certainly not to elaborate on the economic development of China with a comparison between the party lines in Mao and Deng's era, but rather the way that certain apparatuses are utilized for the re-articulation of a dominant ideology for the establishment of a radically new social order. The point here is, both discourses—statistics that show a continuously developing economy (during the Cultural Revolution) and the refutation against the Cultural Revolution as a total disaster—are both "official," i.e., "propaganda" of the same "communist" regime at different conjunctures, or even at the same time (for example, days before the new policy was announced in the end of 1978, the official discourse was still singing high praises of the collectivized agriculture under the communal system). The contradiction is obvious but often ignored between the official discourse about the agricultural reform and the reality that those small number of villages around the country that kept the collective form of economy are the most prosperous ones (See Zhou Yi, 2006, p. 3, pp. 115-120). In many studies (e.g., *Dialectic of Chinese Revolution: from Utopianism to Hedonism*, Ji, 1994), Maoism is presented as a utopian idea—a society in which the possibility of enjoying the result of one's labor is indefinitely put off—despite the existence of first hand material as evidence of the opposite: Mao was the one who insisted on a more realistic goal for economic development and the necessity to reduce the gap between the city and the countryside (see, e.g., the "Request for opinions on the seventeen-article document concerning agriculture" of Mao [1955]; see also the "Outline of agricultural development in 1956-1957" of the Central Committee of the Communist Party of China [1956]). The conditions—agricultural infrastructure and industrial productivity—that the collective economy had created for the fast development in later years had been largely ignored,[4] and the problems of the reform are all attributed to the "insufficient" degree of reform.

---

4   The contribution of Mao's era to the economic development since the reform and opening-up did not get official approval until after the 18th CPC National Congress. In 2013, Xi Jinping pointed out that we should not reject the first 30 years of the People's Republic of China with the achievements of the second 30 years, and vice versa. See http://cpc.people.com.cn/pinglun/n/2013/0510/c241220-21441140.html.

The shift away from Mao Zedong's mass line was first expressed in the form of economic reform in rural China.

In the end of 1978, the policy of rural reform was made and in the following few years, the communes were dismantled and collectivized agriculture abandoned nationwide. In replacement was the "household responsibility system" which divided the land again and gave the use right of agricultural land to individual households. For some scholars, this is a return to "a form of bourgeois property similar in many respects to what had prevailed in 1952 at the conclusion of the land Reform Campaign" (Meisner, 1996, p. 221) that evenly (re)distributed land in countryside. But this policy, according to the official discourse, has tremendously boosted farmers' working momentum. If such individualized agriculture once played a positive role in the development of the rural economy, its negative impact has become more and more prominent after three decades with various social problems arising in rural communities, such as insufficient agricultural labor due to the large population flow to cities as migrant workers, harsh educational conditions with the removal of village schools, low standard of health care, and poverty caused by serious illness, and in political sense, the reduced influence of the Party committees at the village level due to the absence of a collective project of rural economy.

(3) The Urban Reform, or the Privatization of Industrial Production

The appearance of the TV commercials in 1979 also suggests that the reform, despite its popularly perceived beginning in the countryside, was from the very beginning an integral process that incorporated both rural and urban China. The claimed success of the rural reform lies less in the actual wellbeing of the peasants than the ideological preparation for full scale urban reform, i.e., the privatization of industrial production. Ironically, such a strategy of "from rural to urban" testifies to the effectiveness of Mao's line during the revolution before 1949, in an unconventional way, much the same as Mao's strategies are utilized by corporations for internal management today. In the cities, the most distinguishable state action was the separation of political responsibility from corporate responsibility in state owned enterprises, thus reducing, if not completely removing, the control of the Party from the management, so that production and its related process of distribution, exchange, etc., became purely economic activities that must follow the "objective" economic law. It effectively removed the ideological barrier for privatizing the state owned enterprises by neutralizing the production and management, and eventually, the private ownership of the means of production.

Two side notes are necessary here. First, the term state-owned enterprise is used here for the sake of convenience, which in fact is a rather new term that replaced the old "public owned (and state-run) enterprise." The difference is certainly not very difficult to fathom.

Second, large publicly owned enterprises, mainly in strategic areas such as energy, transportation, telecommunication, banking, etc., survived the wave of privatization with the new name of state-owned enterprises (SOEs). The existence of these large SOEs and the social responsibilities that they fulfill (e.g., greater contribution to national tax revenue, employment, better welfare package for their employees, etc.) help China maintain its status of socialist market economy, but has always been the target of criticism for monopolistic advantages in market competition. And the general trend continues in two forms: the continuous growth of various forms of private economy and the development of the "mixed ownership" in SOEs as advocated by government policies since the 18th CPC National Congress.

The consequence of urban reform, i.e., the privatization of formally public owned enterprises, were yet to be felt in the 1990s, especially after 1992, when the Chinese people witnessed the unprecedented development of commercialization and the most dramatic changes in the structure of Chinese society.

In the meantime, under an open and even state encouraged privatization, the control of the state owned enterprises shifted from workers, both materially and symbolically, to the managers, who could now determine with their own will the future of a factory, which, as time proves, often means the shift of collective ownership to private ownership, and the creation of the new class of the bureaucratic-corporate capitalists.

136

(4) The Consolidation Stage after 1992

In 1992, Deng Xiaoping made a series of "history-making" talks during his inspection tour in Southern China. Three things are prominent in his talks. First, the economic development assumes primary importance in all policy making and execution. Even though the "Four Cardinal Principles" (the socialist route, people's democratic dictatorship, Party's leadership, and Marxism-Leninism and Mao Zedong thought) are still part of the official discourse, in actual practice, they are nothing more than a foot note that few would bother to read. Second, he defines the reform as a purely economic act, again, by brushing aside all debates about the nature of the reform as insignificant. He reiterated the principle of "seeking truth out of practice" by Mao, without contextualizing the principle or maintaining the connection between theory and practice. Third, while cautioning against the westernizing tendency of "rightism," he pointed out that special measures should be taken to prevent the effect of "leftism" (in a sense this means the Communist conservatism).[5] For some (e.g., Zhao, 1998), this signifies an unprecedented turn in Party politics, even though correcting the "leftist" mistakes was what Mao had been doing his whole life, including the Cultural Revolution.

---

5   Deng Xiaoping's talks during his inspection tour in Southern China, see http://business. sohu.com/20120113/n332115956.shtml).

For Zhao (1998), these talks also constitute a striking act that eliminated the political barriers for commercialization and explicitly legitimized it. They also defined the new mood of the country and sped up the pace of commercialization. "Now the market had finally triumphed. It was to have a dominant role not only in the allocation of consumer goods and services, but also in the allocation of production goods and resources" (p. 48). Basically, what Zhao (1998) argues is that the official position of the state tilts unequivocally to the right, or the capitalist mode of production.

This summary is quite popular, but lacks historical perspective. There is nothing new in Deng's talks. The ground breaking talks were word by word reiterations of what was already said over a decade earlier. In fact, they were nothing but a confirmation of what had already been started, and they stated nothing but what had already been accepted. To be sure, the intended audience is not the mass of the people, but the Party leaders at the time who felt that the reform should be slowed down in order to avoid political instability. To them, Deng's answer was that we need an overdose of what caused the problem.

In execution, it means a farewell to the explicit "socialist" discourse (the fading out of the "Four Cardinal Principles" for example), which might be considered as "ultra-leftist," and a total recognition of market rules and the "objective" economic law, which is claimed to be neither left nor right, but something neutral. The 14th National Congress of the Communist Party of China, in October 1992, officially adopted Deng's proposal for more economic openness and officially embraced the concept of the "socialist market economy." It is exactly what Gramsci said about hegemony, that one must lead before he can rule. For the market economy to prevail in China, the ideology of the marketplace had to prevail first.

If we want to look for some direct impact of it, we only need to turn on that thing in our living room. Advertising now was not just flourishing, but dominating on Chinese television. Unconstrained by any ideological antagonist—the restrictions laid by MRFT/SAPPRFT were obviously ineffective or insubstantially implemented—it became the major source of financial support for television stations and the primary factor that shaped the content and style of Chinese television, that is, within the parameters set up by the state. Here comes the pitfall for all critiques of Chinese media. They either blame it for being too controlled by the state, or for bending too much towards commercial interests, while in reality commercial interest is itself one of the ways of state control.

Just like the emphasis on the socialist path was put to a footnote-like position in Deng's talks—mainly as a warning against the tendency of bourgeois liberalization at the ideological level but not at the economic level—the same mode of discourse could be seen on various occasions thereafter. Each new generation of leaders has had their own distinctive slogan, which, step by step, pushed the initial "Four Cardinal Principles" to obscurity. Jiang Zemin right after Deng had his theory of the "Three Representatives," that Communists are the representatives of the most advanced productive forces, the progressive Chinese culture, and interests of the vast majority of the people; Hu Jintao, the leader of the new millennium, emphasized "the Harmonious Society." Critiques of these slogans often focus on their hypocrisy, but completely fail to recognize that their significance is precisely their sincerity: what else could represent the most advanced productive force if not the commodity production, and what else is the sign of harmonious society if not the market economy?

While a more detailed review of history is necessary, it is hoped that the above sketch at least presents a sense of continuity in terms of a conscious move—both economically and ideologically—from socialism towards what is called socialism with Chinese characteristics. We should be crystal clear here about the nature of this "transition" in contemporary China. Among both Chinese and Western scholars, this transition is represented as one from planned economy to market economy, from public ownership to the mixed ownership, or from socialism to the co-existence of socialism and capitalism. Whatever it appears to be, in the center of this movement is the state, whose role in this truly effective ideological project has been largely ignored. In this sense, even the critics of this transition miss its most fundamental characteristic and inadvertently conform to the official discourse and dominant ideology. As I will demonstrate below, the ideological reconfiguration in China has so far been achieved with tremendous success through obscuring the distinction between state and (civil) society.

(5) The Central Role of the State

Carl Schmitt (1976) points out the inner contradiction of liberal democracy, as well as the distinction between state and (civil) society. In Hegel, state is universal but not total, which is "qualitatively distinct from society and higher than it" (p. 24). Political science under Hegel's influence used to maintain a clear distinction between the two, which gradually lost its clarity (p. 23-24). Interestingly, the turning point of such a loss for Schmitt is 1848, a time when the first wave of working class revolt swept across Europe, and a time when Marx and Engels published the *Manifesto of the Communist Party*. The development of what Schmitt calls "national-liberal intermediary state" may not be coincidental at all. The development of a capitalist state necessarily requires (and results in) dominant narratives that draw upon categories derived from the domain of the economy, such as freedom, equality, and choice. Marx got to its core in a simple yet decisive way in *German Ideology*, that "the ideas of the ruling class are in every epoch the ruling ideas" (Marx, 1988, p. 64).

There is every reason to believe in a homologous relationship between Europe in 1848 and China in 2018, in the sense that the new form of state demands new dominant narratives, and that such narrative will have to find its vocabulary from the economic sphere as the new legitimizing factor of the state. Of course, such a simple correspondence between two distant historical epochs necessarily misses substantial differences between them. The point is that with an understanding of the (blurred) relationship between the state and civil society, the historical events in China since 1978, including the very conditions for the existence of advertising on television, can be understood in a much clearer way.

Now we can come back to where we began in this section. It is already quite clear that the first critique, i.e., that China is too capitalistic, misses the real target. Even though it recognizes the distinction between state and society, it fails to recognize the relative autonomy of ideology as part of the superstructure—that the "socialist" discourses focuses entirely on the state, and has the potentiality of turning towards genuine socialism despite the current economic growth that is not based on public ownership. The second one, i.e., China is not capitalistic enough, misses the target too, this time deliberately, with the goal of conflating state and society, consciously or otherwise. At a more fundamental level, it demonstrates a total ignorance of what constitutes socialism by equating socialism to communism and then to authoritarianism.[6] The understanding of the "transition" in China as primarily economic is based on the dichotomy between the political and the economic, or, to be exact, on the false assumption that the Party line (the one in practice not the one in rhetoric) and the ideology of global neoliberalism must be mutually exclusive.

As was mentioned above, 1978 was the most remarkable turning point. To illustrate the idea that the "transition" towards a market economy—with the debate over its nature being tabled, for good reason—has its internal coherence and continuity, we might as well go back even further. A movie made during the Cultural Revolution may be quite revealing in this aspect. The movie *Jue Lie* (*The Break*, 1975) depicted a confrontation between the collectivization of agricultural production that would benefit peasants on the one hand and the household based production that a few speculators wished on the other. Clearly a piece of "Party propaganda" at the time, the movie was quite popular between 1975 and 1978, to the extent that even today, people from my generation still remember it from their elementary school movie experience. To people's surprise, this piece of Party propaganda was banned by the Party itself after 1978. The obvious reason is, of course, that it is a product of the Cultural Revolution, which was defined as an unmitigated catastrophe that brought about a halt to the normal functioning of the political and economic system of the state, albeit in a rather ambiguous way in terms of what really happened and who should take responsibility for it. But careful review of the movie reveals an even more substantial cause of its destiny. Situated at a time of struggles between opposing Party lines regarding the development of rural China, the movie in fact features a clear Maoist theme, i.e., that "socialism is the only way to save China." Specifically, it features a victory of collectivized agriculture and rejection of privatization and individualized production. If we remember that what was

---

6 This is much like what Hayek did in the 1940s, though even more confusing without the planned economy as the target of critique like Hayek's critique. See Hayek (2007).

installed in 1978 was exactly what was rejected, first in 1957 movement of collectivization, then in its cinematic representation in 1975, we might be able to see that socialism has never been fully established in China. What had been achieved were only temporary victories. The idea that China is at the primary stage of socialism and the proposal of a socialist market economy precisely indicate the inevitable twists and turns that socialism must experience in its long road of development, with struggles, contradictions and compromises in both economic and ideological terms.

There are many other cases of the same nature which may not be quite noticeable to the public. Supposedly party propaganda magazines like *Zhong Liu* (*The Central Current*) were also banned after the editors openly opposed the acceptance of capitalists into the Communist Party of China. Ironically, the destiny of these cultural (and ideological) products has the same cause, i.e., they tried to stick to what they considered as a genuine "socialist" route and their words are labeled as the expression of "ultra-leftism." Such a label functions in China the same way that the word "communism" does in the West, that simply mentioning the word is sufficient to define something as negative and therefore must be avoided. Contrary to the popular perception about state intervention in the domain of civil society with regards to such cultural products as film, newspaper, and magazine, censorship is not just against representations that advocate the so called Western bourgeois liberalization. In fact, if one looks carefully enough, or if one cares enough to look, the distinction between the two types of censorship is rather slim. Both socialist propaganda—discourses that advocate public ownership, workers as the creator of value, and planned economy—and the intellectual, cultural, and ideological products from the capitalist West or in favor of liberalization in economic and political terms have to negotiate their way into the "market" of ideas in China, which suggests a continuous struggle and contradiction between the socialist and capitalist forces, at both domestic and global levels.

Television advertising, as the primary articulation of the fetishism with the level of exchange and consumption, is undoubtedly the most visible reminder of this redefining of the bottom line of censorship.

Nothing illustrates such struggles in the economic and ideological fields better than education. As a form of the "ideological state apparatuses," school is the primary location where a particular philosophy becomes part of common sense through curriculum design. In 2007, a middle school exam on economics, students were asked what the correct understanding was of the newly passed legislation on private property ownership, to which the credited answer was that property rights were the number one human right and the foundation of all other rights. Under a centrally controlled exam system, such a non-Marxist and non-socialist education could be understood as an institutionalized effort to universalize the bourgeoisie property relationship. The actual Property Law, of course, did not place property right at the position of the "number one human right," but nonetheless points to similar direction. It is at the same time a testimony of Alain

Badiou's idea that any universal claim is based on particular needs. A seemingly innocent act in the realm of education may well function as an effort to construct a new superstructure, making it a political act precisely because it is a state action, no matter how resentful one may feel towards such a categorization.

Education certainly does not take place only within the confines of school. Now that children grow up with television as one of their primary sources of information, and that they are able to recite words from television commercials before they enter the school, the ideological shift is quite clear. Speaking of education, we might as well continue this discussion with the focus shifted to civil society, with special attention to Chinese intellectuals, who are playing a pivotal role in educating the public for consensus in the establishment of a new social order.

7.2.2 Civil Society and Chinese Intellectuals

(1) The Case of a TV Documentary and Beyond

The 1980s must be remembered as a very special period in the history of People's Republic of China for being the times when intellectuals have their voice heard in a "political" way, in various forms of high culture from literature to visual arts. One prominent example—also a case that combines intellectual work with broadcasting media—was the 6 episode TV series of *He Shang* (River Elegy, or literally The Death of the Yellow River) in 1988.

As Zhao (in Wasko, 2005) rightly points out, no single media text than the *He Shang* series "more forcefully expressed the ideological orientations" of the "reformist ethos" and the intellectual preoccupation in China of the 1980s. The social context for Chinese television in the early 1980s was full of uncertainties and possibilities—a propaganda mouthpiece, "a promotional instrument for the Chinese state's modernization program," and the "primary site of contestation for different political and social ideas". *He Shang*, as a sign of the culmination of the so called "Second Enlightenment" in the 1980's—to be exact, the second wave of Western liberal thought since 1919—also constitutes an elegy of Chinese television as a "serious medium of political communication" (p. 525).

Created by a group of young university lecturers, writers, and television producers, *He Shang* examined Chinese history and tried to address the question of why modern industrialization and a democratic state never happened in China. Discursively and visually, the world cultures were roughly divided into two fundamental prototypes, i.e., "Yellow Civilization," which is river-based agricultural culture, and "Blue Civilization," which is ocean-based commercial (Western) culture. By categorizing China as the representative of the "Yellow Civilization" that is politically backward and intellectually suffocating (as inevitably fostering authoritarianism, insularity and fatalism), it was concluded that the most urgent task of China today was to give up the ethos of its "Yellow Civilization" that had become an obstacle to Chinese modernity and democratization, and to fully embrace the inherently more dynamic "Blue Civilization" of Anglo-American origin and fully integrate with global capitalism.

The success of *He Shang* was noticeable. It was broadcasted on the CCTV newwork twice in prime time due to public demands. Its powerful rhetoric and images created a sense of national crisis over Chinese culture among intellectuals and urban dwellers, who were invited to ponder seriously about what political changes must be made so as to move beyond the "dead" yellow culture. Even though there was no evidence about its direct impact, the student movement a year later undoubtedly constituted an enactment of what had been promoted within *He Shang*, and again, with the help of television as an important medium for political communication.

The *He Shang* fever and the student movement have been considered to be the result of an ideological divide. Just like among scholars in the West, representation of what happened in China in the end of 1980s and subsequent critique of China usually follows the line of a binary opposition between an authoritarian force on the one hand, and liberal democratic reformists on the other. However, easy conclusions always mislead and are by no means helpful. This can be demonstrated by the fact that the "urgent" task of embracing the "Blue Civilization" (labeled by the state propaganda as "total Westernization") as advocated by *He Shang* has already been fulfilled (within less than ten years after the student movement) by state implementation of what appeared to many as neo-liberal policies—mainly the extent of privatization and the opening of the vast Chinese labor market to global capital. Liberal intellectuals back in the 1980s were advocating political reform and freedom of speech, as liberal intellectuals would do today. But if political reform means to establish a state in which free competition widens the gap between the haves and the have-nots, then isn't it a mission already accomplished in the decade immediately before 1989? If freedom of speech eventually means the freedom to rule the people with the ideas that legitimize social inequality—that only rich people can have their own houses, as some real estate guru argued in his blog—then what is political reform if not the establishment of the bourgeois rights of property and a whole set of theories to valorize this property relation?

This is not to argue that political reform—with a socialist orientation—is not needed in China, but rather to point out that the ideological consistency (between the state and civil society) has always been ignored. The divide is superficial in spite of its appearance of radical opposition. In retrospect, many demands in the social movement in the late 1980s can be heard in a loud voice today, again, in public, and it is not because China is more tolerant to these ideas, but because they have always been part of the "political" reform. All intellectual efforts to disseminate alternative political ideas in the 1980s, including *He Shang*, in spite of their appearance of belonging to the realm of civil society, are nothing but transformed expressions of a political design of the state. The fact that the demands for political reform—with a liberal democratic orientation—still exists simply means that the struggles between the socialist and capitalist forces are still going on and that the potentiality of a socialist economy remains, even though the possibility appears less strong and only remains more at the level of superstructure at the present stage.

The "high culture fever" (Wang Jing, 1996), or the "second enlightenment"—the obsession with Western philosophical, political, economic, and cultural thoughts that culminated in the TV series of *He Shang*—demonstrated a problematic intellectual project under pressure. With possible benign intentions, Chinese intellectuals in the 1980s failed to recognize the complexity of both Chinese and Western culture. In some sense, philosophical, political, and economic ideas were consumed much the same way as McDonald's and the KFC's fast food were consumed. What they provided was the spectacle of active thinking, rather than genuine insights for social changes. In reality, the route that China has taken is the one that has been recognized by the state, against which many Chinese intellectuals gained their identity. So far, the state and the civil society were heading towards the same destiny, and the difference was that of a detour. The "enlightenment" project of the Chinese intellectuals in fact failed the very moment it began, due to the lack of concern about the people at the bottom of society—workers and peasants—and without identifying the real problems and truly urgent task in China.

If we try to incorporate the intellectual debates and social movements in the second half of the 1980s into the narrative of the actual transformation of Chinese society, they would appear to be rather insubstantial, in the sense that they cannot possibly be used to identify any real changes. For example, did these events actually change the direction of the reform? The answer could not possibly be affirmative if we simply look at it beyond 1992, only three years after the movement.

143

The same analysis applies throughout the 1980s and 1990s. For example, the divide of contemporary Chinese history into the pre- and post-1989 eras is fundamentally flawed. As Wang Hui rightly points out, what happened in 1989 did not change the fundamental reform path that China has taken since 1978, since it didn't oppose the contemporary market system (Wang, 2003, p. 141). In retrospect, the apparent opposition between the State and the civil society is less important than their common request: the market economy, if not straight forward the rule of capital. The only and real difference lies in whether changes should take place predominantly in the superstructure, or first and foremost in the economic base. Eventually they will come to an agreement, which has already happened, for the reason explicated in the Marxian proposition, i.e., that social existence determines social consciousness.

What followed in the early 1990s turned out to be nothing but a temporary setback in the process of marketization and commercialization, due to the concern of losing control of the ideological terrain. And precisely because of this awareness of the real cause of the chaos in the late 1980s, namely, the loss of control in the ideological field, that politics in China finally shifted from its negative form—rejection of the Cultural Revolution—to its positive form of direct promotion of the market economy and the construction of a whole set of new discourses to accompany the process of marketization. Those discourses, I argue, have articulated the already ongoing ideological project in contemporary

China. That is to say, the genuine ideological control is now switching openly (yet in a less visible manner) to the more effective way of building consciousness and engineering consent, using market rules to regulate all social life. The traditional party propaganda, still highly visible at the dominant position, can no longer function as the mainstream with genuine hegemonic power in the Gramscian sense. In spite of its distance from the heart of the people, it plays the role of a guard that ensures the process of building a new superstructure, which may have different ideological ends. That is why the state maintains a token subsidy to CCTV, even though its advertising revenue reached RMB 12.4 billion Yuan as early as in 2005[7] and maintains a double digit growth rate with a revenue of RMB 26.98 billion Yuan in 2013[8] even under the tremendous impact from the Internet.

Continuity overshadows (the fabricated) breaks. It is only on the basis of this recognition that the year 1992, instead of 1989, constitutes a turning point in contemporary Chinese history. In the same year, the state redefined the role of a traditionally state-subsidized media institution, which was to be operated under the new principle of self-financing and profit-making (see Zhao and Gao, in Wasko, 2005, p. 527). This is by no means coincidental. Advertising, already playing a prominent albeit controversial role in relation to Chinese television, now became the dominant factor with official endorsement of its function, both economically and ideologically.

144   (2) A New Intellectual Trend

The turn of the century thus witnessed two prominent things, equally recognized in a conscious way at the level of the state and civil society alike. The first one is the dramatic economic growth, which has been talked about too much. The second one is the rediscovery of Chinese culture in canonical works of literature and philosophy, which constitutes a shift from the West back to the Orient, a return to the Chinese tradition, and surging of national dignity among the Chinese people.

The counterpart of this "rediscovery" in popular/consumer culture can be easily seen in the content of television advertising. Representations of familial piety, gender roles, children's education, food, the game of Chinese chess and its philosophy, gift culture, drinking culture, patriotism, and so on, distinguish Chinese television advertising today from its early stage (the 1980s) not only in its aesthetic quality, but also in terms of its articulated confidence in the Chinese culture and national identity. This is by no means insignificant if we remember that 30 years ago the cultural trend was "complete westernization" and total embracement of the "blue civilization."

---

7 "Advertising income in 2015: 12.4 billion Yuan for CCTV, only 600 million for the Hunan TV" (2005年广告收入央视进账124亿，湖南卫视仅6亿元), http://finance.sina.com.cn/roll/20060215/1109551399.shtml.

8 "Increase of the advertising revenue of the CCTV, only half of that of provincial networks" (今年央视广告收入显疲态，增速仅省级卫视一半), http://money.163.com/14/0604/11/9TT2MCFE0025260O3.html.

The return to the Chinese tradition by both intellectuals and advertising agencies should not be characterized as merely an "intellectual adjustment" and "academic professionalization" (Wang Hui, 2003). Rather, it is part of a larger social development, a structural change, which requires new ideological configuration. Specifically, it is the symbolic requirement of a country that has regained its national pride through economic development. As the official government reports put it, China has always dreamed of its national rejuvenation. When it sees the light of such a hope as it gets stronger economically, politically, and militarily, it needs to reestablish a whole set of cultural superstructures to represent the Chinese nation symbolically. Quite predictably, there should be a resurgence of rediscovering national traditions and ancient culture within China; and not surprisingly, this will be reflected in advertising.

That is why we have seen Chinese power (economically, politically, and militarily) growing hand in hand with the rediscovery of the value of Chinese tradition, which feeds into the resurgence of nationalist discourse. The two are mutually constitutive.

Consequently, for the first time in modern Chinese history—the beginning of which is set at 1840, the Opium War—modernization and tradition are no longer incompatible concepts. They are harmonized in the totality of a new social structure, of which advertising is the most prominent symbolic order. I already dealt with the "return" to the "traditional" value in the content of Chinese television advertising. Such a return would not be possible in a society where social hierarchy is largely destroyed.

145

This is a look at the so called transitional era in China from a new perspective. Given that the Chinese government was already leaning toward a much more tolerant position towards capitalist components such as private ownership and wholly foreign owned enterprises (WFOE), which in certain cases, e.g., real estate policies, looks much like a liberal corporate regime (which was hard to find in the end of the 1980s and the early 1990s), it is very likely that even without the advocacy of the Chinese liberal intellectuals, or even without the 1989 student movement, both advocating a Westernized market system with corresponding ideologies of democracy and freedom, China would still move towards what those intellectuals were advocating, i.e., a regime that rules predominantly by consensus, rather than coercion (the moment of failure). In other words, the tightened control between 1989 and 1992 was only a hesitation, while the speeding up after 1992 did nothing new except on a much larger scale.

With this perspective, the student movement in 1989 can no longer be seen as a disruption, which can be illustrated by what happened in 1992, i.e., the end of political debate and the expansion of the market economy and commercialism based on the recognition of a more effective way of control. The student movement was subdued precisely because it was pursuing political reform in the "wrong" way—beginning at the level of superstructure rather than the base level—thus threatening the very condition for the integration of China into a new global order in which China would play a more and more significant role.

(3) A Critique

It is a bit depressing to see that the process of commercialization was accompanied by the fading away of the critical discourse among Chinese intellectuals. Take the study of television advertising for example. Academic publications on this subject are next to none up till the first decade of the new millennium. What can be found is a complete list of "how to" programs for producing "good" advertisements with higher aesthetic quality and commercial value, or reconciling the interest of transnational capital with indigenous culture. Not only is there a lack of reflection within academia upon the political implications of all the "pure economic" and "commercial" practices such as advertising, but the very act of such critique has become impossible due to the disdain accumulated in the past three decades towards "ideology" and "politics."

When critique does arise, it mainly focuses on one aspect, namely, the political control of news and individual freedom of expression. Such a concentration does not necessarily constitute a problem in itself. But when it becomes the only major complaint, and when such complaint is distancing itself farther and farther from the majority of the suffering people (urban working class and migrant workers), two problems are obvious. The first, as Wang Hui (2003) points out, is the replacement of Marxism with a humanistic Marxism, and Marxist (or Maoist) critique of capitalist modernization with an "ideology of modernization." Wang Hui rightly points out that such a replacement, and the consequent critique of the "traditional socialist historical experience" as its primary target is obsolete "in a context in which the market society and its norms are increasingly dominating discourse" (pp. 152-154). I will not digress by talking about "humanistic" Marxism, but rather want to point out that Wang Hui's critique of the "new" socialism is far from sufficient. To say that its problem is its obsoleteness is focusing on its trivial aspect. It is not only obsolete, but deliberately misleading. The critique of the "traditional socialist experiences," i.e., the age of material and spiritual scarcity as well as Maoist totalitarianism, is based as much on fabrication as it is on facts, as was illustrated by my discussion of agricultural production before 1978. Secondly, the replacement model that truly dominates today is the market model, which is to use one Party ideology to oppose another. If analogy can be made, this is exactly the same logic underlying the marketing strategy of the transnational corporations such as the Procter and Gamble (P&G), which uses its own product (Head & Shoulders) to compete with its other brand (Pantene).

Such misconception is partly due to the unwillingness of Chinese intellectuals to connect their works with social reality, and partly due to the double marginalization of intellectuals, first during the Cultural Revolution and then during the first two decades of the economic reform. The first marginalization resulted in the genre of "traumatic literature" in the 1980s, and the second one led to deliberate efforts by intellectuals to attach themselves to what is deemed the real power, which could be either the state or the market force, further proving the consistency between the two. The (re)insurgence of the study of Western philosophical and social works, rather than providing inspiration for a better understanding of the current social structure and collective action, practically functions to depoliticize a political project with new, definite, political goal. Thus, while Chinese intellectuals on the right have tried to push for democratization of the Chinese political system, they have inadvertently (or intentionally) collaborated with the political force that advocates the logic of market and the authoritarianism of capital.

Even the so called "leftist" scholars can be seen to join the chorus without any skepticism about the way history is (re)written and knowledge is disseminated.

For example, popularly perceived as the leader of the "new left" in China, Wang Hui completely accepts the existing parameters in discussing contemporary China, i.e., that the devastated economy makes the reform a natural thing to happen (Wang Hui 2003). More interesting, while insightfully pointing out that the occurrence of the reform should be attributed to no individual but rather a group of pragmatic leaders of which Deng is a member, such subtlety has never been bestowed upon the analysis of Mao's relation to the Cultural Revolution and the economy during that time. It is often considered to be a tragedy that during the Cultural Revolution, the whole society went crazy with one idea of one idolized person. What happened after the Cultural Revolution was the unanimous agreement on the economic conditions by the end of the Cultural Revolution and the "natural" occurrence of the reform due to "dissatisfaction over the existing economic and political system, burgeoning access to information, as well as human nature" (Wang Hui, 1994, p. 58, note 7). The aim of this critique is certainly not to defend the Cultural Revolution or characterize it as a successful movement that benefited the Chinese people in an all-around manner. What I am interested in is the unusual extent of ideological success among the intellectuals and ordinary citizens alike with regard to the root of the reform and opening-up, which was in many respects contextualized by people's perception of the immediate history before.

147

Another example from overseas Chinese scholars is more illuminating. In *Television in China: History, Political Economy, and Ideology*, Zhao and Guo (Zhao and Guo, in Wasko, 2005) present a critical reflection of the history of Chinese television. In this very informative and much inspiring piece, a tiny, even unnoticeable (due to its always being taken for granted nature) piece of information is found to be the most revealing about the modes of critique by Chinese intellectuals. Within the smooth flow of historical narrative, the authors stated that in the first period of Chinese Television, "…human interest news stories were non-existent…" (Wasko, Ibid, p. 522). To avoid taking a statement out of context, let us look at the quote in its full detail:

"From its inception, Chinese television was institutionally and ideologically incorporated into the Party's pre-existing media system as a propaganda mouth-piece. Inadequate production capacity limited the activities of early Chinese television to the transmission of existing media content, such as newsreels produced by film studios. Self-produced content was limited to feature stories about communist role models, and live broadcasts of children's and other cultural and educational shows. Entertainment programming in China consisted primarily of feature films. Because of the small audience and the lack of independent economic interests under the planned economy, film studios often showcased new films on television either simultaneously with or even ahead of cinema releases... In fact, because human interest news stories were non-existent at the time and news content was limited to major political events and state policies, television's entertainment function was hardly explored, and, later, explicitly suppressed. (Zhao and Guo, in Wasko, 2005, pp. 522-523)

This narrative has a familiar vocabulary that has been used to evaluate almost all aspects of Chinese society between 1949 and 1978. Every word of it—propaganda, mouthpiece, lack of independent economic interests, no entertainment, etc.—resonates so naturally with common beliefs that it has become the only truth about China during that period of time.

Familiarity, however, by no means guarantees the validity of a historical narrative. The above description, implicitly based on a set of universally accepted judgments, is certainly not an innocent documentation and objective representation of history. What I will do is not to argue with facts that demonstrate a different life experience, which is possible (only in another separate study) but not truly productive. The real question is, what kind of ideology makes it possible for the state, intellectuals, and men on the street alike, to think and express themselves in such a consistent way about history and their own life, in spite of constant self contradictions in their own efforts of re-presentation, and in spite of the appearance of radical antagonism among themselves? Apparently, in such a narrative, "human interest" is reduced to entertainment, and entertainment to an unspecified, everyone-already-knows concept, which, if I may speculate for a moment, refers to a kind of "non-political" and "non-propaganda" content sponsored by "independent" economic interests, i.e., advertising. In the meantime, education, cultural performances, children's shows, feature stories about communist role models, political events, state policies, are all excluded from the category of "human interest" content. The sense of urgency to disclaim/discard the ideas of a particular historical era is constantly felt by Chinese intellectuals, consciously or subconsciously.

In the post-revolution and "post ideology" era in China, "human interests" appear to be unequivocally equated to, or connected with, "entertainment," which is not "political," but personal, individual, and independent, in short, trivialities of everyday life that are free of the grand narrative of revolution. Along with the creation of this popular sentiment, is the marginalization—if not complete exclusion—of the educational programs, the commercialization of children's programs, and the replacement of the "communist role model" with celebrities from popular culture. Behind every single act in this line stands commercial sponsorship. From the very first commercial on Chinese television in 1979—immediately after the state cracked open the door towards market economy and non-public mode of production—to the new millennium when the advertising supported television system is unanimously acknowledged by Chinese intellectuals as finally representing "human interests," a complete picture can be drawn of an ideological reconfiguration in contemporary China. Television advertising, as the embodiment of "independent economic interests," presents the objective economic law and defines the new mainstream culture.

It is often held that with the development in the economy and new information technologies, a civil society has been formulated in China, which has more and more become a force that balances the power of the state. It is also held that the ideology of the civil society (which originally means "bourgeois society", *bürgerliche Gesellschaft* in German but was mis-translated and thereby neutralized as "civil society"[9]), is presenting a paradoxical co-existence with the political propaganda of socialism.

The very existence of advertising on Chinese television is a sign that at the most fundamental level, the dominant (state) and the mainstream (the civil society) are highly consistent with each other. The socialist discourse appears to be dominant, but should not be considered to be ideological when there is no project of collective economy at the base level, nor does it function as ideology. Looking at television advertising, an illustration of the very idea of fetishism with the exchange level that Marx critiqued, it is quite obvious that the relationship between the dominant and the mainstream ideology is not antithetical, but dialectical, structurally different from the commonly perceived antithesis between them. They are conditional upon each other. Neither the official discourse nor the popular perception has a stress on the communist and the socialist project, and both have kept a distance from public ownership of the means of production with the increase of private ownership in the economy, for which advertising appears to be a necessary element for both economic and ideological purposes. It is the stunning sameness between the dominant and the mainstream that reveals the reality of Chinese society today. The new ideological project is the implicitly redefining of friend and enemy, a reversion of what Mao said in 1926 about the primary task at the time: to distinguish who is our friend and who is our enemy. It is a project that was initiated at the state level, and completed within civil society, with the aid of Chinese intellectuals, both right and left ones. Chinese intellectuals must be considered to be the true functionaries of propaganda for the state. The conformity with the state, despite their self perceived resistance, is the sign of a formulating hegemony in Gramscian sense, that a particular philosophy—that of the market—becomes part of common sense, and apparently liberating discourses have led to genuine enslavement.

149

---

9   My thanks to Roland Boer for letting me know about the original German term and its translation into English.

Chapter 8. Conclusions: The Political and the Ideological

8.1 A Summary

I have reviewed the institution, content, and audience of Chinese television advertising. After that, the exploitative nature of advertising was explored, and the political conditions were discussed that have made it possible for Chinese television to rely on such an exploitative institution.

Every aspect of Chinese television advertising points to one thing: the pervertibility of a newly emerged commercial culture.

The legitimacy of the existence of advertising as an institution relies upon the idea of "free" programs, an idea which is destroyed by the commodity transaction as well as the labor of the audience during the process of television viewing. The content of advertising happily presents images and narratives with the appearance of universal appeal, which at the same time must presuppose the exclusion of working class "consumers." The audience of television advertising is capable of recognizing all the problems of advertising, but nonetheless cannot imagine a life without it, while those who can are neither seen nor heard. Finally, the kind of advertising today that is based on visuality and symbolic production of meaning necessarily divides a commodity into two indissociable yet heterogeneous things, the product, and the brand, with the symbolic existence of brand, which assumes central significance upon which the values of material products must depend.

A brand has a fake value, and along with it, the fantastic relations that are called the brand loyalty. Fake, because it does not deliver what's promised, e.g., love, friendship, family, status, etc. Even the perceived informational function becomes dubious given that only a very small fraction of the audience is influenced in terms of their perception of the advertised product and consequent consuming behavior. The pervertibility of branding constitutes the ultimate stage of advertising, which dictates the inversion of the relation between social existence and social consciousness and the society as whole is now standing on its head, once again after the Chinese revolution and its subsequent economic designing was labeled as anti-human interests.

For someone who is concerned about the social transformation in contemporary China, the significance of Chinese television advertising, as this book has illustrated, lies in its ideological function. Television advertising, particularly from the West, presents an image of material prosperity, which looks more like what is promised by socialism. Being exposed to such images, it has been quite convincing for the Chinese people that China and all socialist countries are lagging behind in this great world of consuming products. More than that, television advertising has been more powerful in its capacity to reach the vast majority of Chinese people than any other form of communication. It has been the only conveniently accessible source in the two decades of the 1980s and the 1990s that informed and enlightened the vast majority of the people about capitalism, which is no longer perceived as the embodiment of a sweatshop but rather as a synonym of material prosperity, political freedom, and at the most fundamental level, a system that represents "human interest."

Eventually, the displacement of social needs into the realm of consumption has more effectively (than coercive power of the state and well crafted arguments of liberal intellectuals) performed the role of an educational apparatus that incorporates the vast majority of urban residents in China into the grand march towards a consumer society and integration into the "global village."

Progress is now conflated with merely moving forward in time, as from the cultural revolution to the reform and opening-up, so that it is capable of being further reduced into a taken for granted movement towards a market oriented system ruled by the logic of capital. In terms of the values conveyed in the Chinese television advertising, there is really nothing new in this "new" phenomenon, not only because it had happened before, for example, in the 1930s in Shanghai, but also because its own internal coherence and consistency since its (re)appearance in 1978, when the economic reform was launched.

The very concepts to reflect upon, therefore, are the ideas of change, transition, trans-formation, etc. These ideas presuppose some before and after, past and present, clearly distinguishable breaks within continuity. But more important are the dialectics between those antitheses: a dispersed, permeated connection between the apparently contradictory past and present, old and new, mainstream and dominant. Something pervert about contemporary China is that often times continuation (e.g., of socialism) is a break while transformation (e.g., towards a market economy) simply means to resume an interrupted process (by the founding of People's Republic of China and by the Cultural Revolution, respectively).

In this sense, television advertising cannot be viewed as merely an economic element of a commercial system, albeit a structuring element of that system. With its capability to create desire and manipulate conceptions, television advertising has been—from the very first moment of it's (re)inception in the post-Mao China—an integral part of a hegemonic force, which has been in constant contradiction with the vision of a socialist future for China.

Therefore, I would argue that the economic function of television advertising in China is nothing but a perverted expression of a political act, i.e., the transformation from the revolutionary Maoism towards a compromise to capitalism, something comparable to Lenin's New Economic Policy, but with much bigger vision, farther reaching consequence and longer struggles involved, the nature of which has been concealed precisely because of its obviousness. The transformation of the watching class into "working" class at the discursive level and the consequent invisibility of the real working class is part of a process that is shaping the social structure of contemporary Chinese society. It is a political process that has been depoliticized through articulating (as Althusser and Hall put it) culture with propaganda, civil society with the state, and the economic with the political.

The prevalent critique of China among scholars in the West, either from the right of the left, needs to be critically reflected upon. First, the critique often focuses on political authoritarianism, occasionally accompanied by a benign commendation on its economic achievements. Such a combination makes the whole critique irrelevant at its best, since it assumes that economic development is just economic, thus missing the point that what is labeled as "authoritarian" politics is the very condition of what is conceived as "economic" achievements. The distinction sheds light on neither the economic nor the political. It is missing the real target. Contrary to the popular belief in the West, the real obstacle to political democratization in China is not the socialist state that is often labeled as authoritarianism, but the seemingly uncontrolled expansion of the rule of capital. To put it simply, the condition of the authoritarianism in China is not communism, but the potential restoration of capitalism. Other than what appears to be the obvious, there are two more reflections based on this discussion, the first on the concept of the political, and the other on the concept of ideology.

8.2 Redefining the Premises of Inquiry

(1) The Concept of the Political, and the State as the Site of the Political

To fully understand the pervertibility of television advertising as an institution and discourse, it is imperative that we move beyond the confines of the conventional analysis of political economy, which focuses primarily on the economic, and by doing so, undermines its own foundation that stipulates its primary concern, i.e., the commodification of (audience) labor as the inherent political nature of the economic. What we have seen so far in every aspect of Chinese television advertising— institution, content, audience—can be described as an act of "hospitality," if I may use this term in a very loose sense, which, according to Derrida (2000), is characteristic of pervertibility (Ibid, p. 79). As illustrated in the case of Chinese television advertising, it is an unconditional yet at the same time transgressed hospitality, towards commercialism and the totalizing logic of capital. Such an act has normally been understood within a purely economic dimension, as both conventional wisdom and scholarly consensus that once prevail in the West. When it does come to be connected with the realm of the political, such wisdom and consensus often translate into a vision that political change will some day happen in China with economic development as the motive force that fosters a democratic political agenda.

It is quite obvious that the political reform in China, if any, has not followed the path as envisioned by politicians and political scientists in the West. Some, like Zizek, have already recognized the fact that political democratization is not a natural result of economic development. Under certain circumstances, political authoritarianism is not antithetical to economic development; in fact, the political stability of an authoritarian state may reduce the cost of social transformation—such as many other third world countries had experienced—thus making economic development possible in the first place. Such a perception does have its resonance within the Chinese context even though contradiction remains over the nature of its reform. In the very least, if we do take seriously the critique of the Chinese authoritarianism, we will also have to face an even more serious challenge: what if "democracy" is not an impetus, but rather an obstacle to economic development? This question, apart from its rhetorical force, leads us to consider a different relationship between the economic and the political. In the present study, this relationship has been expressed in the following process.

154

The act of hospitality towards capitalism is fundamentally a perverted one, in the same way that a host becomes hostage and a guest becomes the host. In China, television advertising (as in 1979) was but the nose of the camel in the tent, which might soon find itself comfortably settled in the tent. And capitalism is a process of automation that never stops. It may first subsume old socialist modes of production, only humbly settling itself in seemingly harmless areas such as television advertising. But with the expansion of not only its mode but the very condition of its existence, it will inevitably take over and transforms socialism into capitalism. In this sense, the success of the socialist mode of production in China will depend upon the extent of compromises towards capitalist components at the primary stage of socialism, as well as the result of struggles in the ideological sphere.

Therefore, it is imperative that this act of hospitality be taken as a concept that describes a political situation—hospitality as an act of "the political." Here by "the political" I am not referring to the much corrupted term of "politics," which has been equated to struggles for control within a hierarchical governmental structure. Rather, it is a concept that would truly unite the economic and the political in the domain of "political economy," thus making it possible to have a political analysis of the economic. That is to say, to add the missing half (the political) to the analysis of political economy in general, and the political economy of communication in particular.

But what is it that we call a political act? What is "the political?"

The word political is often used negatively as being antithetical to a series of other categories such as religious, cultural, legal, scientific moral, aesthetic, and most prominently as well as most relevant to the present discussion, the economic. Despite all of the confusions and self-contradictions in the popular conception of the political, and the effort to blur the boundary between the state and civil society (e.g., that the state should only govern in such a way that market is the determining force), the persistence of the antithesis between the political and such categories as the economic does point to an unambiguous fact, that the political is itself a category that has its own criteria which express themselves in a characteristic way.

Carl Schmitt (1976) in *The Concept of the Political* points out in a decisive way that in order for the political to be a category in itself, it must rest upon its own "ultimate distinctions," to which "all actions with a specifically political meaning can be traced" (pp. 25-28), just like morality rests on the distinction between good and evil, aesthetics on beautiful and ugly, and economics on profitable and non-profitable. In spite of all his negative connection with the Nazis, Carl Schmitt's efforts to define an important category deserves our attention:

155

> The specific political distinction to which political actions and motives can be reduced is that between friend and enemy... The distinction of friend and enemy denotes the utmost degree of intensity of a union or separation, of an association or dissociation. It can exist theoretically and practically, without having simultaneously to draw upon all those moral, aesthetic, economic, or other distinctions. The political enemy need not be morally evil or aesthetically ugly; he need not appear as an economic competitor, and it may even be advantageous to engage with him in business transactions. But he is, nevertheless, the other, the stranger; and it is sufficient for his nature that he is, in a specifically intense way, existentially something different and alien, so that in the extreme case conflicts with him arc possible. (Schmitt, 1976, pp. 25-28)

Three things must be clarified about this distinction. First, the distinction (between friend and enemy) is to be taken in its concrete and existential sense. Second, the enemy is necessarily a public enemy. Third, the state is the political entity that decides for itself the friend-enemy distinction. I believe that this is what the Chinese television advertising tries to inform us: the return of the political, or, in Freudian term, the return of the repressed.

Why would the audience insist upon the identity of consumers rather than that of the audience? How have they come to love what they hated? What ideological conditions have made it possible for the audience of Chinese television to express hospitality towards an utterly "non-traditional" value system yet at the same time believe it is an act with no political meaning whatsoever?

These questions are only approachable when there is a consciousness about their being political in nature. They are questions about who shall be treated with hospitality, and who shall be represented in effect as unwelcome and is consequently excluded from public discussion. Ultimately, it is asking: who is the friend, and who is the enemy? Again, the distinction between friend and enemy is not used metaphorically, but in its "concrete and existential sense."

The economic shall certainly never be discarded. Quite obviously, in the relationship between the political and the economic, it would be equally mistaken to conceive that there exists a political act only, or an economic act only; that a political agenda can succeed without its economic expressions, and an economic agenda can be just economic and can possibly depend on conditions that are purely economic (such as the market). The former leads to the perceived "failure of the Cultural Revolution", while the latter leads to the fantastic understanding of the social existence today. However, this does not mean that the two are indistinguishable, or that such distinction is no longer informative. The relationship between the two categories is dialectical, which must be treated as indissociable, but at the same time heterogeneous. The case of Chinese television advertising clearly illustrates a distinctive political agenda carried out as a series of decisions in the realm of the economic. In the present study, television advertising is certainly an economic act, but it says nothing if we stop right there. It is meaningful only when we recognize the fact that it is the articulation of the political in the domain of the economic. Here is the dialectic relation between the political and the economic. The real reform in fact began at the political level, which endorsed advertising and a series of other discourses that compromises socialism as a legitimate political option. Eventually, or, "in the last instance," the contradiction is between the socialist and the capitalist modes of production, the outcome of which will come to be the determinant of political perceptions, thus completing the circle with a reversion of the relationship between the base and superstructure.

A clear distinction needs to be made here. When it is said that television advertising in China is fundamentally a political act, this has nothing to do with the values as expressed in individual commercials or any amalgam of commercials, as many would argue in the area of cultural studies, which falls victim to the consumption model that they set off to resist.

What I am trying to draw attention to is the ideology of advertising as such, the ideology of the very existence of advertising on television. For that reason, the "economic" act of television advertising, along with the reform in general, needs to be carefully examined in a way that does not miss the aspect of central importance, namely, the concept of the political, which has been assumed as an unquestionable, default presence in the studies of *political* economy. This also applies to the way that Chinese culture is discussed.

(2) The Cultural

Academic inquiry should not be simply regarded as innocent. The very idea of *Chinese* television advertising tends to be assumed as having certain uniqueness in comparison with its counterpart in the West, which is the de facto state of existence for television advertising per se. The analysis in this study has very likely failed in this line, since I have deliberately avoided the idea of having "Chinese" as a necessary prefix for the primary category under discussion, which, though not possible because of the constraints of language, must be clarified even at the risk of redundancy.

In 2005, I made a presentation on the audience of Chinese television at a conference, after which a scholar from the UK approached me and asked me if I was interested in writing something for their upcoming journal in the Chinese media. The topic would ideally be comparative study of the Chinese and the US audience, or of the Chinese audience living in China and the United States.

This encounter strikes me in terms of how strong the temptation is to take Chinese culture as the primary factor, or one of the primary factors in understanding the "uniqueness" of television broadcasting and television advertising in China. Its institution, content, audience, and particularly, its political implications, etc., are necessarily approachable only with a cross cultural perspective. When I actually started to develop research on Chinese television advertising, comparative studies is the one focus that stands out as the major concern among media scholars. Only then did I realize the significance of the previous encounter.

157

Such a concern over Chinese culture has two specificities. First, Chinese culture is unique and therefore determines the characteristics of the content of Chinese television advertising. Second, China is ruled by an authoritarian regime which determines the nature of its media institution, content, and audience, in short, everything. Such an effort to approach Chinese television advertising, media or China in general, on the basis of some imaginary presuppositions about China, will not be as productive as is expected by many scholars in cultural studies or China studies. Their questions, based on the two specificities, are not as straightforward as they look at first glance. There were simply too many unexamined assumptions.

At the very moment when questions are raised about how Chinese culture determines the unique content of television advertising in China, one is confronted with a more fundamental question, namely, what do you mean by "Chinese" culture or "Chinese" tradition, and which Chinese culture or Chinese tradition are you referring to? Are we talking about the agricultural tradition that is supposedly looking down at commercialism as inherently degrading humanity, or the socialist tradition that defines the workers as the master of the country and the exploitation of them as unacceptable? In either case, the fundamental principle of advertising is antithetical to the so-called "Chinese tradition." This is already a very rough categorization. Even so, it clearly shows that very first demanding task is to find an appropriate—which often means arbitrary—cutting point that marks the epistemological boundary between the present and the past, transgression and tradition. There are simply too many of them. For example, in reverse chronological order, there can be 1978 (the "beginning" of the Reform and Opening-up—the "beginning" has to be in quotation mark), 1949 (the founding of the People's Republic of China), 1911 (the end of Monarchy), or 1840 (the first Opium War when China was forced to open its gate to global capitalism), and I can keep going further for quite a while in the search for a beginning.

The way that "culture," and "cultural difference", are used today, with their Anglo-American heritage, essentializes and marginalizes cultures that are non-White, systemizes and neutralizes violence under the name of "cultural tolerance," and renders impossible critical thinking and radical alternatives. Speaking about culture in the Anglo-American context may be different from speaking about it in the Chinese context, but what underlies both is a hierarchical structure, noticeable among both tourists/scholars from the West and in the nationalist sentiment within China. The consequence is by no means trivial, for the confusion of political economy and cultural studies makes it impossible to clearly see either the political or the cultural.

158

On the one hand, even though culture as a universal concept does not appear to have any specific ideological connotation (everyone is a cultural existence), such a universal concept must be articulated through each distinctive culture, the discourse of which is inevitably contaminated by ideology (of hierarchy). This can be seen from the different focus in the studies of television advertising in the Euro-American context and in the Chinese context, the latter of which always has to "naturally" include a "cultural" perspective as compared to a pure political/economic analysis.

On the other hand, not without some sense of irony, when culture is talked about, living experiences of Chinese people today are often excluded from the realm of "cultural studies". In *Writing Diaspora*, Rey Chow (1995, p. 126) talks about the "institutional Orientalism" that privileges European literature as "the objects worthy of study" vis-à-vis Asian literature, and the accomplice to the same logic within the "native elitism" in the study of Ancient Asian literature vis-à-vis modern Asian literature. The same logic applies in the area of film studies too (Rey Chow, 1995, p. 27). More often than not, as could be seen in Chinese scholars as well as Western sinologists (see Rey Chow, 1995, introduction; 2002, Chapter 1), it is imperative that Chinese culture remains ancient, or backward in time, and contemporary experiences are pushed into such areas as anthropology, sociology, economics, or political science. That is to say, when "the political" should be the central concern of theoretical intervention, culture is often amplified in the picture, while when culture should be the focus of investigation, attention is often consciously shifted towards the political categories. Not surprisingly, neither may achieve the lucidity necessary for such scrutiny, though sometimes it does inadvertently hit the target.

It is certainly impossible to argue for a clear distinction between the study of Chinese culture and political economy in China. However, one should be cautious about conflating categories and the risk of missing the real question about contemporary China. It is especially important to recognize the emergence of a new social order through capitalizing on the so-called Chinese "tradition" that fosters nationalist sentimentalism and displaces internal conflict outward. This confusion about the cultural and the political is the same as the confusion about the economic and the political (valorizing values that stemmed from marketplace discourse such as individuality, freedom, choice, etc.), and both are reflected in scholarly research as well as popular perceptions. The reason for such confusions is ideological. What Chinese television advertising informs us is exactly the ideological process that depoliticizes a distinctive political process.

Therefore, as was shown in previous chapters, the only way to avoid the confusion in cultural studies and China studies is to get to the real question, i.e., what is the political? In contemporary China, it means to identify the political process and its expressions in economic and cultural dimensions. Culturalism is misleading at best for the analysis of the political process of restoring capital- ism, while many political (or economical and sociological) analyses of Chinese culture today are simply complacent with the seemingly smooth conclusion regarding the coexistence of economic capitalism and political "communism."

At the fundamental level, Alain Badiou (2002) speaks about cultural difference in a very powerful way. According to Badiou, contemporary discourses about "cultural difference," or "ethics of difference," have their origin in the conceptualization of the "other" (as in Levinas). The problem is: the phenomenon of the other is confronted with a difficult task of attesting to "a radical alterity which he nonetheless does not contain by himself." There is no ontological guarantee for alterity to be experienced as "an essential non-identity." What has been ignored by such discourses as the "recognition of the other," or "ethics of difference," or "multiculturalism," is the fact that their philosophical foundation is in principle a religious one. The "Altogether Other", which "transcends mere finite experience," and which constitutes "the principle of alterity" in Levinas to carry the concept of the Other, is obviously "the ethical name of God." The consequence is that philosophy is "annulled" by theology, and ethics becomes "a category of pious discourse" (Badiou, pp. 18-23).

When "every effort to turn ethics into the principle of thought and action is essentially religious" (Ibid, p. 23), those discourses on "cultural difference" without its religious character necessarily become "pious discourse without piety" (Ibid, p. 23), and function only as a means of concealment of the truly disturbing problems of the world. By focusing on local, microscopic unique-ness of each "community," it constitutes a digression away from real totalitar-ian power. In the case of China, the problem is not only that the "self declared apostles of "ethics" and of the "right to difference" are clearly horrified by any vigorously sustained difference" (Ibid, p. 23), but the conflation of totalitar-ianism and communism in describing China demonstrates a lack of genuine concern about the truth of our time: the systemic violence that masks itself with a "fake sense of urgency" (Zizek, 2008, p. 6) in humanitarian acts against various kinds of bloody violence and inequality, while in the meantime making it impossible to ponder the very conditions that make violence and inequality possible. As this study of Chinese television advertising has shown, culturalism is obviously irrelevant, as could be seen in the superficial distinction between the local and the global in advertising. What really becomes dominant is the totalizing logic of global capital, which only accepts a "good other," or differ-ences that are acceptable.

Differences, according to Alain Badiou, are nothing more than "the infinite and self-evident multiplicity of human kind," and precisely what truths "render insignificant" (Badiou, 2002, p. 27). Philosophically, difference is simply what it is. The difficult yet necessary task lies in the recognition of the same. Here we can approach the concept of sameness in two steps. First, it is the sameness achieved by the logic of the totalizing capital. As was demonstrated in the case of Chinese television advertising, the superficial appearance of difference—in brand names, choices of consumers, and expressions of different values—brings about the truly homogeneity among consumers, in both consumption behavior and political imagination. Second, and more important, is the same which occurs in regard to truths in the plural. A truth, as "the coming-to-be" of what is not yet, can only be a process, in which there is no ethics, but only ethics of, of "the labor that brings some truths into the world" (Ibid, pp. 26-28). During such processes, the political is one of the fundamental subjective types as procedures of truths. For the present study, the political subject is the one that labors to bring truths into the realm of the political, which means to illumi-nate the exploitative nature of advertising, and the very political condition that makes possible such an unethical form of communication.

8.3 The Sublime Object of Ideology

Having said so much, I would like to go back to a question that drove me to this study in the first place: why are such ill-grounded and unreal claims as those made in advertisements acceptable, and why are such nonsensical con-nections between a product and personal happiness persuasive in terms of not only the merit of the product but also the legitimacy of its very existence? It certainly can be explained through the large investment by advertisers that ensure aesthetic quality and narrative relevance. The reason may also lie in visuality, the fundamental concept that makes television a unique form of me-dia. A picture is more eloquent than a thousand words, and a motion picture is even more powerful since the representation is so "real"—and for that reason intrusive—that it simply cannot be ignored. Its sheer visibility is the proof of its existence and in that sense content is largely irrelevant during the production of the objective watching time of the audience. Or, from an anthropological point of view, relations with objects have always been an indispensable part of how human beings make sense of their life (see Jhally, 1990, p. 1-22).

In this study, however, the issue is addressed through the connection between the fundamental principles of advertising (the perverted relation between material production and symbolic production as in branding) with the political conditions that have made advertising itself possible in Chinese society. The educational/ideological function of advertising ensures the prevailing of a set of new discourse about love, friendship, family, social recognition, etc., which in turn sets up new standards of what is acceptable and what is not. Such an ideological transformation is consistent with the political project of the primary stage of socialism, with compromises to capitalism made at the economic dimension, that is initiated at the state level. Advertising and the new social order are therefore mutually constitutive and mutually enhancing as parts of the same process.

Unlike the history of Western capitalism as Raymond Williams (1980, pp. 177-178) has described, in which advertising was the result of particular economic requirements by an economic "base", advertising in China in the post-Mao era (re)appeared and (re)developed without a pre-existing economic base. 161 Or, to be exact, television advertising (re)appeared as both the result of and a necessary condition for the (re)appearance of the economic base that would soon in turn naturalize advertising as something that *should* be there if we are going to talk about the economy in a "rational" way. Without the political decision to take the turn—to allow the coexistence of multiple modes of production—advertising would not be possible on Chinese television, while without the effective ideological reconfiguration through advertising and a consequent series of market related discourses, the return of non-pubic ownership and private economy lack the legitimacy that is essential for the dramatic social transformation.

This leads to a different angle to look at television advertising in China, which suggests that advertising is working in the same way that ideology does. The watching process, or the production of meaning for a brand name appears effortless, yet the consequence cannot be overstated.

The moral of the Nike example is that the value created by watching as working might as well be called fake value. This is not, as Marx (1912) and Zizek (1998) point out, to discover the hidden secret of commodity exchange that is the surplus value extracted from workers' labor, something that had already been discovered by classical political economy. The real question rather concerns the *commodity form* that the act of watching must take, just like factory labor must take the form of commodity.

Unlike material production, such production of meaning, and consequently the value it produces in the form of increased capital, is based entirely on faith. It is a kind of faith of the audience that supports the very existence of a brand name, just like the faith that makes possible the replacement of all exchange between goods by the exchange between all commodities with money (Zizek, 1989, pp. 11-53).

This is what the audience of Chinese television advertising informs us. For example, can the audience escape commercials? When commercials are between programs in China—when the audience knows that they have 5 or 10 minutes before a show resumes (note: in fact, it is a common practice now on the CCTV that the time span of a commercial slot is specified on the screen at its beginning), does it change the way advertising and commercial media work effectively? We can push it even further by asking whether digital technologies such as TiVo make it possible for the audience to escape commercials? The answer is no. It does not change a thing, and it is not just because advertisers are becoming more creative, such as in Zillion TV that customizes commercial watching and rewards the audience for it, or in the potential of turning all programs into commercial slots through product placement. The possibility of escaping does not translate into actual (effective) act of escaping, as has already been proven by those audience who claim that they never watch commercials but know as much as those who love to watch commercials. Psychologically, it is much like what S. Zizek describes as the "compulsive" act, such as what someone in an elevator would do, namely, to keep hitting the close/up/down button, even though it does not make it arrive any faster. The audience, in a similarly compulsive way, would return to that channel to check if their show is back, even though they know exactly when it will be back, be it the highly standardized 6 minutes in the US, or the sporadic in length but explicitly announced 1 minute 30 seconds (or 8 minutes) on the China Central Television.

This fact can never be overstated: ideology is a concept in the domain of action, not the domain of ideas.

The effects of advertising are first and foremost instructional. To borrow George Gerbner's idea, it tells people what to do, except that we are not just talking about the act of buying here. Everyone hates advertising at certain moments, but everyone keeps returning to the point where they act exactly as advertising asks them to do. This is how ideology works. It acts against one's will. It tells us to do what we hate to do, and in so doing, love to do it. As Zizek rightly puts it, it is this "I know, but...." moment when ideology is illustrating its ultimate success.

The act of watching television commercials thus constitutes an articulation of both a specific commercial ideology and ideology in general. As such, it is an act in the realm of the political, which at the same time depoliticizes itself. Or, the reversion should make it even clearer, the act of de-politicization—the self-claimed act of 'just watching television" or "it's the economic law"—is itself an act of the political, of befriending capital and setting up public owner-ship as a public adversary. This "hermeneutic circle" is just like the oedipal circle that Zizek describes, i.e., the effort to avoid the tragic end turns out to be the very effort that leads to the tragic end. Isn't this also true in China, where intellectuals have to resort to the means of "democracy," e.g., free elections, when they are incapable of making a political judgment about what is just and what is good? Their means, i.e., demand for political rights based on the dis-course of freedom, stems from the self-destructive system of the marketplace, in which freedom means the freedom to subject oneself to enslavement.

To conclude, I would like to point out three things about television advertis-ing in regard to ideology.

1. Advertising must be looked at as a whole in order to understand its gener-ative power and persuasiveness in principles of necessity, freedom (of choice), and equality (in exchange), in short, the defining element of contemporary society, in China or otherwise. Just like the Freudian use of the term *dream work* (not dream), advertising should be understood as a term different from individual advertisements. There is also a three fold structure in advertising: the content, the desire, and the unconscious desire (the desire of desire). The real secret about advertising is not the values it conveys, but its very existence.

2. The way that advertising functions illustrates an important characteristic about ideology. That is, ideology does not have any internal substance, nor does it lie at a deeper level behind what is seen on the screen. It does guide consumers to act, but in doing so, it exists only with the narrative through im-ages. It exists only when it is attached to those images. The visual, the pure visibility, the superficial, is where ideology is. It is invisible precisely because of its obviousness.

163

3. The externality of ideology also adds to the critique of advertising as religion. As Jhally (1990) points out, advertising is a secularized religion in the (post) industrial age that makes choices for people when it is impossible for them to make their own choices, much like what religion did in the pre-in-dustrial world. Now with the expansion of global capitalism when advertising dominates the symbolic environment of everyday life with its radical visibility, a Lacanian turn is illuminating for the well known Marxian proposition that social relations between human beings are replaced by social relations between things. A commodity, the object that embodies labor, now becomes the radical exteriority where beliefs reside (see Zizek, 1989, pp. 34-35). This is not psy-chology, for it has nothing to do with what people think they believe. And there is little difference between watching a TV program and watching commercials. Just like the laugh track in sitcoms laughs for the audience, commercials not only tell the audience what to believe, but actually believe for them, in their place. In the same way that the act of going to church makes one believe in God, it is the ritualistic performance of watching that makes them what Badiou would call "political" subjects in the process of social transformation. You

follow the rituals and then you are a believer. All these are only too familiar in China—practice proceeds theory, the slogan accentuated by Deng Xiaoping inadvertently strikes the cord by revealing the whole secret about ideology and its "sublime object," object in its abstract sense, as an object in what Deleuze (1998) calls the "symbolic space," in which "it is not itself—it has no self— it is every thing and nothing—it has no character" (Keats, 1935, p. 226, in G. Agamben, 1999, p. 112).

Advertising is beautiful, yet stupid. It is perverted, yet is teaching the norms of behavior. It is dominating, yet parasitic. No matter how (cultural) resistance can be maneuvered at various levels, the defining logic of capital cannot be escaped within the parameters set up by capital itself, and by the same token, neither can the commercials be escaped by the television audience. Within such confines, what can and will be changed is only the way of advertising: the working environment for the audience labor. Ultimately, the audience may not even want to stop watching, since to stop watching means to stop working, which eventually would mean to stop believing.

8.4 Some Final Words

As an effort to provide as much information about Chinese television advertising as possible, and at the same time to be as analytical as possible about its relation with the political transformation in China, the present study inevitably contains descriptions and propositions that may sound hasty and require further elaboration and empirical support. Specifically, the following technical and conceptual reflections and clarifications are crucial for future research.

1. The present study includes generalizations about China based on commercials on the CCTV network. One important fact about the CCTV network is that its influence, despite the self-claimed high ratings nationwide, gradually diminishes when one travels from North to South, and from the 20th century to the 21st century. Southern Chinese provinces, Guangdong for example, may not feel the impact of the centralized propaganda machine (in both political and commercial sense) at all. Speculations can certainly be made about advertising and its related categories in Southern provinces. For example, even though television in Guangdong may not have experienced the political zeal that was seen in Beijing temporarily in the 1980s, it is rather ahead of the Northern provinces in the process of commercialization, and in that senses, it led the country in what was to come anyway. But I would remain cautious about any specific claim at this stage.

2. The content analysis provides some contextual information regarding the values that Chinese television tries to convey, and the kind of symbolic environment that is being established in contemporary China. In retrospect, some categories that could have been coded were not coded. For example, the theme of nationalism was not included in the coding process, but was later found to be a quite visible factor with a closer look at some individual commercials,

and highly relevant in the discussion about the "transition" in China. This must be dealt with in the next project about China, with or without advertising involved. Besides, procrastination makes the project last longer than it was initially planned. In practical terms, this means the sample commercials coded in this study are too old when it is completed. Even though I am confident about the general argument in this study, it would be no surprise if developments in Chinese television and advertising industry make some concrete examples less relevant than they used to be.

3. The section on the new social order, though consistent with what comes before, has its experiential nature and is also rather sketchy. Relying on some snapshots, it is more of a logical refutation of some fundamentally flawed assumptions in the narratives and interpretations about the reform in China, than a presentation of the results of systematic and empirical research. A significant portion of it relies on personal memories and second hand material to argue against those who use the same type of material to support arguments in different directions. This is the part that needs to be singled out and really developed into a full fledged project, with support of first hand material.

4. This project initially began with the ambition to be extensive, which would cover every important aspect—institution, content, audience, and ideology of Chinese television advertising. Recognizing how unpractically large that task is, I scale it down to focus on the basics of advertising. This goal was only partially achieved—"partially" because of the nature of writing and language as an "automation machine" that expanded beyond the tightly set up boundary. In practical terms, it means things that are deemed relevant along the process were also included, even though they had not been conceived as the focus of this study. One of the consequences, of course, was the difficulty of maintaining a balance between inclusiveness and the depth of analysis. As already implied above, each major chapter may be singled out and developed into a bigger project, or even a monograph.

165

That being said, I hope that these limitations, monstrous as they are, have not stopped me from making the point clearly about Chinese television advertising, that during the so-called transitional period in contemporary China, the economic and the cultural must be both understood as integral parts of a political agenda, consciously or otherwise. Television advertising, as the process of depoliticizing the political, constitutes the primary ideological apparatus in contemporary China. By the same token, it is the task of the political subject to take television advertising as a departure point to launch the project of a genuine critique of capitalism, which will then lead to the beginning of a radical alternative of social transformation.

Bibliography

Adorno, T. (1954). How to look at television. *Quarterly Review of Film, Radio, and Television*, 8(3), 213-235.

Amin, S. (2017). "The October 1917 Revolution started off the transformation of the world." *International Critical Thought* 7(3), 364-384.

Althusser, L. (1970). *For Marx*. New York: Vintage Books.

Althusser, L. (2001). *Lenin and philosophy and other essays*. New York: Monthly Review Press.

Badiou, A. (2002). *Ethics*. New York: Verso.

Barthes, R. (1968). *The elements of semiology*. New York: Hill and Wang.

Barthes, R. (1973). *Mythologies*. London: Paladin Grafton Book.

Barthes, R. (1983). *The fashion system*. Berkeley: University of California Press.

Barthes, R. (1988). *The semiotic challenge*. Berkeley: University of California Press.

Baudot, S. B. (1989). *International advertising handbook*. Massachusetts: Lexington Books.

Benjamin, W. (1968). *Illuminations*. New York: Schocken Books.

Bennett, T., Martin, G., Mercer, C., & Woolacott, J. (1991). *Culture, ideology and social process*. London: Open University.

Bishop, R. (1989). *Qi lai! Mobilizing one billion Chinese: The Chinese communication system*. Ames: Iowa State University Press.

Broadcasting & Cable's TV International. (1999), 7, 5.

Button, G. (1993). Ads for the sets of China. *Forbes*, 151(9), 12-14.

Carver, T. (Ed.). *Marx: His later political writings*.
London: Cambridge University Press.

Chaffee, H. S. & Hochheimer, L. J. (1982). The beginnings of political communication research in the United States: Origins of the "limited effects model." In Rogers, M. E. & Balle, F. (Eds.), *The Media Revolution in America and Western Europe* (pp. 267-296). Norwood: Ablex.

Central Committee of the Communist Party of China. 1956. "Outline of agricultural development between 1956-1967 (draft)". [In Chinese] https://baike.baidu.com/item/一九五六年到一九六七年全国农业发展纲要/5803423#4.

Chan, K.W. K. (1995). Information content of television advertising in China. *International Journal of Advertising*. 14(4), 365-374.

Chang, T., Wang, J., & Chen, Y. (2002). *China's window on the world: TV news, social knowledge and international spectacles*. Cresskill, NJ: Hampton Press, Inc.

Chang, W. H. 1989. *Mass media in China*. Ames: Iowa State University Press.

Certeau, M. de. (1984). *The practice of everyday life*.
Berkeley: University of California University Press.

Cheng, H. (1996). Advertising in China: A socialist experiment. In Katherine Toland Frith (Ed.), *Advertising in Asia: Communication, Culture, and Consumption* (pp.73-102). Ames: Iowa State University Press.

Cheng, H. (1997). Toward an understanding of cultural values manifest in advertising: A Content Analysis of Chinese Television Commercials in 1990 and 1995. *Journalism and Mass Communication Quarterly*. 73(4), 773-797.

Cheng, H. and Schweitzer, C. J. (1996). Cultural values reflected in Chinese and U.S. television commercials. *Journal of Advertising Research*, 36: 27-45.

Cheng, X. (2017) The weakness and innovation in the creative television culture (电视广告文化创意中的短板与创新). *Contemporary TV*, no 11: 67-68.

Chow, R. (1991). *Woman and Chinese modernity*.
Minnesota: University of Minnesota Press.

Chow, R. (1993). *Writing diaspora*. Bloomington: Indiana University Press.

Chow, R. (1995). *Primitive passions*. New York: Columbia University Press.

Chow, R. (2002). *The Protestant ethic and the spirit of capitalism*. New York: Columbia University Press.

Ci, J. (1994). *Dialectic of the Chinese revolution: from utopianism to hedonism*. Stanford: Stanford University Press.

Cruz, J. & Lewis, J. (Eds.). (1994). *Reading, viewing, listening*. Boulder: Westview.

Deleuze, G. (1998). How do we recognize structuralism? In Stivale, C., *The Two-fold Thought of Deleuze and Guattari, Intersections and Animation* (pp. 251-282). New York: The Guilford Press.

Derrida, J. (2000). *Of hospitality*. Stanford: Stanford University Press.

Dong, H., and Liu, Y. (2016). The role of regional culture in television advertising (地域文化在电视广告中的运用). *Journal of Contemporary TV*, no. 10, 67-68.

Dou, L., Sun, X., and Lin, S. (2012). Cultural values in Chinese television advertising: A comparative study (中国电视广告中的文化价值观：基于横向与纵向的比较). *Journalism & Communication* (新闻与传播研究), 19 (03), 42-51.

Duan, R., Zhong, S., Wang, X., & Li, T. (2002). *Social stratification during the Chinese modernization* (中国现代化进程中的阶层结构变动研究). Beijing: People's Press.

Duncombe, S. (2002). *Cultural resistance reader*. New York: Verso Press.

Fan, W. Current situation and strategy of television advertising communication in the age of new media (新媒体时代电视广告传播现状及策略研究). *Communication and Copyright*, no. 2, 74-75.

Fisk, J. (1987). *Television culture*. New York: Methuen.

Frith, T. K. (Ed.). (1996). *Advertising in Asia: Communication, culture, and consumption*. Ames: Iowa State University Press.

Gao, X. 2014. The dilemma of television advertising and marketing innovation (浅析电视广告困境及营销创新). *Contemporary TV*, no. 12: 104-105.

Gao, Z. (2008). Controlling deceptive advertising in China: An overview. Journal of Public Policy & Marketing, 27(2), 165-177.

Garnham, N. (1979). "Contribution to a political economy of mass-communication." *Media, Culture and Society*, no. 1: 123-146.

Gerbner, G. (1973). Cultural indicators: The third voice. In G. Gerbner, L. Gross, & W. H. Melody (Eds.). *Communications Technology and Social Policy* (pp. 555-573). NewYork: Wiley.

Gerbner, G., Gross, L., Morgan, M. & Signorelli, N. (1994). Growing up with television: The cultivation perspective. In J. Bryant and D. Zillman (Eds.), *Media Effects* (pp. 17-41). New Jersey: Erlbaum.

Goodman, D. (Ed). (2008). *The new rich in China*. New York: Routledge.

Gramsci, A. (1992). *Prison notebooks*. New York: Columbia University Press.

Ha, L. (1996). Concerns about advertising practices in a developing country: an examination of China's new advertising regulations. *International Journal of Advertising*, 15, 91-102.

Hall, S. (1977). *Re-thinking the base-and-superstructure metaphor*. The Communist University of London.

Hall, S. (1980). Encoding/decoding. In S. Hall et al. (Eds.), *Culture, Media, Language* (pp. 128-138). London: Hutchinson.

Hall, S. (1982). The rediscovery of ideology: The return of the repressed in media studies. In Gurevitch et al (Eds.). *Culture, Society and the Media*. London: Methuen.

Hall, S. (1994). Reflections upon the encoding/decoding model: An Interview with Stuart Hall. In J. Cruz and J. Lewis (Eds.), *Reading, Viewing, Listening* (pp. 253-274). Boulder: Westview.

Hao, X. (2000). Party dominance vs. cultural imperialism: China's Strategies to Regulate Satellite Broadcasting. *Communication Law & Policy*, 5(2), 155-182.

Hayek, F. A. (2007). *The road to serfdom*. Chicago: The University of Chicago Press.

Head, S., Spann, T., & McGregor, M. (2001). *Broadcasting in America: A survey of electronic media* (9th Ed.). Boston: Houghton Mifflin Company.

Herman, E. and McChesney, R. (1997). *The global media*. Washington: Cassell.

Hirschman, C. E. (2003). Men, dogs, guns, and cars: The semiotics of rugged individualism. *Journal of Advertising*, 32(1), 9-23.

Hong, J. (1994). The resurrection of advertising in China: Development, problems, and trends. *Asian Survey*, (34)4, 326-343.

Janus, N. Z. (1980). *The making of the global consumer: Transnational advertising and the mass media in Latin America*. Unpublished dissertation.

Jenkins, H. (1988). "Star Trek" return, reread, rewritten: Fan writing as textual poaching. *Critical Studies in Mass Communication*, 5(2), 85-107.

Jhally, S. (1987). *The codes of advertising*. New York: Routledge.

Ji, F. M. & McNeal, U. J. (2001). How Chinese children's commercials differ from those of the United States: A content analysis. *Journal of Advertising*, (30) 3, 79.

Kanso, A. & Nelson, A. R. Advertising localization overshadows standardization. (observations). *Journal of Advertising Research*, 42(1), 79.

Katz, Z. (1987). Communications research since Lazarsfeld. *Public Opinion Quarterly*, 51(4), S25-S45.

Katz, E. & Lazarsfeld, P. (1995). *Personal influence: The part played by people in the flow of mass communication*. New York: Free Press.

Kellner, D. (1990). *Television and the crisis of democracy*. Boulder: Westview Press.

Kilbourne, J. (1999). *Deadly persuasion*. New York: The Free Press.

Klein, N. (1999). No Logo. New York: Picador USA.

Leiss, W., Kline, S., & Jhally, S. (1997). *Social communication in advertising*. New York: Routledge.

Levi-Strauss, C. (1963). *Totemism*. Boston: Beacon Press.

Lacan, J. (1997). The agency of the letter in the unconscious. In *Ecrits*. New York: W.W. Norton & Company.

Lee, C. (Ed.). (1994). *China's media, Media's China*. San Francisco: Westview Press.

Lewis, J. 1991. *The Ideological octopus*. New York: Routledge.

Li, S., Zhao, H. and Lin, S. (2017). A second by second analysis of the rating for advertising inserted within television program— The influence of length, order and position (电视节目插播广告收视率的逐秒分析—长度、顺序、位置的影响). *Journalism & Communication* (新闻与传播研究), 24(03), 42-63.

Lin, A. C. (2001). Cultural values reflected in Chinese and American television advertising. *Journal of Advertising*, (30)4, 83-95.

Liu, S. (2000). *Electronic engineering times*, January 17, p. 30.

Lowery, A. S. & Defleur, M. L. (1988). The Payne Fund studies: The effects of movies on children. In *Milestones in Mass Communication* (2nd Ed.). New York: Longman.

Macdonald, D. 1957. A theory of mass culture. In B. Rosenberg & D. M. White (Eds.). *Mass Culture: The Popular Arts in America*. New York: Free Press.

Mao, Z. (1955). "Request for opinions on the seventeen-article document concerning agriculture". In *Selected Works of Mao Tse-tung*, vol. 5. Beijing: Foreign Languages Press. https://www.marxists.org/reference/archive/mao/selected-works/volume-5/mswv5_49.htm

Marx, K. (1912). *Capital* (Vol. 1). Chicago: Charles H. Kerr & Company.

Marx, K. (1964). *Karl Marx: Early writings*. McGraw-Hill Book Company.

Marx, K. (1970). *The German ideology*. New York: International Publishers.

Marx, K. (1996). Introduction to the Grundrisse. In Terrell Carver (Ed.), *Marx: Later political writings*. London: Cambridge University Press.

Mattelart, A. (1991). *Advertising internationally: The privatization of public space*. New York: Routledge.

McChesney, R. (1993). Telecommunications, mass media, and democracy. New York: Oxford University Press.

McChesney, R. (1999). *Rich media, poor democracy: Communication politics in dubious times*. New York: The New Press.

McQuail, D. (1991). Reflections on uses and gratifications research. In R. Avery & D. Eason. (Eds.). *Critical perspectives on media and society*. New York: The Guilford Press. Beijing.

Ministry of Radio, Film, and Television (1991). *Proclamation No. 5.: Regulations on the management of cable television*. Beijing.

Ministry of Radio, Film, and Television (1994). *Proclamation No. 10: Regulations on the import and broadcasting of the television programs from outside People's Republic of China*. Beijing.

Ministry of Radio, Film, and Television. (1994). *Proclamation No. 12. Regulations on Cable Networks*. Beijing.

Morley, D. & Chen, K. (1996). *Stuart Hall: Critical dialogues in cultural studies*. New York:Routledge.

Mouffe, C. (1991). Hegemony and ideology in Gramsci. In T. Bennett, G. Martin, C. Mercer & Ja. Woollacott (Eds.). *Culture, ideology and Social Process*. London: Open University.

National Bureau of Statistics. (1999-2017). *China statistical yearbook*. Retrieved October 10, 2018, from http://www.stats.gov.cn/tjsj/ndsj.

Neuendorf, K. A. (2002). *The content analysis Guidebook*. Thousand Oaks: Sage Publications.

Nie, G. (2017). The creative expression of the Chinese elements in liquor advertisements on television (酒类电视广告的中国元素创意表达). *Contemporary TV*, no. 11, 71-71.

O'Donnell, V. (2007). *Television criticism*. Los Angeles: Sage.

Prendergast, G. & Shi, Y. (2001). Client perceptions of advertising and advertising agencies: a China study. *Journal of Marketing Communications*. 7(2), 47-63.

Radway, J. (1983). Women read the romance: The interaction of text and context. *Feminist Studies*, 9, 53-78.

Radway, J. (1988). Reception study: Ethnography and the problems of dispersed audience and nomadic subjects. *Cultural Studies*, 2(3), 359-376.

Radway, J. (1986). Identifying ideological seams: Mass culture, analytical method, and the political practice. *Journal of Communication*, 9, 93-123.

Raskin, M. (2004). Liberalism. New York: Rowman & Littlefield Publishers, INC.

Rubin, A. M. (1984). Ritualized and instrumental television Viewing. *Journal of Communication*, 34(3), 67-77.

Schmitt, C. (1976). *The concept of the political*. New Brunswick: Rutgers University Press.

Sciulli, M. L. & Taiani, V. (2001). Advertising content for the global Audience: A Research Proposal. *Competitiveness Review*, 11(2), 39.

Silverstone, R. (1989). Let us then return to the murmuring of everyday practices: a note on Michel de Certeau, television and everyday life. *Journal of Theory, Culture and Society*, 6(1), 77-94.

Sinclair, J. (2008). Globalization and the advertising industry in China. *Chinese Journal of Communication*, 1(1), 77-90.

Sinclair, J., Jacka, E., & Cunningham S. (Eds.). (1996). *New Patterns in Global Television*. Oxford University Press.

Smythe, D. (1977). Communications: Blindspot of Western Marxism. *Canadian Journal of Political and Social Theory*, 1(3), 1-27.

Smythe, D. (1980). *Dependency road*. Norwood, NJ: Ablex.

State Council of People's Republic of China. (1982). *The Interim Regulations for Advertising Management*. Beijing.

State Council of People's Republic of China. (1987). *The Regulations for Advertising Management*. Beijing.

State Council of People's Republic of China. (1994). *The advertising law of People's Republic of China*. Beijing.

State Council of People's Republic of China. (1997). *Proclamation No. 228: Regulations on radio and television broadcasting*. Beijing.

Streeter, T. (1996). Selling the air. Chicago. University of Chicago Press.

Ubios, J. (1994). TV China. *Digital Media*, (4), 7.

Variety. (2000, April 3), (378)7, 76.

Wang, D. (1996). *Dictionary of advertising in China* (中国广告词典). Chengdu: Sichuan University Press.

Wang, D. L. Current situation of television advertising in the age of new media and its counter measures (新媒体时代电视广告传播现状及对策). *Journal of News Research*. 7 (20): 267-268.

Wang, H. (1994). *The gradual revolution*. New Brunswick: Transaction Publishers.

173

Wang, H. (2003). *China's new order: Society, politics, and economy in transition*. Cambridge, Mass: Harvard University Press.

Wang, Jian. (1997). From four hundred million to more than one billion consumers: A brief history of the foreign advertising industry in China. *International Journal of Advertising*, 16(4), 241-261.

Wang, Jian. (2000). *Foreign advertising in China*. Ames: Iowa State University Press.

Wang, Jing. (2008). *Brand new China*. Cambridge, Mass: Harvard University Press.

Wang, Jing. (2008). The language of chopsticks. *Journal of Advertising Research* (Special issue: *The Challenge of China*), (48)4, 1-3.

Wang, L. (2016). The corporatization and capitalization of the operation of television advertising (浅谈电视媒体广告经营的公司化与资本化). *Journalism & Communication* (新闻传播), no.20: 79-80.

Wang, R. (2003). *Advertising Laws and Institutions in China* (中国广告法律制度研究). Han Kou: Hubei People's Press.

Williams, R. (1980). *Problems in materialism and culture*. London: Verso.

Williams, R. (1961). *The long revolution*. New York: Columbia University Press.

Williamson, J. (1978). *Decoding advertisements: Ideology and meaning in advertising*. London: Marion Boyars.

Wu, D. and Wang, J. 2007. New crisis of television advertising and its countermeasures (电视广告面临的新危机及其出路). *Sociological Study*, no. 5, 185-187.

Xu, Z., and Yan, F. (2016). Advertising industry in developing countries and the opportunities for China (当前世界发展中国家广告产业发展态势及其中国机遇分析). *Modern Communication* (*Journal of the Communication University of China*), 38(10), 114-121.

J. Zhang, J. & S. Shavitt (2003). Cultural values in advertisements to the Chinese X-generation: Promoting Modernity and Individualism. *Journal of Advertising*, (32) 1, 23-34.

Zhao, X. & Shen, F. (1995). Audience reaction to commercial advertising in China in the 1980s. *International Journal of Advertising*, (14)4, 374-391.

Zheng, Y. (2004). Globalization and state transformation in China. Cambridge: Cambridge University Press.

Zhong, Y. (2003). In search of the loyal audience – What did I find? An ethnographic study of Chinese television audience. *Journal of Media & Cultural Studies*, (17)3, 233-247.

Zhao, S., Yin, X., and Zeng, X. (2017). Study of contextualized marketing based on cross-screen interaction on television (电视跨屏互动场景化营销研究). *Modern Communication (Journal of Communication University of China)*, 39(5), 119-123.

Zhao, Y. (1998). *Media, market, and democracy in China*. Urbana: University of Illinois Press.

Zhao, Y, and Guo Z. (2005). Television in China: History, political economy, and ideology. In J. Wasko. (Ed.). *A Companion to Television*. Malden, MA: Blackwell Publishing.

Zhao, Y. (2008). *Communication in China: Political economy, power, and conflict*. New York: Rowman & Littlefield Publishers, Inc.

Zhou, N. & Belk, W. R. (2004). Chinese consumer readings of global and local advertising appeals. *Journal of Advertising*, (33)3, 63-77.

Zhou, S., Zhou, P., and Xue, F. (2005). Visual differences in the U.S. and Chinese television commercials. *Journal of Advertising*, (34)1, 111-120.

Zhou, D., Zhang, W. & Vertinsky, I. (2002). Advertising trends in Urban China. *Journal of Advertising*, (42)3, 73-82.

Zhou, Yi. (2006). *Hua Xi village: Post-collectivism in a transitional economy*. Hong Kong: Oxford University Press.

Zizek, S. (1989). *The sublime object of ideology*. New York: Verso.

Zizek, S. (2008). *Violence*. New York: Picardo.

175

www.ingramcontent.com/pod-product-compliance
Lightning Source LLC
Chambersburg PA
CBHW031152020426
42333CB00013B/625